We Ran Away to Sea

WE
RAN AWAY
TO SEA

A Memoir and Letters

GEORGE KENT KEDL

PAMELA THOMPSON KEDL

Jacana Press
Albuquerque, New Mexico

Front cover illustration: Pamela Kedl

The cover is an adaptation of a collage Pam made using her favorite images
of the family. She slouches in a chair, the boys sit on a log, and the cats play
on the floor. Kent is the inflexible preacher, Cotton Mather, and she is
pulled between Kent, home, family, art, and life on the boat.

Book design: Sara DeHaan
Maps: Doug Nelson, DCN Maps

Publisher's Cataloging-in-Publication Data

Names: Kedl, George Kent, author. | Kedl, Pamela Thompson, author.
Title: We ran away to sea: a memoir and letters / George Kent Kedl and
Pamela Thompson Kedl.
Description: Includes bibliographical references. | Albuquerque, NM:
Jacana Press, 2023.
Identifiers: LCCN: 2023900017 | ISBN: 9798987009703 (paperback) |
9798987009710 (ebook)
Subjects: LCSH Kedl, George Kent—Travel. | Kedl, Pamela Thompson—Travel. |
Sailing. | Seafaring life. | BISAC BIOGRAPHY & AUTOBIOGRAPHY /
Personal Memoirs | TRAVEL / Essays & Travelogues |
SPORTS & RECREATION / Sailing
Classification: LCC G540 .K43 2023 | DDC 910.9163/09²—dc23

For two adventurous and loving women:
Pam, whose letters inspired this book,
and Linnea, who helped me complete it.
—George Kent Kedl

Contents

Maps

Prologue

Fools rush in where angels fear to tread.
—ALEXANDER POPE, *An Essay on Criticism*

The yellow house was a delight to me. The life that I'd
envisioned for my family and me was coming true. I'd always
wanted to be a professor's wife and live in a university town
with all the liveliness of students and the opportunities such
a town provides. I enjoyed taking classes and could take as
many as I wanted. I had two boys, the ideal number and sex of
children for me. The house itself was more than I'd ever hoped
to possess.

I used to wander through the yellow house at night when
everyone was asleep, feeling the space and looking at the
things we'd done to make it unique. Kent had a workshop and
tools, and projects. By the time we'd finished, I had a snazzy
kitchen, a pottery studio, most of the antiques refinished and
glowing, and a garden that could still use some improvement.
The wonderful walk-up attic was filled with both Kent's and my
childhoods—dolls, Lionel trains, typewriters, books, toys, and
projects begun and never completed.

We had plenty of friends. We had the cabin in the Black
Hills for the summers, a pleasure that I can't think about
without crying. I sang, "We all live in a big yellow house, a big
yellow house, a big yellow house."

One night Kent said, "If I don't get away from here, I think
I'll die."

I asked if I wouldn't leave with him, would he go without us?
He said, "I don't know."

I was scared beyond writing about it.

Because I was content and not sensitive to what was going on in Kent's life, I didn't realize that he was miserable at the university. He didn't feel he could be the kind of teacher they expected. He was frustrated by the indifference of the students and the general population's attitudes about education. Each time his contract came up for renewal, he worried that they'd let him go. Or maybe, he hoped they'd let him go so he could put an end to his anguish about what he saw as his inadequate teaching and get on to something more suited to him. Even after he'd gotten tenure, he couldn't shake the feeling of inadequacy, and it was eating him up. I should have been more aware of what was happening, but I was so blinded by my own interests in the kids, pottery, and the house that I didn't look carefully. I felt so secure once he got tenure that I was thankful to think we could keep what we had and what I thought was important.

Nevertheless, we began to look for other ways of living.
(Pam's Reflections on Home, 2003, unpublished)

I had fine ideas about leading a simple, honest life, but our family was not living that way. We did not live lavishly by American standards, but even Americans of modest means consume an excessive proportion of the world's resources. Everything from the foods we eat to the way we travel requires a shameful share of scarce and non-renewable resources. I talked the talk, but I did not walk the walk.

Living in the United States, we were small cogs in an enormous machine. We fit into established ways of feeding ourselves, traveling, earning our livings, and associating with others. We were also paying for warmongering, bullying foreign policies we did not support.

A friend mentioned that her sister was living aboard a sailboat and cruising the Pacific Ocean. I glommed onto the idea of life on a sailboat and could not let it go.

On a boat, we could feed ourselves without supporting the huge agricultural industry that was eating up and destroying the land. We would travel without consuming non-renewable energy, and we could live with little money, minimal taxes, no utilities, no house/yard maintenance, and few expenses for entertainment.

Unlike many who run off to sea in a sailboat, we had no love or knowledge of either the sea or sailing. I was free to imagine an idyllic life at sea. I read all the sailing books in the public library, including the accounts of Joshua Slocum (the first person to sail around the world single-handedly in a small boat), Eric and Susan Hiscock, Miles and Beryl Smeaton, and Bernard Moitessier. Instead of worrying about promotions and paychecks and complaining about the latest news events over which they had no control, they lived unconventional lives, pursued adventurous travels, and wrote about their experiences.

I naively thought a sailboat would be an ideal vehicle for our new life. On a boat, we would depend on each other for what mattered. The wind would blow us about. Each person's task would be essential when we needed to change a sail or move the anchor. A modest boat would be our home and means of transportation. Every port in the world would be at our doorstep. We could create a little island world of sanity, feed ourselves from the sea, get along with little money, and, if necessary, find work.

The boys would study, help sail the boat, and meet children around the world, all the while having adventures, diving on reefs, learning foreign languages, and forming broad world views. When not engaged in great father-son adventures, I would write profound philosophical papers. Pam would share my enthusiasm and keep the family together. Admittedly, seeking adventure was also part of my motivation, and I was, no doubt, going through

a mid-life crisis. Pam explained our decision in a letter written in
1985 to her godparents, Bill and Marie Ray:

> About two years ago, Kent got fed up with teaching phil-
> osophy to disinterested twenty-year-old kids at South Dakota
> State University. I was teaching one first-year composition
> class and began to realize what an embittering thing it was for
> him. We started to cast about for some solution. We'd love to
> travel, and we wanted the kids with us. We couldn't afford to
> quit work, but we hated the idea of waiting twenty-five years
> for retirement and then finding we'd lost our enthusiasm or
> our health. Finally, we decided we'd become ocean voyagers.
> Only someone living in South Dakota—as far from the sea
> as possible—and with no sailing experience—could so
> cavalierly contemplate doing what we did.
>
> Last June, we sold the house, auctioned the furniture,
> cars, and appliances, garage-saled the books, records,
> kids' toys, and clothes, bought a camper, and headed east
> searching for a sailboat we could live on.

Our friend Terry Branson took us sailing a few times in his dinghy-
sized sailboat on the small prairie lakes near Brookings, South
Dakota. I grew up thinking that sailing was an art that took years
of experience to master. However, once I grasped one or two
elementary principles and learned to say *port, starboard, luff, and
leech* with hardly a stumble, I did what novices often do: I jumped
to the extreme opposite view. Sailing was simplicity itself; any
fool could do it. To make sure we could handle a sailboat without
getting too seasick, we chartered a small sloop for two days on
Lake Superior; half-a-day with an instructor and one day on our
own. A little knowledge is, indeed, a dangerous thing.

I don't think that Jake, aged fourteen, and Andy, ten, realized
what a revolutionary change we were planning. We were giving

Jake, Pam, Andy, and Kent on trial sail, Lake Superior

up the only way of life we'd ever known. My department chairman talked me into taking a year's leave of absence without pay instead of resigning, in case things did not work out. I went along with that, although I was sure I would not return. But, leaving this door open may have been a mistake.

We looked in cities along the Great Lakes—no luck. We looked in New York—nothing. In Annapolis, we decided that boats in the United States were too expensive. Since the dollar was strong against European currencies, we put the small Mobile Traveler camper in a sales lot, put what remained of our belongings into a Goodwill donation bin, put backpacks on the boys, and put ourselves on a plane to England. We no longer had a key to put in our pockets.

Now I, like the sailors whose tales I so admired, have gathered my stories and Pam's writings about our lives on two boats.

We have changed a few names to protect the guilty, the innocent, and ourselves. Our story is told in two voices; Pam's, through her letters because she is no longer here to speak for herself, and mine, written at various times and places.

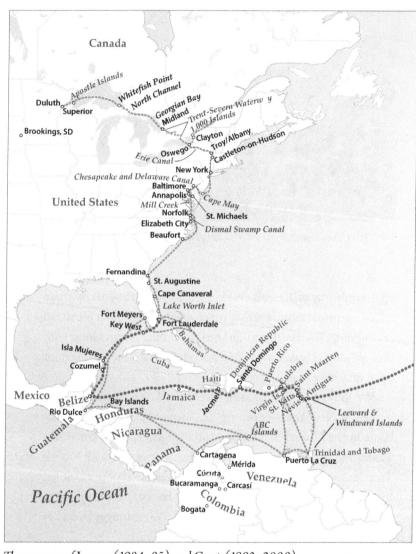

The voyages of Jacana *(1984–85) and* Coot *(1993–2000)*

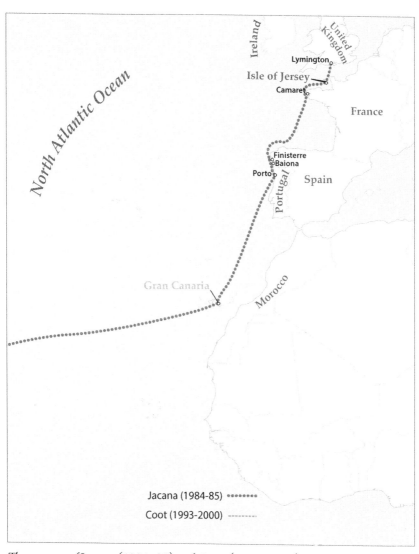

The voyages of Jacana (1984–85) and Coot (1993–2000), continued

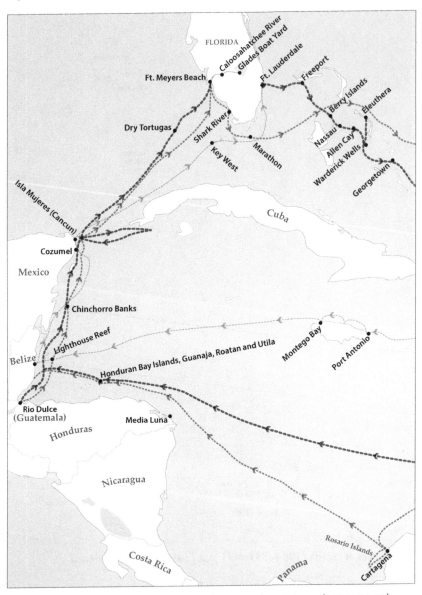

Caribbean routes: the voyages of Jacana *(1984–85) and* Coot *(1993–2000)*

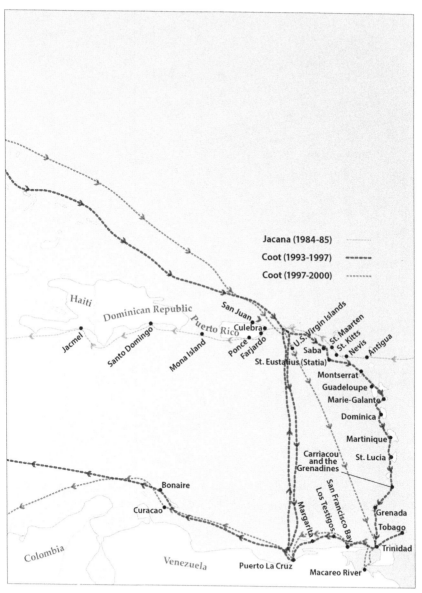

Jacana (1984-85)

Coot (1993-1997)

Coot (1997-2000)

Caribbean routes: the voyages of Jacana *(1984–85) and* Coot *(1993–2000),*
continued

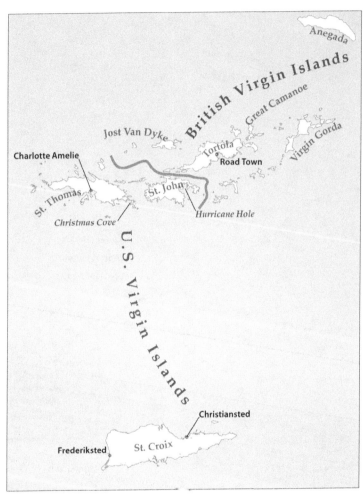

U.S. and British Virgin Islands

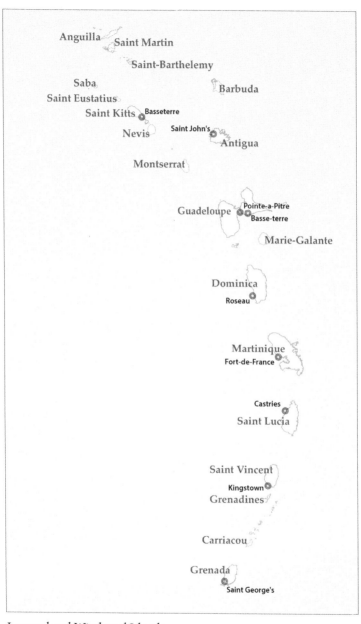

Anguilla
Saint Martin
Saint-Barthelemy
Saba
Saint Eustatius
Saint Kitts Basseterre
Nevis Saint John's
Antigua
Barbuda
Montserrat

Guadeloupe Pointe-a-Pitre
Basse-terre
Marie-Galante

Dominica
Roseau

Martinique
Fort-de-France

Castries
Saint Lucia

Saint Vincent
Kingstown
Grenadines

Carriacou

Grenada
Saint George's

Leeward and Windward Islands

I

Jacana

June–September 1984

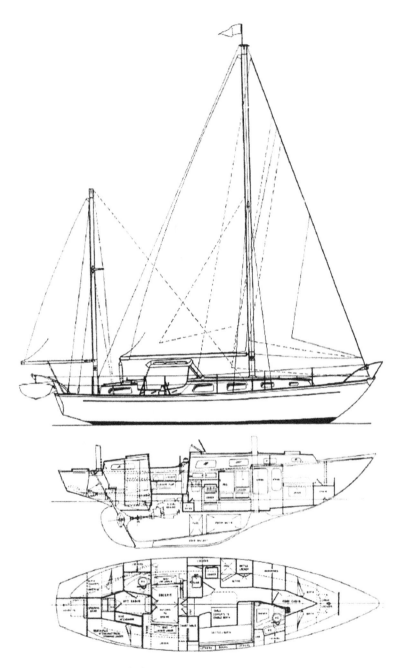

Jacana 2, *Camper Nicholson 38*

Chapter 1

Getting Our Feet Wet

June–September 1984

*He that will not sail till all dangers are over
must never put to sea.* —THOMAS FULLER

Do not let a mid-life-crisis male, intent upon changing his life, see that you think he is a fool. It will only get his back up and make him move forward with even more determination. The British boat brokers' startled expressions proclaimed more clearly than words, "You fool! Do you have any idea what you are doing?" I took no heed and, jaw firmly set, carried on. We already knew we didn't know what we were doing, and insofar as we had one, our plan was, "We'll buy a sailboat and figure out the rest as we go along."

While traveling around England by car during our search for a boat, we stopped in quiet cemeteries where Jake and Andy could run around. While we picnicked on pub sandwiches or fish and chips, Pam read the headstones and the markers for those lost at sea. Many said, "Lost in the Bay of Biscay in September . . ." During the September equinox, the bay invariably experiences severe gales. We were warned not to sail then, but that was when we needed to set out to avoid a northern winter. Pam grew increasingly nervous.

3

She also had to contend with her mother's disapproval. What was her inexperienced philosophy-professor-son-in-law thinking to take her only daughter and grandsons across the Atlantic in a small boat? During our time in England, Pam developed a mysterious, debilitating illness with fever, indigestion, and a loss of appetite. A doctor came to our hotel room, found nothing seriously wrong, and gave her medicine to ease her symptoms. He could do nothing about me and my obsession.

Pam said I sometimes proceeded like a blinkered mule. That was certainly the case now. I saw Pam's seasickness, nervousness, and recurring illnesses as temporary inconveniences. I had no health issues, misgivings, or surviving parents, and I was occupied with the sheer effort required to make our new life happen. Was the philosophy professor and advocate of critical thinking blinded by his own ideas?

After a month of searching along England's south coast, we finally found *Jacana 2*, an affordable and suitable thirty-eight-foot ketch (a two-masted sailboat; see the diagram for details) on the Isle of Jersey. My fantasy was to sail to the Caribbean and go through the Panama Canal toward my Hollywood-formed vision of the sun setting behind palm-lined beaches in the South Pacific. After we agreed to buy *Jacana* and settled on a price, the seller suggested we sail back to England to complete the purchase for reasons relating to the English VAT (Value Added Tax). He was willing to pay for the passage across the Channel and back with a hired skipper, and we were delighted to take an excursion on the soon-to-be-our boat.

However, it began to sink in, even to me, that we were foolishly irresponsible to set out without actual ocean-sailing experience and no real plan. The money from the sale of the house and our possessions, plus the interest on our savings, would pay for the boat and allow us to live on it for the foreseeable future. We didn't think seriously about the long-term sustainability of our chosen way of life, but reality would give my fantasy some rude jolts early on.

Because the harbor dried out at low tide, the hired skipper asked us to fill the fuel and water tanks and take the boat to a mooring outside the harbor where he would join us. We motored to the fuel dock, and the wind pushed us gently alongside. It was as easy as could be. A large French ferry tied up in front of us, and the passengers watched us from above. We felt like real sailors, although we hadn't the foggiest idea of what we were doing.

When we cast off, there seemed to be plenty of room between us and the ferry. I started forward and turned the wheel, but nothing happened. I sped up and turned the wheel hard over. Nothing! The boat scraped along the wall, heading straight toward the ferry. I hit the throttle in a panic, thinking I needed more speed to activate the rudder. By the time I realized we were not pulling away from the wall and reversed the engine, it was too late.

Jake ran forward to try to stop our ten-ton boat with his hands. Our bow pulpit rammed the ferry's towering hull, took the shock of the impact, and bent to one side. Nothing else was harmed, although my ego sported a serious bruise.

There is a trick to getting a boat off a dock when the wind is blowing it on.

"This is how you do it," explained the gas pump attendant,

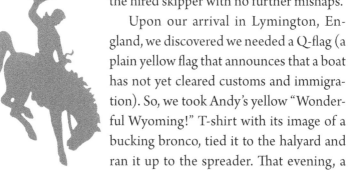

and we managed to leave the dock and meet the hired skipper with no further mishaps.

Upon our arrival in Lymington, England, we discovered we needed a Q-flag (a plain yellow flag that announces that a boat has not yet cleared customs and immigration). So, we took Andy's yellow "Wonderful Wyoming!" T-shirt with its image of a bucking bronco, tied it to the halyard and ran it up to the spreader. That evening, a fellow on the quay strummed his guitar and serenaded us with "Home on the Range."

Because we had children on board and had put up the U.S. ensign, people were curious about us. Fourteen-year-old Jake hated the attention and wanted to be left alone: "Mom, everybody's looking at us!" It was the first time I noticed he was unhappy.

Our little bank in Brookings promptly wired money to buy the boat, and we were able to complete the paperwork. We had our boat, and it was time to celebrate! But we had not yet sailed on our own, and the boat needed to be readied for long-distance voyaging. Pam's mysterious, debilitating symptoms increased, and Jake began treating our grand adventure as an ordeal. Nevertheless, I was elated. My dream was coming true!

We sailed back to Jersey with the hired skipper and began working on the boat in the St. Aubin harbor. The crooked bow pulpit constantly reminded me of my inexperience, so that was the first job on my list. I disconnected the lifelines but left them running through the stanchions instead of removing them.

At low tide, the boat settled into thick, gooey mud. While I worked on the pulpit, I heard Pam down in the galley talking with Andy on the deck above. Suddenly, I heard a zipping sound, and Andy's voice vanished. Pam rushed on deck and discovered him waist deep in the mud, looking startled and confused. He had leaned back against the unsecured lifelines, somersaulted backward, and fortunately landed feet first. We pulled him out with difficulty.

One morning shortly after this, Pam announced, "I'm going back to Brookings. You can stay here to work on the boat."

We sat around the table in the cabin to discuss our options.

"Who wants to go home with me?"

I assumed that Andy would return with Pam. But I desperately hoped Jake would stay.

Then Jake said, "I want to go with Mom."

I left the boat without a word and walked for the rest of the day, seeing nothing. I wondered if Pam was leaving me and the boat permanently. When I returned, I could tell they were worried about me, but we didn't talk about my feelings. And I couldn't give up my dream. It was only later, when we corresponded by mail, that I was sure Pam was planning to return to the boat. After she and the boys left, the momentum of the work that I had already started and the unrelinquished image of our future idyllic life got me through my depression and feelings of abandonment.

Pam flew to Washington, D.C., and drove the boys to Brookings after purchasing a used two-door Ford sedan that left them stranded on the road more than once. They lived in a broken-down house trailer, and Pam, no longer a faculty wife, earning pin money by teaching freshman composition, paid the rent by slinging hash at Country Kitchen. Before long she decided she'd rather meet me in the Canary Islands in November than in the Caribbean in December. Jake begged to finish his fall semester in eighth grade, so Pam arranged with friends to look after him when she and Andy returned to the boat.

Several people offered to house Jake, including Terry and his wife Ruth, who had a daughter close to his age. However, to Pam's surprise, Jake chose to stay with three young, single women (one an assistant director at the Art Museum and the other two graduate students). They turned out to be good "moms." One helped with homework, a second made sure he got fed, and the third attended his parent/teacher conferences. Jake probably thought he could get away with more with the "moms," and from stories we heard later, I think he did.

Pam wrote to Bill and Marie Ray:

The boat needed some work, and the kids and I began to get homesick and nervous about a trip down the west coast

of Europe toward the Canary Islands in September during
the equinoctial gales, so we jumped ship and went back
to Brookings, leaving Kent to carry on with a hired crew.
We'd planned to join him at Christmas when he reached the
Caribbean. Kent managed to outfit and provision *Jacana* and
get her to the Canaries through a nasty gale. By then, Andy
and I were so lonely for him that we decided we'd join him
in the Canaries for the Atlantic crossing. Jake stayed behind
with friends in Brookings to finish the fall semester.

Pam's letter minimizes the difficulties she faced after leaving
me and the boat and fails to mention that her decision to leave
traumatized me and called into question her commitment to our
new life.

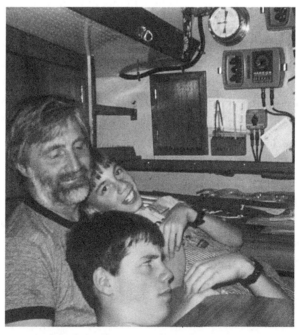

Kent and the boys in Jacana *cabin*

Chapter 2

To Sea!

June–September 1984

The cure for anything is saltwater—sweat, tears,
or the sea. —ISAK DINESEN, Seven Gothic Tales

Once Pam had gone, all thoughts of spending the winter sailing the Mediterranean and traveling in Europe vanished. I spent weeks in St. Aubin preparing for the Atlantic crossing. I needed help, so I found two Jersey men in their early twenties to accompany me to the Canary Islands. David Sandeman[1] had sailed his family's boat, a sister to *Jacana*, as he was growing up. When he was seventeen, he sailed across the Atlantic single-handedly. Even though he was too young to enter the 1976 trans-Atlantic OSTAR race officially, he met all the other qualifications and unofficially took off with the rest of the fleet. When he arrived in Rhode Island, he set a record as the youngest person to sail alone across the Atlantic and beat about half the official entrants in the race. David taught me how to navigate with a sextant on our

---

1. For more information about David Sandeman, see the section on the 1976 Ostar Race in Wikipedia, "Single-Handed Transatlantic Race." Last Modified 2 October 2022.

passage to the Canaries in the days before modern electronic navigation.

Gary Picot, the son of a Jersey fisherman, had no experience with sailboats but had spent time on fishing boats and knew what to expect from the sea. He had trained as a chippie (ship's carpenter) and was building GRP (fiberglass) surfboards. He also had a car, which was very helpful. His skills with GRP and carpentry would prove extremely useful.

We installed an Aries windvane to make the boat self-steering, made a bottled gas locker on deck to replace the dangerous one inside the cabin, reinforced the deck under the mizzen (aft) mast, added two more cockpit drains, installed a radar reflector, and modified the mainmast and rigging to take a second genoa (a large foresail). We bought provisions, and the boat was finally ready.

The workers and shopkeepers in St. Helier came by with their tabs, and I wrote checks from our Lloyd's bank account. David thought we needed dry ice to keep our meat supply cold, so just before we departed, we waited for a huge truck to unload its supply of meat and give us a block of dry ice. It was September 18, 1984, just days before the dreaded equinox.

I looked forward to battling the elements and imagined myself as Spencer Tracy at the wheel in *Captains Courageous.* I had read about the passage and the danger of becoming embayed (trapped) in Biscay Bay should we visit the French coast. However, David wanted to stop at the lovely French village of Camaret-sur-Mer. He was not concerned about becoming trapped, and since he was an experienced sailor, I deferred to his judgment.

After one night in the postcard-pretty village (my first experience of continental Europe) we headed into the Bay of Biscay and the Atlantic Ocean. The wind picked up and continued to build. Four separate gales were predicted over the next few days. We sailed as close to the wind as possible, hoping to make the Finisterre light at the end of the bay in four days without tacking. The seas rose, the motion and crashing of the boat increased, and the wind began to howl. I was finally getting started on an adventurous new life!

The bow plowed into the waves, sending water cascading over the length of the boat. During the night watch, my Wyoming blood got the best of me. I yelled like a cowboy on a bucking bronco, but the noise of the wind and sea completely drowned my "yahoos." I doubt Pam would have been as thrilled as I was.

Although Gary was used to being at sea in such conditions, he was concerned. From his spot in the forward berth, he could see the bulkheads jump as they broke away from the fiberglass hull when the bow oil-canned (flexed) with each pounding wave. He feared the boat might collapse. We woke David, who was not concerned. I was excited and too ignorant to grasp the seriousness of our situation, so poor Gary worried alone.

A crack like a rifle shot shook the boat, and the foresail flogged like a flag in a hurricane. The force of the wind on the sail had torn the winch off and catapulted both winch and mount into the sea. We jerry-rigged the sheet to another winch and fell off the wind to relieve pressure on the sails and reduce the pounding that was breaking the boat apart.

During the fourth night, we strained to see the Finisterre light. I will never forget my relief when I saw it twinkling in the distance, signaling the spot we could finally turn south and away from the eye of the wind. Years later, while walking the Camino de Santiago, my arrival on foot at this lighthouse at the end of the earth meant more to me than my arrival at the cathedral in Santiago.

We cleared into Spain at the village of Baiona on the afternoon of September 24. I was anxious to use the long-neglected

Spanish I had learned as a Peace Corps Volunteer in Colombia in the 1960s. As the boat came to the dock, a fellow looked like he was waiting to take a line. I threw him one and asked him in Spanish to tie it off. After I jumped ashore, I noticed he still held the line. Had I lost my Spanish? I took the rope, tied it off, and talked to him again very slowly. He replied, *"Je ne parle pas espagnol!"* He was a Frenchman looking for a ride back to France.

David, Gary, and I cleared in, walked through the town, and enjoyed long-awaited beers in a cozy bar. Neither Gary nor David spoke Spanish, and although mine was rusty, I could ask questions, conduct necessary business, and get us where we wanted to go. After our evening meal, Gary and David headed to shore, looking for a good time and leaving me, the old (mid-forties) married man, alone on the boat. "Don't expect us back tonight!"

I thought I'd look around, too. Baiona was a beautiful little village, and aside from the brief stop in France, it was my first experience of continental Europe. I found myself in the same bar again and chatted with some Spanish fishermen—young kids like Gary and David. They invited me to go with them in their car, and I went along without knowing where they were going. We stopped at a discotheque in the countryside that may also have been a source of drugs. The eyeballs of one of my companions started rolling in opposite directions.

The fishermen were having a good time, but I began to long for the boat and bed. However, they drove further into the country, searching for some *vino verde* (green wine) from a place that one of them knew. One had passed out in the back seat by the time we arrived at what looked like a shabby farmhouse by the side of the road. The eastern sky was beginning to lighten as we knocked at the door, which, to my surprise, opened at once. We sat on low three-legged stools around an equally low table in a dirt-floored room. The woman who brought a jug of wine and bowls told us the wine was "fresh." My companions put spoonfuls of sugar in their bowls, but I didn't think that was the proper way to drink wine. However, after one sip, I, too, added sugar to make the vinegary bite palatable.

When the jug of *vino verde* was finished, my new buddies proposed a cookout with the fish they were carrying in the trunk of the car. Exhausted, I begged off, saying my crew would be worried about me. The fellows wanted to see the inside of a yacht, so I invited them to stop by the boat the next day (and they did).

When I stepped on board the boat at six in the morning, Gary and David accosted me.

"Where have you been?"

I had to laugh. They had told me not to worry, but when I, the old man, stayed out late, they scolded me like the parents of an errant teenager. I grinned because I had made connections during our first night in Spain, leaving the two "stay-out-of-my-way" kids to worry. The little night out with the boys made me feel young and independent. I engaged with local people and moved out of my comfort zone. I wanted experiences like this for the whole family. I wrote a detailed account of my little adventure to Pam, hoping she would find it enticing.

We made quick, temporary repairs to the loosened bulkheads, and I bought a winch in nearby Vigo to replace the one lost in Biscay Bay. We built a temporary wooden mount for it and sailed south to Portugal, where we entered the Rio Douro at Porto. David had been there before and knew how to negotiate the river's bar. We tied up to the river wall in the heart of town, just downstream from the double-truss Luis I railway bridge designed by Eiffel (of the tower fame) across the river from the Sandeman Port warehouse.

David was related to the founders and owners of the Sandeman port and sherry business, one of the oldest and most prominent in the country, and he wanted to visit the winery. The door was locked when the three of us arrived, so David pushed the buzzer.

"Who is it?" came a voice on the intercom.

"David Sandeman."

"Oh! Just a moment."

Minutes later, the door swung open, revealing the entire office staff lined up to greet us. The staff manager looked at us, puzzled.

"Who did you say you are?"

"David Sandeman—I am related to the owners."

"Oh! The president of the company is also named David Sandeman, and we thought we were receiving a surprise visit from him."

We were welcomed with laughter and invited to take a private tour. I had never visited a winery before, so I found the processes and distinctions among the various wines fascinating. One barrel was about 200 years old, and although its wine was no longer considered drinkable, tiny amounts were added to flavor certain special wines.

After the wine tasting, we made our way back across the bridge to *Jacana*. Porto's ancient, tile-roofed buildings climbed the hills along steep, narrow streets that begged to be explored. I went alone because David and Gary wanted to visit the English Club rather than go for a walk. Relieved as I was that Pam had not been on the stormy trip across Biscay Bay, now I wished she was with me. She, too, would have been entranced by this picturesque old city. I struggled to capture my feelings in a letter, but Writing for Engineers, my only college English course, failed me.

When we cast off to head out to sea, a local fellow looked down at us and said, "The wind is blowing up the river." Since we were using the engine, I didn't think that mattered. When I translated for Gary and David, they shrugged, not knowing the significance of the remark either. We held close to one side as we headed toward the bar at the mouth of the river. There was no room for error. David was at the helm, and I was below when I saw him through the companionway hatch turn pale and exclaim, "Oh, my God!"

Suddenly the boat was under water, engulfed by a huge wave. It hit with a thud, almost knocking me off my feet. The engine hesitated and almost quit, which would have put us into the wall in seconds. Another wave hit, but not so hard. David thought we were goners, then the engine sputtered back to life, taking us over the bar. Had the engine died, it would have been catastrophic. At least a foot of water filled the mostly enclosed cockpit, and several stanchions had bent 40 degrees. I wish I had seen that wave, as well as felt it.

I learned that I should ask questions when someone tells me something about the wind that I don't understand. The Oporto bar was notorious when the wind was against the current. I later learned to expect danger at any river bar in similar conditions. David wrote in the logbook, "Very rough over the bar in S or W winds. Not advised."

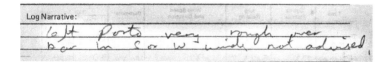

Chapter 3

Canary Island Interlude

October–November 1984

If at first, you don't succeed, try, try again.

—TRADITIONAL

We arrived in the Canary Islands on October 5. David returned home to Jersey, and Gary and I spent the next five weeks fiberglassing the forward bulkheads that had broken loose in the gale and installing new stainless steel winch mounts to avoid losing winches in another storm. We straightened the stanchions bent by the wave at Porto and reinforced an attachment that controlled the rudder.

Although these projects kept me busy, I had plenty of time to ponder why I was alone on a small island in the Atlantic Ocean covered by dust blown from the Sahara Desert.

Once before, I had upended my life to pursue a passion. As an undergraduate engineering student, I gave up my scholarships and quit school in my senior year. I joined the Peace Corps in Colombia. Two years later, I returned to school and changed my major to philosophy, a choice that disappointed my working-class family. Engineering was a respected, lucrative profession, but what good was a degree in philosophy? They would have been aghast to see me now.

When I returned to school, I met Pam, who struggled through a logic class despite earning a Phi Beta Kappa key. Already smitten, I volunteered to tutor her. We married when I was in graduate school, and she supported me by waitressing while I acquired a Ph.D. in philosophy.

After the anxious years of job-hunting and the arrival of our son Jake, Pam and I were eager to settle down. There were hundreds of applicants, even for temporary, one-year appointments. I got a couple of those before finally landing a permanent teaching position at South Dakota State University. Pam was happy, as she later wrote, to have a cellar, firmly, permanently under her feet, "the one thing that could never be put on a truck and moved cross-country."

I enjoyed teaching philosophy. I approached it as an intellectual puzzle. A few students enjoyed this game, but most did not, which was okay with me. Then, David Nelson, my South Dakota colleague, convinced me that philosophy was important for everyone, especially those least inclined to enjoy it. So, I tried to reach the students who fell asleep in the back rows of my classes. However, in the process, I lost the interest of the few students who had once made teaching a pleasure. I began to feel like an imposter. I did more preaching than teaching.

Besides my frustration with the university, Pam and I felt confined by small-town South Dakota. We did not want our boys to grow up thinking that living well meant getting all the material things they wanted. They were influenced by the other children's materialistic, racist, sexist, and homophobic notions. They thought they needed $100 pairs of athletic shoes to fit in, and they were probably right.

I was influenced by Henry David Thoreau, who preached,

Kent in Peace Corps 1963–65, top; Pam and Kent wedding picture, 1966.

"Simplify, simplify, simplify!" and E. F. Schumacher, who argued that *Small is Beautiful*. Dismayed by American materialism and consumerism, I wanted a simpler life that made a small footprint on the earth. My ideas came not only from books but from experience, especially from my years as a Peace Corps volunteer in the remote village of Carcasí in the mountains of Colombia. I wanted Pam and the boys to experience the changes of perspective that come from living in other cultures. Like Socrates, I believe an unexamined life is not worth living.

—

I was heartened that Pam was returning to me and our grand experiment despite her mother's disapproval and her discomfort at sea. Now that I was an experienced sailor, she was willing to try life on the boat again.

I was eager for Pam and Andy to return, and I wanted to look my best when they arrived. Pam had cut my hair for 20 years, and I had now been without my barber for several months. So, I sat down on the foredeck and attacked my hair with a pair of scissors. I didn't anticipate how difficult it would be to look in a mirror and cut. I did my best, trimming the back of my head entirely by feel. Gary smiled oddly when he saw me but didn't say anything.

At the small airport, I saw the silhouettes of the arrivals behind a window. Andy appeared to be accompanied by a tall, slender teenager with a crew cut. I could not see Pam. Where was she? Then, I recognized her. She had cut her hair with clippers in preparation for life on a boat in the tropics. After almost squeezing the life out of each other with hugs, we backed off for a good look.

Before I could say anything about her hair (or lack thereof), she laughed, "What have you done to your hair?"

Pam handed me the box full of Andy's schoolbooks, several duffle bags, and her purse, which held a two-speed, self-tailing bronze winch, padded by her underwear. The winch was a match for the one I bought in Vigo. The expensive winches, additional airline tickets, and the numerous repairs on the boat made a large dent in our budget, but I anticipated that after these setbacks, our frugal life would begin.

I managed to get all the stuff to the rental car and wondered how Pam had made it through airports with her load. When we got back to the boat, one of the first things she did was even-up my hair. There was nothing I could do to hers.

The town of Puerto Rico on Gran Canaria was built to service Europeans on holiday. One week was German, and all the signs and notices were German. Subsequent weeks were Swedish, French, and English. Even the Senegalese kids hawking their wares on the streets switched languages from week to week. The area included a topless public beach and a waterslide that Andy figured out how to ride forever on one ticket.

The local markets and nearby towns had everything we needed. I bought small loaves of bread, milk, and a chunk of the best blue cheese ever in the early morning, then returned to the boat and woke Pam and Andy by unwrapping the blue cheese.

"Who died?" were the first English words I heard each day.

We adopted a stray gray tabby kitten. When Pam and Andy fed her, she decided to stay. She wandered at night but always returned by morning We named her "Canary Cat," or "CC" for short.

One day while the cat was hopping about on the boat, a voluptuous Swedish blond in a teeny bikini stopped on the dock and asked if the little kitten was ours. It was the first time she had acknowledged my existence, although I had been aware of hers for several weeks. She sometimes wore a bikini top with a thong, and sometimes she was topless with a bikini bottom. I waited for the day she came topless in the thong, but she never did.

She purred in her broad Swedish accent, "I want that cat—I must have it!"

I was about to reply, "Of course, anything you want—thank you so much for stopping to speak to me!"

But Pam was right there, seemingly immune to the Swedish charm.

"No. She's ours. Why do you want her?"

"Every night, your kitten comes to my boat and sleeps in my hair." She gave her head a toss to emphasize how great that was. "I don't think I will be able to sleep without her!"

Pam replied something like "rough rocks" and sent her on her way.

After Pam and Andy arrived, Gary told us he had to return to Jersey to care for his sick dog. He was too polite to tell us he had second thoughts about crossing the Atlantic with people as inexperienced as we were. So, we posted a notice at the local chandlery for a crewman. We wanted someone to take the third watch because ten-year-old Andy was too young.

Young men and women hung about the Canary docks, looking for a chance to crew and get passage to the Caribbean and beyond. We chose Jeremy, a young Englishman in his early twenties with no sailing experience. He wanted to cross the Atlantic and get to Brazil. Pam would have preferred someone with more experience, but she went along with my choice. I was afraid we would become mere passengers taking orders if we chose a more experienced sailor.

Jeremy was personable and willing to do what we needed, although Andy resented being treated like a little brother again. Unfortunately for all of us, Jeremy and Pam were both smokers. When we left the Canaries, they agreed to leave their cigarettes behind. Pam saw this as an opportunity to stop smoking. Unfortunately, Jeremy and Pam fed on each other's misery, and Pam never had a chance to think of herself as an ex-smoker. She was just a smoker out of cigarettes. I came to regret our choice of Jeremy for that reason because I, too, wanted her to quit.

—

Andy and Jeremy shared the aft cabin with two berths and a toilet accessed from the rear of the center cockpit. Pam and I slept in the forepeak's 'V' berth. The main 'head' with a toilet, shower (hot and cold pressure water), and a lavatory was located starboard, opposite a wardrobe between the forepeak and the salon/galley. The aft-facing chart table and instruments were starboard of the companionway, opposite the galley. One of the seats for the dining table was also used for the chart table. The settee converted into a double berth where Pam and I sometimes slept when we were at anchor. The four-cylinder, 36-horse-power diesel engine was located beneath the cockpit sole (floor).

Jacana had three fresh-water tanks, about 120 gallons, and one 40-gallon diesel fuel tank. We would bathe using a bucket of salt water with just a quick rinse in fresh water. We would run the diesel engine mainly to charge the batteries and when entering and leaving a port. We figured we could make the fuel last since we cooked with butane and used kerosene lanterns for light. We wouldn't run the engine often. We would have books to read and a cassette player for music.

—

We waited for what we hoped would be the worst of the hurricane season to pass and said goodbye to the solid earth beneath our feet, the lovely blue cheese, the fresh fruits and vegetables, and the Swedish family next door who helped cast off our lines. We set forth into the Atlantic with our adopted kitten and small crew of woefully inexperienced sailors. I wasn't afraid or nervous, but maybe I should have been.

Chapter 4

The Atlantic Crossing

November–December 1984

To young men contemplating a voyage, I'd say go.
—JOSHUA SLOCUM

We left the Canary Islands on November 14, 1984, setting out for the island of Antigua, a common destination for British sailors, over 3,000 miles away. Our instructions for finding the trade winds that would blow us to the Caribbean were, "Sail south until the butter melts; then turn right."

We set out in light airs in Gran Canaria's wind shadow, having put up all the sail we could carry. We were relaxing into easy sailing when we reached the end of the wind shadow, and a first stiff gust caught us unprepared.

I shouted, "We need to reduce sail, NOW!"

With Andy at the helm, Jeremy, Pam, and I scrambled to the pitching foredeck, tripping over each to take down the genoa (large foresail) and put a reef in (shorten) the mainsail. In the confusion, someone let go of the halyard, the line we needed to raise the working jib (small foresail). The halyard flew up to the top of the mast, where it stuck in the block (pulley). Somebody would have to go up in the bosun's chair to bring it down.

Because I was the only one who knew how to navigate, Pam and Jeremy refused to let me go. They couldn't survive without me. So, we tied Jeremy into the chair and raised him to the top of the mast. Swinging wildly, hanging on for dear life, it was a baptism into sailing he said he would never forget. He freed the halyard from the block, and we all breathed a sigh of relief when he returned to the deck.

I was excited and invigorated, but when I looked at Pam, her eyes said, "What have I gotten myself into? Let me off this boat!"

Our Atlantic crossing had begun.

Both Pam and Andy were prone to seasickness. Pam barfed over the side for the first few days but never missed a watch. Andy stayed in the aft cabin and only showed his head when he came up to vomit. He could not keep food down and stayed in his berth for several days. We gave him water with electrolyte tablets, but it came back up as fast as the food. After those painful first days, both Pam and Andy recovered and said they'd never felt better.

For most of the passage, the gentle trade winds pushed us to the Caribbean. Our days became routine. With the self-steering windvane, we did not need to stay at the helm. When we were all up and about during the day, we didn't keep formal watches, although one of us kept an eye on the compass and logged our speed and course each hour. We made no adjustments to the sails for days and wallowed downwind at 4-5 knots (5-6 miles per hour). The back-and-forth motion of a boat sailing downwind is called the "downwind wang." Most sailors detest that motion, but we didn't know better. We got used to the rhythm of the 20-30 degree off-vertical swing. It accompanied everything we did.

We waited until the companionway hatch was vertical, took a quick step, grasped a handhold, waited for the boat to right itself, then took the next step and handhold. Like automatons, we moved at a synchronized, rhythmic pace. We could read and write comfortably by wedging ourselves into tight places.

We organized our days around navigation, watches, meals, and Andy's schooling. Jeremy, Pam, and I divided the three-hour night watches, rotating so nobody was stuck with the same one every night. We each had three hours on and six hours off.

At dusk, we turned on the tricolored light at the top of the mainmast to make us visible. The nights were black, except for the moon, the stars, and a tiny red compass light in the cockpit. The night watches were pleasant, with Canary Cat purring on our laps and soft music from the radio-cassette player. Barber's "Adagio for Strings" was a favorite, and when I hear it now, I think of those peaceful times at sea.

The gentle rolling motion, the cat purring, the water gurgling, the soft music, and the heavenly lights gave me a sense of peace and comfort that made the world we had left behind seem crazy and chaotic. We stayed in the cockpit, going below each hour to grab a snack and log the boat's speed and heading. There was no place I would rather be. I enjoyed watching the sun rise and set. In the morning, my head filled with theories of celestial navigation, I sometimes visualized the sun resting while the horizon dropped beneath it, giving me a sensation of pitching forward, like going over the top on a Ferris wheel.

Andy and I were perfectly happy during the crossing, and Pam and Jeremy were too, except for yearning for cigarettes. Cooking, eating, navigating, schooling, sailing, reading, bathing, and napping filled our days.

We had cartons of long-life milk to put on our breakfast cereal. Unwashed, unrefrigerated eggs kept for months. A dense, twice-baked German bread from the Canary Islands stayed fresh for the whole crossing. We used dried and canned goods to make casseroles, stews, and tuna sandwiches. A pressure cooker took care of dried beans. I enjoyed spooning canned peas out of the can for a snack, but nobody else did. Potatoes and carrots kept well. We ate canned fruit, chicken, tuna, beef, pork, ham, and butter. We bought enough food in the Canaries to last three or four months, much longer than our anticipated three-to-four-week crossing.

During the crossing, I worked with Andy on history and math. After a couple of hours, I would be tired. Then Pam worked with him on English, art, and geography. When she'd had enough, I drilled him on his multiplication tables or started another lesson.

Pam and I were worn out after a solid day of teaching, but we didn't think about how Andy was faring with only a short break for lunch. Then we found a note on the back of an envelope waiting to be mailed to friends.

"Help! I am being held hostage on a school ship by two teachers!"

After that, we decided to add a couple of short recesses to the day.

Schooling Andy was one of the best things we did. Andy found rote memory difficult. He had been placed in a remedial math class at school, which surprised me because I knew he had a good mathematical mind. He could figure things out, and when I explained math problems, he caught on amazingly quickly. He probably had a more natural aptitude for math than Jake, who whizzed through his classes.

I discovered Andy did not know his multiplication tables, so I began to drill him. It was painfully difficult at first. I taught him all the tricks I knew. Eventually, through steady drilling, he learned. By the end of the year, he knew his tables well. While working with Andy, I realized I had some of the same problems myself. I had always been embarrassed to admit that I didn't learn the alphabet until I was in the 10th grade and that learning my students' names was difficult. I realized that my father had suffered from the same problem. He was a typographer for the Sheridan, Wyoming, newspaper, and although he spent his life putting words together in type, he was a poor speller.

To augment Andy's math lessons, I made him the backup

navigator. In these years before GPS, satellite communication, and electronic navigation, we used the same tools sailors had used since the eighteenth century. Each day we took sun sights at 10:00, 12:00, and 03:00 local time and reduced the sights by using the *Sight Reduction Tables for Air Navigation* and a current ephemeris to determine our position. I had two sextants: a good bronze one and an inexpensive plastic one for backup. Andy noted the time when I took a sight with the good sextant; then, I did the same for him when he used the plastic one. Afterwards, we went below to reduce our sights independently, looking up seven and eight-digit numbers in tables and doing lots of arithmetic.

Andy with sextant

We never used a calculator, and our fixes were usually close. The one time we differed wildly, Andy was right, and I was wrong. He was triumphant! It was the best mistake I ever made. I wish I could say I had done it intentionally.

Andy and I marked our positions on a chart of the Atlantic Ocean that was folded in half to fit on the chart table. With each sight, we moved about a quarter of an inch. We celebrated by opening a can of ham on the day we reached the fold, halfway across the ocean, and called the day "Crease-mas." When we turned the chart over, we focused on going toward the New World rather than away from Europe. Until Crease-mas, we measured our progress by how far we had come, but afterward, by how little distance remained. The occasion was much like life itself. In our early years, we note and celebrate our accomplishments, but by midlife, we begin to focus on what remains to be done and on how little time is left in which to do it.

We were becalmed several times. Without wind, we simply bobbed and swayed in the waves. There was no point in motoring because there was nowhere we could reach with the amount of fuel we carried. During one of those times, we encountered the first and only ship of our crossing, a Korean freighter several miles away. We radioed for a time check and received an answer giving the correct time within a minute or two. We concluded that this ship did not rely, as we did, on celestial navigation that required accuracy within seconds.

We were glad the ship had not come a couple of hours earlier and witnessed our only attempt to fly the spinnaker (a large, often colorful, balloon-like foresail that will move a boat forward in light airs). I had never set a spinnaker, and Jeremy, of course, had no experience. One of our books explained the procedure, so we gave it a try when the wind was dying.

As the boat swayed back and forth, the spinnaker partially filled, then collapsed, tangling the lines and wrapping its halyard around the forestay, so it was impossible to lower. To untangle the mess, we started the engine and drove in circles until the halyard unwound. We put the spinnaker back into its bag, where it served as a bed for the cat for the duration of the voyage. It was unfortunate that we gave up on the spinnaker because it would have increased our speed.

Shortly after the Korean freighter passed, a small sailboat hove over the horizon. Because it was motoring, it gradually closed the distance between us. The crew radioed from half a mile away and asked to come alongside. We were delighted since we had seen no one since leaving the Canaries.

It was a French hard-chine (hard-edged) steel boat, not much bigger than *Jacana*, operated by an older man and four younger ones. They were out of cooking gas. Did we have any to spare? I wondered why anyone would take off across the Atlantic without plenty of fuel for cooking, but we had more than enough, so we strung a line between the boats and exchanged a full bottle for an empty one. They seemed ill-prepared to be in the middle of the Atlantic. They may have gone out for a day's sail, drunk too much cognac, and decided to set out across the ocean.

"What can we give you for *le gaz*?" the older man asked.

"Thank you, but I think we have everything we need."

As we spoke, I noticed Pam and Jeremy's shadows. Behind my back, they pantomimed their desperate desire for cigarettes, but I ignored their silent pleas and, relishing my role as captain, denied we had any needs. After this encounter, Pam and Jeremy never stopped talking about how good a cigarette would be when we reached Antigua. The Frenchmen sent over a half bottle of cognac before we dropped the lines; I didn't object to that.

Jeremy wanted to go swimming mid-ocean. So, one day when we were becalmed, he tied a line around his waist, just in case a breeze came up. He jumped into the water, took a few strokes, and made a couple of shallow dives. He was nervous, although he was a good swimmer. No doubt, he thought about the thousands of feet of water below him, the great distance from land, and the mysterious creatures in the sea. He didn't go very far from the boat and didn't stay long, but we were relieved when he climbed back on board.

Minutes later, a huge swordfish, as long as the boat, emerged from the deep, exactly where he had been swimming. The fish lay on its side inspecting the four of us with one perfectly round, unblinking eye, impressing upon me that I was trespassing in a fantastic, strange world. I was suddenly ashamed of the audacity that had gotten me there in such ignorance. I knew that angry swordfish occasionally attacked wooden boats, driving their swords through the planking on their hulls. Were we in danger? I had no idea. The swordfish lost interest in us and, after a few minutes, slowly sank into the deep. Jeremy decided one swim was enough, and no one else wanted to take a dip.

One of the joys of the passage was the return of a breeze after a calm spell. When we were becalmed for an hour or a day or more, we sheeted the mainsail hard to the center to dampen the effect of the swells that could vigorously rock the boat and cause the sail to whip and slam from one side to the other. The boom would jerk, and the running rigging shake and bang. Although the boat was becalmed, the noises and commotion were wearing. When the breeze returned, the sail filled, the rigging grew taut, and the boat moved forward. Then the only sound was the water reassuringly gurgling along the hull. We felt we'd awakened from a bad dream.

Canary Cat adapted to the boat remarkably well. She delighted in the flying fish we found stranded on the deck in the mornings. She perched on the point of the bow watching the dolphins and grew so excited we feared she would dive overboard. We made her a small harness and tether and looped it to a jack line, so she could move around on the deck and yet be tied to the boat. Alas, we were too generous in giving her places to wander.

The afternoon before we made landfall, Andy and I predicted that the person on watch would see the lights of Antigua off the port bow at 3:00 am. That night, Pam was on watch, and within minutes of three am on December 7, she woke us, calling, "Land ho!" We crowded onto the bow to see the faint twinkle of lights of what I hoped was Antigua. It was the first confirmation that our navigation was correct after sailing for over three weeks without sight of land.

After a little celebratory shouting and, in my case, a Columbus-like sigh of relief, we returned to the cockpit, but not before Pam noticed the cat's tether stretched tightly over the side. She pulled in the line, and sure enough, CC had gone over. The line was long enough to reach the water, and she had been dragged until she drowned.

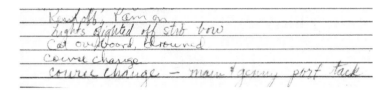

The elation of making landfall turned into guilt and remorse at the loss of the sweet little kitten who had been such delightful company during the crossing. We vowed we would never keep another pet on board, despite having lived with cats since the first days of our marriage.

We remembered our old cat Jessica, who was like our child before we had children. She came to live with us just after we were married and was still with us when we prepared to leave Brookings. By then, she was too old and weak to bring along or give away. What would we do? Then, just weeks before we left, she died in her sleep. It was her last and kindest favor to us. We buried her in the garden with a ceramic plaque Pam had made with her name.

The people who bought our house had a young daughter also named Jessica. Imagine their surprise when they discovered the buried plaque bearing their daughter's name! The acquisition or loss of a cat has always seemed to signal a change in our lives.

Antigua's high hills gradually emerged from the darkness – our first Caribbean Island! We circled to the south, giving the surrounding reef a wide berth before dropping anchor in English Harbor. It was the first time I entered a harbor on my own and Pam's first time anchoring the boat, although she had already sailed across an ocean! The scent of land and busy sights and sounds assailed our senses after the peace and isolation of the ocean crossing.

Customs and immigration officials came aboard even before I had the sails stowed. I went below to fill in the forms, which took ten minutes. Then, while I put on the mainsail cover, Pam and Jeremy raced to pump up the inflatable dinghy. Before I could say, "Wait for me!" they rowed toward shore, marooning Andy and me on the boat.

Upon their return an hour later, they each held two cigarettes, one in each hand, laughing and flaunting them in derision. Judging by their behavior, they also had more than one cold beer in their bellies. They thought themselves funny and were not apologetic about leaving us behind. I figured Pam was paying me back for sending the French boat away without cigarettes. Their desertion struck me as funny, but I deeply regretted that Pam had not taken advantage of her opportunity to quit smoking.

Chapter 5

The New World

December 1984–February 1985

Oh, brave new world / That has such people in it!
—WILLIAM SHAKESPEARE, *The Tempest*, 5:1

We were full of ourselves after our Atlantic crossing. We anchored amid the many boats in English Harbor and assumed we fit right in. We had unknowingly arrived during Nicholson's Boat Week when expensive yachts kept pristine by hired crews came from all over the Caribbean to show off to prospective chartering agents.

We walked through the 18th-century ruins of Admiral Nelson's dockyards, completed chores, and thought ourselves among a fraternity of fellow cruisers. Then we climbed to the top of a hill high above the harbor and tried to pick out *Jacana* among the boats below.

After a long time, Pam whispered, "I think I see her."

"Where?"

"Right there behind the blue-hulled schooner."

I saw the schooner's dinghy but no *Jacana*. Then it dawned on me. That was no dinghy; it was *Jacana*! We were as out of place at Nicholson's Boat Week as a mouse at an elephant's convention. We had no idea how small we were compared to the other boats. The people we assumed to be other cruisers were professional crews. We may have been the only cruising boat in the harbor. We had anticipated sitting around a table exchanging stories of our crossing with fellow cruisers, but nobody paid attention to us.

Jeremy left us for another boat, hoping to get to Brazil. He had been a fine crew member and companion, but I wasn't sorry to see him go. I looked forward to sailing with the family and Jake's arrival in January.

We island-hopped west toward the Panama Canal and our rendezvous with Jake in the Virgin Islands. Our first stop after Antigua was Nevis. We soon learned why we were the only boat anchored off Charlestown. The waves wrapped around the island and set up a motion in the open roadstead that discouraged most cruisers. But we were too ignorant to know that anchoring was not supposed to be that way. We put up the lee cloths that kept us from being bounced out of our berths, just as if we were at sea.

A big sign on the dock announced: "Birthplace of Alexander Hamilton," a fact we had not known and were delighted to learn. We cleared in and wandered through the open-air market, where we learned about a small cooperative pottery near a village named Newcastle. Since Pam had been a potter and was a native of New-castle, Wyoming, we thought we ought to visit. We waited for a bus in the square.

The "bus" turned out to be an International Travelall (like one we had once owned) with two wooden bench seats running its length. It drove around the square, stopping for anyone who waved. When it got to the three of us, I thought it was full.

"Not at all," the driver said.

Everybody squished down to fit us on, and the bus picked up two more passengers. I was handed a baby, and we lifted our feet when someone scooted lumber down the middle. An elderly woman got on with three or four cases of empty bottles and jars that the driver stacked on the roof. When the bus stopped to let her off, I helped others get the jars and bundles to her door. The friendly passengers asked where we were from, how we got there, and why. Upon our arrival in Newcastle, the driver directed us to the pottery and instructed us to meet him at four o'clock for the ride back.

The pottery was closed, but we happened upon a quiet seaside resort that had once been a colonial estate. We bought bottles of cold ginger ale at the veranda bar and sat on the beach to drink them while Andy waded and made sandcastles. We lost track of time and realized we had missed the bus. We walked along the road toward town, and half an hour later, the bus showed up.

The driver had come looking for us. He was on his way around the island. Would we mind going along? Mind? Not at all. We were eager to see more of Nevis. The drive over the island's central ridge reminded me of the rolling foothills of the Big Horn Mountains in Wyoming, where I grew up. A few small houses and the occasional horse or cow dotted the landscape. Except for the ocean surrounding us, we could have been in the inland American West.

We arrived at the neighboring island of St. Kitts to find one other boat. *Hirta* was a British, turn-of-the-century Bristol Channel Pilot Cutter sailed by Tom Cunliffe[1] and his wife, Rosalind (Ros). We rowed the dinghy over for a look at this unusual boat and ended up spending a couple of days with Ros and Tom. Their daughter, a little younger than Andy, was the only child we'd met so far. Tom, a great storyteller, had sailed a Camper Nicholson 38 like ours.

"Do you still carry your cooking gas bottles under the sink?" he asked.

---

1. Tom Cunliffe is a well-known sailor, writer, and storyteller. For more about his accomplishments and adventures, see his website, entertaining and practical short YouTube videos, and Wikipedia, "Tom Cunliffe." Last Modified 17 January 2022.

"No," I replied. "I moved them to a locker I built on the deck."

"Wise move!"

Tom and Ros once had a job in Brazil taking care of a Nic 38. One day, when they were getting the boat ready for its owner and his guests, Tom decided to replace the cooking gas bottle. Unfortunately, when he tightened the regulator, the valve broke off, emptying the entire contents of the bottle into the boat. Had there been an open flame, the boat could have exploded. That didn't happen, but how could the heavier-than-air butane gas be removed from the bilges and other places where the wind could not blow it out? Tom flooded the bilges with seawater, which forced the gas to rise to a level where he could bail it out through the companionway with a bucket.

While he was bailing, the owner and his guests arrived on the nearby shore, shocked to see the boat half sunk and Tom madly bailing with an empty bucket. As Ros rowed to pick up the visitors, she ran explanations through her head, none of which seemed quite right. It all seemed hilariously funny, especially since they had unwisely consumed a bottle of wine with their supper.

Hirta was one of the few authentic Bristol Channel Pilot Cutters still afloat. They had found her in Scotland and put her in deep sea order. When they sailed into the harbor of her old home port in the Bristol Channel, 60 years since she had last been there, an elderly fellow sitting on the dock identified her by her original name. The town dismissed school so the children could see the boat.

We explored the old fort on Brimstone Hill with Tom and Ros and enjoyed dinner at an Indian restaurant that Tom knew. It was wonderful to meet another cruising family, which helped us feel less isolated and unsure of ourselves.

—

We woke late on our first morning at Gustavia on St. Barts, a short hop from St. Kitts, puzzled to find ourselves alone. The harbor had been full of boats when we'd arrived the evening before. Thinking this strange, we dinghied to the port captain's office, which was closed. A weather forecast in French was posted in the window, and we could read enough to understand that an out-of-season hurricane was pointing our way. Four or five boats were washed up on shore, left over from a storm that had hit the island a month earlier when we had been in the Canaries waiting out the hurricane season. We realized we were not anchored in a safe place.

Because most of the other boats had left, we found a spot in the more protected inner harbor, where we tied the boat to anchors, trees, and buildings. One of the few remaining boaters told us that the others had moved to the lagoon at St. Maarten, just a few miles away, which was considered safe. But it was too late for us to leave now. Fortunately, the storm veered away, although we now felt vulnerable in our new floating home. Ten years later, Hurricane Luis would hit St. Maarten directly, sinking almost every boat anchored in that "perfectly safe" lagoon.

Once the danger of the storm passed, we did a little Christmas shopping and decorated a palm frond with homemade paper chains and brightly foil-wrapped chocolates that we ate before they melted.

We stopped briefly in St. Maarten before facing the notorious forty-mile Anegada (oh-my-god-a) passage to the Virgin Islands. We made the dreaded crossing at night with an unexpectedly light breeze and hardly enough wind to fill our sails. We began to think the dangers of sailing were exaggerated. How little we knew!

We nonchalantly headed up the rather long channel into the harbor of Charlotte Amalie, St. Thomas, U.S. Virgin Islands. When a large cruise ship came up behind us, I pulled to the side of the channel and motored in a circle to let it go ahead. I was unfamiliar with the harbor and had not carefully studied the charts, so I had no idea where the cruise ship was going. When it was a couple of cables (500 yards) ahead of us, it turned sideways and appeared to stop.

When we caught up to the ship, I noticed a group of anchored boats in the distance, so I headed straight toward them, crossing in front of the enormous ship that was now twenty yards away. Then I saw it was making a small bow wave. The vessel had not stopped! The bow loomed overhead as we cut across its path, barely slipping beneath it. Workers in a powerboat roared by, shouting things I was thankful I couldn't hear. Had I studied the chart more thoroughly, I would have known the ship had not stopped but was making a right turn into the cruise ship dock.

What a way to finish this momentous year! It was December 31, 1984, my forty-fourth birthday. I'd left my job and South Dakota's brutal winters behind, bought a boat, learned to sail it with some competence, and successfully crossed the Atlantic. Pam and Andy were back after their temporary desertion, and Jake would be with us soon. What could possibly stop us now? I looked forward to a fantastic 1985.

Playing pirate

I woke each morning eager to see what the day would bring. I basked in the sun, swam in the clear Caribbean water, and no longer stewed over the world's problems or the fate of my reluctant students. I was responsible only for those in my little world of the boat.

We arrived in St. Thomas a week before Jake. I had not seen him for almost five months and Pam for nearly three. So far, our life on the boat had been disjointed and hardly a family venture. I hoped that was about to change.

Jake came with our friends Hugh and Diana Randall on January 5, 1985. He and I had never been separated before. Even when Pam flew ahead during some of our moves, Jake accompanied me in the rental truck. I potty-trained him in a U-Haul during our move from Reno to South Dakota. But now, he was glum and unresponsive to my enthusiasm. Maybe he was missing the good times with the three moms back in Brookings. Or perhaps he felt overlooked with so many people crowded on our small boat.

We took our guests on a fun two-week sail through the Virgin Islands. We danced at Rudy's on Jost Van Dyke, sailed across the Anegada passage and back again, and visited St. Maarten, Île Fourche, and St. Barts, where we restocked our now depleted liquor cabinet. During these weeks, Jake was unusually subdued. He stepped on a sea urchin at the Baths in the British Virgin Islands and drove several painful spines deep into his foot.

It was Super Bowl Sunday when we returned Hugh and Diana to the St. Thomas airport after two weeks of good times. We took the dinghy ashore in Lindbergh Bay and walked our guests to the terminal, where we said goodbye.

I knew Jake wanted to see the game. He loved football, kept track of all the professional teams, and knew the names of the players and even the numbers on their jerseys. He had an incredible memory for trivia. So, we took the boat around the corner to Charlotte Amalie, where I hoped to find the game televised. Pam and Andy stayed on *Jacana*, and Jake and I left in plenty of time to find a bar with a television.

We noticed a conference room with rows of chairs facing a large television screen in a hotel next to the dinghy dock. This must be for the Super Bowl! We grabbed seats in the front row and waited. As game time approached, the room filled with cigar smoke and loud, beer-drinking men. Indeed, this was the place! Jake was quiet, and we both felt awkward, wondering if it was okay for us to be there.

At last, the game between the Miami Dolphins and the San Francisco 49ers started. I knew Jake felt out of place and missed the comfort of our old home, but he didn't want to miss the game. At half-time, a fellow started a sports quiz. The first question stumped the audience. Which Miami Dolphin player caught a career-high number of passes in 1968 and made All-Pro that year? The loudmouths who had been showing off their football knowledge shouted out names

"Mercury Morris!"

"Jim Kiick!"

"Larry Csonka!"

They must have named every player on the roster, but none were correct. As the room quieted, Jake tugged on my sleeve and whispered, "Karl Noonan"—a name I did not know. Because we were in the front row, and the fellow with the microphone was standing almost on my toes, he heard Jake.

"What's that? What did you say?"

He put the mike in Jake's face. With his head down, wishing he could disappear, Jake mumbled, "Karl Noonan."

"You're right! Come up here, young man!"

He almost lifted Jake out of the chair. He asked Jake who he was and where he was from. Then came prizes, including an official NFL T-shirt he assured us could not be purchased in any store. Jake was beaming.

Then the speaker said, "I would like you to meet this man."

A tall man walked up to Jake, shook his hand, and said, "My name is Karl Noonan."

He removed his Super Bowl championship ring and put it on Jake's finger.

"How does that feel?"

By now, Jake was so excited he could hardly talk. The Dolphins lost the game. I doubt Karl Noonan was pleased, but Jake was happy.

When Pam saw us return, she noticed Jake was so energized that he appeared to be riding on air above the dinghy. He was the happiest we had seen him since he joined us. I doubt any of his friends in Brookings enjoyed that Super Bowl more. When we packed up to move again ten years later, that old worn-out, too-small t-shirt was one of the items he chose to save.

Years later, when Pam and I were on the second boat, we were in Charlotte Amalie again at Super Bowl time. The hotel where Jake and I had watched the Super Bowl was now derelict from hurricane damage, so Pam and I watched the game at an outdoor bar on the grounds. We remembered that long-ago day and wrote to Jake about what we had done.

Sadly, the change in Jake after the Super Bowl was not permanent. He was eager to enter high school and play football with uniforms and all that good stuff. He resented being dragged away from his friends and saw himself as an innocent victim imprisoned on a 38-foot sailboat with only his parents and a little brother/cellmate for company.

The Sisyphean struggle we'd waged to break away had worn Pam down, but I still dreamed of the Pacific. It might take a bit longer for the others to fall in love with our new life, but I was sure that after a month or two of cruising, Jake's attitude would change, and we would head toward the Panama Canal as a family of enthusiastic and seasoned sailors.

When I began to read Pam's letter to Bill and Marie right after
she wrote it in February 1985, my delight in her enjoyment of our
adventure turned to dismay at its conclusion:

I still can't believe it, but this ole Wyoming girl with dust
and cactus in her soul made an Atlantic crossing in a small
sailboat. We reached Antigua on December 7, 1984, after
23 days at sea, and have spent the last two months cruising
north through Nevis, St. Christopher (St. Kitts), St.
Bartolomé (St. Barts), St. Martin, and the U.S. and British
Virgin Islands.
It is so lovely. I can't quite believe it all. I didn't think
the white sand beaches, palm trees, and underwater reef life
existed outside travel brochures or National Geographic
covers. Jake joined us the first part of January, and we're
having school by correspondence on board.
We're in Charlotte Amalie Harbor, St. Thomas, USVI,
awaiting parts from England for our self-steering vane. We
plan to head west to Puerto Rico, Hispaniola, Jamaica, Belize,
the Yucatan, and then north to either New Orleans or the
Florida Keys.
Once back on the U.S. mainland, we'll try to sell *Jacana*.
Jake is the wrong age (fourteen) for this venture—his school
and friends are just too important to him now—and we don't
think we could manage to make a living afloat and still do
the things we want to. Kent hedged his bets and took a year's
leave of absence from the university so we can go back. But
it's been a hell of a year—at least this half so far has been. It's
not been particularly comfortable, and I sometimes think
I'm developing an ulcer when we're navigating reef-infested
waters, but it's been worth it. (*Conclusion* of *Pam's Letter to
Bill and Marie Ray, Charlotte Amalie, St. Thomas, U.S. Virgin
Islands, February 4, 1985*)

I was shocked to learn that Pam had already decided to give up the boat. She loved much that we were doing and was proud of all we had accomplished. We had talked about Jake's discontent, but I didn't think we had made any decisions. Because I don't like confrontation, I didn't challenge her. I thought I could change her mind if I caught her on a good day. After all, we had a month or two of sailing to the west end of Jamaica, where we would have to decide whether to head south to Panama or west to Belize and home. So much could happen during that time!

Chapter 6

Disappointment

February–May 1985

Alea iacta est. (The die is cast)
—attributed to Julius Caesar

Charlotte Amalie was a good place to do schoolwork, and shopping was convenient. While we waited for a part to repair the windvane we'd somehow damaged, we hung our laundry on the rigging to dry, slung a hammock between the mast and the forestay to make a place where the boys could read and relax, and fly kites off the stern when the wind picked up. It was, all in all, a good catch-up time.

Once afternoon I noticed a middle-aged couple in a dinghy motoring slowly through the anchorage. They went by a couple of times, and I caught their eye the third time. They called out, "Do you take free food?" I was puzzled, but I invited them over.

They were getting ready to return their boat to a charter company and preferred to share their food with needy cruisers rather than give it back. We must have looked like the neediest boat in the anchorage. I was not flattered, but I hesitated to turn down free food. They had a freezer full of steaks, roasts, and ice cream, which we had not seen for months but could not take because we

Andy in Hammock with Kent and Pam

did not use the refrigerator. However, we did take two full dinghy loads of canned and packaged goods.

It was true that we were not like the other boats in the anchorage. We were not sailing for sport or pleasure, nor were we trying to make a living with our boat like those who ran charters. Our boat was our home: we were not taking an extended vacation but were trying to make a life of cruising.

We continued sailing west, island hopping. At Fajardo, Puerto Rico, we left the boat and took a bus to San Juan. The boys delighted in exploring El Morro, the old Spanish fort, and I kept hoping each good experience would bring Jake around.

I thought we would pay import duty on the boat when we cleared into Puerto Rico at the tiny island of Culebra, but the fellow who stamped our papers shrugged as if he did not know and did not care. When we arrived in Ponce a month later, I called the customs office on our radio late one afternoon and learned that if I didn't pay the duty immediately, they would impound our boat!

It was a long dinghy ride from our anchorage near the yacht club to the customs office, but if I didn't waste a second, I could get there before the office closed. The dinghy's fuel had not been topped up, but I couldn't contend with that now. I grabbed Andy to come along for the ride. There were derelicts hanging about the customs house, so I left Andy to watch the dinghy while I ran into the office.

"How long have you been in American waters?"

"I cleared in at Culebra on February 9."

"It's now March 9! Why haven't you paid your duty?"

I tried to explain and turned over my English bill of sale and the papers from the American Embassy in London. But, despite my valiant effort to get there, it was too late in the day for them to process the paperwork.

"Come back tomorrow. Your boat's impounded, and don't move it."

I returned to Andy and the dinghy, and we headed back to *Jacana*.

About halfway there, we ran out of gas in a strong outgoing current. I rowed, but one of the oarlocks was worn, making a difficult situation worse. Could I reach one of the big ships docked along the edge of the harbor before the current had its way with us? I had never rowed so hard in my life.

I snagged the anchor chain of the last ship before the open sea and managed to pull the dinghy to the side of the vessel.

I shouted, "Help!"

After a long time, a face appeared above us.

We were barely hanging on. The dock was too high to reach. The only way to get there was to climb up the ship's ladder. We were obviously desperate, and I'm sure having a kid with me helped.

"It's against the rules, but come up, and I'll let you cross."

We climbed up the ladder and crossed the ship to a warehouse and industrial area. Several guard dogs ran loose, but they didn't bother us. Eventually, we reached a road, where a man named Richard stopped, gave us a ride to a gas station, and then drove us back to the docked ship and our dinghy. We motored back to *Jacana* without incident. By the time we arrived, Pam was about to call the Coast Guard to look for us.

Richard invited us to have dinner with his family the next day. He picked us up at the yacht club at the appointed time and took us to his home. It was a delight to visit a local family and enjoy a meal away from the boat. How lucky we were and how little we knew! This was one of several times when we were helped by the kindness of strangers. We did things we should not have done but also had a good time doing them, partly because we didn't have enough sense to realize how foolish we were.

We were blissfully unaware of the dangers of our next adventure, too. A sailor we met at the Ponce yacht club encouraged us to visit Mona Island, a Puerto Rican nature preserve halfway to Hispaniola. He had often sailed there, and his instructions for getting through the break in the reef were straightforward. The anchorage was inside the reef on the island's western side, and because the wind typically came from the east, it was usually protected from the wind and waves.

As we approached the reef, we lined up the third palm tree from the left with the stick in the water we thought was the mark. Pam was on the bow watching the water when a coral reef suddenly rose from the bottom. We barely skimmed over it. The depth sounder read zero. Then just as suddenly, we were floating in fifteen feet of crystal-clear water above sugar-white sand studded with colossal coral heads.

We managed to maneuver between the coral heads and set

the anchor without swinging into them. We were the only boat visiting this beautiful spot. The water was so clear and calm that it was almost invisible. When we were onshore and looked back, the boat, full keel and all, seemed to float in the air.

We saw iguanas, birds, and pirate caves; the weather was beautiful. The only residents were park rangers. We got up before dawn in search of turtles coming ashore to lay their eggs. We noticed a stack of wire traps we thought might be used to catch the large rats we sometimes saw, but one of the rangers told us they were for catching feral cats. The rats were native, but the cats were not, and the aim was to restore the island to its pre-settlement habitat. We spent several carefree days at anchor, relaxed and, we thought, secure; swimming, schooling, hiking, and having a good time in this island paradise.

There must be a God who watches out for fools. Even though the winds usually come out of the east, they do not always, and had they shifted just a little in the wrong direction, we would have been trapped. We could not have crossed the reef had there been any waves at all. Anchored as we were, an onshore wind would have driven us into coral heads and damaged, if not sunk, the boat. Our Puerto Rican friend must have gone there for short visits, and his boat must have been smaller and shallower than ours. To anchor there for days as we did, sleeping through the night without an anchor watch, was foolish. "Fools rush in where angels fear to tread" was never truer.

Since one of the reasons for taking the boys out of school was to give them a perspective on the world they would not get in South Dakota, we thought a visit to Haiti would be enlightening. We approached Hispaniola, a tall verdant island shared by Haiti and the Dominican Republic, from the east, so we stopped first in the Dominican Republic. In addition to visiting the tomb of

Christopher Columbus and some of the first European homes in the new world, we caught the tail-end of a student riot and whiffs of tear gas. In the secure yacht club, employees with sub-machine guns slung over their shoulders struggled to keep them from tangling with our lines as they helped us dock.

As we approached the nearly empty anchorage of Jacmel, Haiti, a man named Marcel ferried out in a dugout canoe and hailed us, "Ahoy, captain. You must let me board. I am your pilot to direct you to the anchorage."

"I have a good chart of the harbor. I know where to go."

"You don't understand. A pilot is required by authorities."

I didn't believe him, but I thought, why not, and invited him on board.

We didn't need him, but Marcel spoke passable English that he had learned while working on ships. And he performed a helpful service by telling us about the town and giving us the opportunity to get to know a local. Marcel had a wife and half-a-dozen children to support, and we were grateful to him.

Baby Doc ruled Haiti, then. Everywhere we looked, signs proclaimed him "President for Life." Haiti was by far the most impoverished country we visited. Most of the children on the street had the bloated bellies of the malnourished. People sold a dozen green beans laid out on a scrap of paper at the market. Many sold bits of charcoal they had made from pieces of salvaged wood. Our guidebook described the city of Jacmel as the San Francisco of Haiti—a small city of culture and the arts. However, we saw nothing of culture and arts, only a town of starving people and relentless poverty.

Marcel told us there were small pools and waterfalls in the hills above the city. With his help, we rented some skeletal horses, and Jake, Andy, and I took a day's ride into the hills. Pam had pulled her back, so she stayed on the boat and kept an eye on things.

The countryside was grim. Almost every tree had been cut

down, and the topsoil was eroded. Children held their hands out, hoping for salvation from us. We were uncomfortable. What could we do, confronted with such desperate need? We took a short swim in the pools under the waterfalls and had lunch at a nearby house. The food was meager, but it was a lot more than the local people had. Those clustered around us, who watched our every bite, fought over the leftovers on our plates. As I prepared to pay for our lunch, so many hands were thrust at me that I had no way of knowing what I owed to whom. I emptied my pockets and let them grab the money—hoping the ones who fed us got paid.

I lived with poverty in Colombia in the Peace Corps, but I had never encountered the desperation we witnessed in Haiti. When we took a garbage bag to shore for disposal, we were met at the dock by a crowd of children wanting to take it. At first, we thought they were seeking a tip to dispose of it for us, but then we realized they wanted the garbage. Even the plastic grocery store bag in which we carried it was of value to them.

Every morning we watched fishermen sail out in crude dugouts with outriggers, sporting sails made of sewn-together plastic scraps of tablecloths, garbage bags, and even grocery bags— anything that could catch and hold a bit of wind.

While the boys and I were in the hills, Pam observed life on shore. A hotel that catered to white guests had a fenced-off beachfront where no blacks were allowed, a sad situation in the first Black republic in the world. A well-dressed white-haired gentleman left the hotel area and came to the dock, where a group of local youth surrounded him. They parleyed for a short while, and then the gentleman departed with one of the kids. Pam was concerned about what might be going on.

Marcel was willing to tackle any task. We needed courtesy flags for Jamaica and Belize, and he said he could get them for us. He needed pictures, so we showed him our atlas and let him take it with him overnight. The next day he presented us with two strange-looking flags. He had sewn together bits of fabric that roughly matched the colors in the illustration. The flags were charming, and we gladly paid what he asked, although we were not sure they would be officially acceptable.

We appreciated all Marcel did for us, and we left some shoes, tee shirts, shorts, and canned food for him. I wish we could have done more to alleviate the suffering we saw. We have not returned to Haiti, but the news over the years does not give us hope that things have changed for the better. Our visit had a lasting impact on our boys and widened their horizons (as well as Pam's and mine). I suspect that the tourists behind the fences of the beach hotel experienced a Haiti that was vastly different from the one we saw.

From Haiti, we sailed to a cozy little bay in Jamaica just off the town of Port Antonio, where we arrived on March 30, anchoring closer to shore than the other two boats in the anchorage. Jake and Andy slept in the aft cabin while Pam and I slept in the main cabin on the settee made into a double berth. During our second night at anchor, I was still caught up in the passage we had made to get there, dreaming that we were at sea. I felt Pam lying asleep next to me and thought, "What is she doing here—she should be on watch!"

A bit vexed, I climbed out of bed. As I stepped through the companionway and into the cockpit, a dark figure emerged from the aft cabin. I had been worrying about Jake's unhappiness, and when the figure dived over the side, I thought we were still at sea and that Jake had just gone overboard.

In a dreadful panic, I shouted, "Jake! Don't! Come back, Jake!"

My shouting woke me and everybody else on the boat. Now awake, I realized what was happening and, almost mid-sentence, began shouting, "Come back here, you SOB!" The thief disappeared into the night with a cheap plastic flashlight we kept in the cockpit. Nothing else was missing. I had been walking in my sleep!

In the morning, we asked the proprietor of the small nearby marina for advice. He told us that thieves boarded anchored boats now and then and that they could be very skillful. One had stolen a purse from under the pillow of a woman napping on her boat in broad daylight. Would it be helpful to report our incident to the authorities?

"Do what you think best," he said, adding that the last time somebody notified the police about a theft, they quickly found a suspect, took him behind a bush, and shot him through the head! Thinking that was a little severe for a lost flashlight, we decided not to report it but warned the other boaters.

When we were planning our life on the boat, I told Pam, "Look, if we run short of money, I'll get a job wherever we are and earn enough to renew the cruising kitty." That was easier said than done. In all our years on two boats, I spent a lot of money but never earned a dime from working. But Jake did.

The anchorage at Montego Bay, Jamaica, was like a circus. Boats pulled tourists up in parachutes, and jet skis raced around our boat, which had apparently been chosen as one of the marks in a racecourse. Speedboats tore by so often that an excursion to shore in our little putt-putt inflatable dinghy meant risking our lives. Bright pink tourists roasted themselves on the fenced-off beaches in front of hotels.

Jake was fourteen but looked older. Wherever we went, young men pestered him to buy ganja (marijuana). Kids who were not old enough to hawk ganja sold aloe vera lotion, but because they were black, they were not allowed to go onto the private hotel beaches. So, a group of boys set Jake up to sell the lotion where they were not allowed to go. He split the earnings with them and hoped to earn enough to pay for a parachute ride behind a speedboat. I was pleased that Jake was meeting locals on his own.

As we island-hopped west, it became increasingly clear that Pam was set on leaving the boat until Jake finished high school. She pointed out how low the balance in our savings account had become, resisted purchasing anything new for the boat, and refused to consider my suggestions about equipping the boat for the Pacific. When we left Jamaica and headed for Belize, I knew she wouldn't change her mind. Hard as it was, I relinquished my dream of continuing our life on the boat, at least for now. We were returning to our old life rather than creating a new one.

The temptation of my old job waiting for me was hard to resist. Returning to Brookings was an easy way out. Although I could have looked for a new, more satisfactory position, my heart was still set on a life at sea. I could bear four more years of teaching while Jake attended high school, and then, having shored up our savings, we would set out again.

After Montego Bay, the path to Panama turned south, but we did not. We would not be cruising the Pacific. I was defeated and exhausted. The past year of momentous decisions, nerve-wracking uncertainties, and challenging responsibilities had come to nothing. On the other hand, the thought of an easy life back home was not so bad. I was too exhausted to resist Pam's decision to return, so I acquiesced without an argument. The mid-life crisis of my male ego had cost the family enough.

We rented a car in Belize and explored our first Mayan ruins. With its pine forests, small towns with false-fronted buildings, and dusty roads, Belize reminded us of our childhoods in Wyoming. We enjoyed our excursions away from the boat, and home was calling us.

We met the unusually friendly Captain Bob, a delivery captain from Key West in Cozumel, Mexico. He had flown there to sail a small boat back to Florida. He gave us a chart for Key West, told us to call when we got there, and he would meet us at the dock and pick it up.

Several weeks passed before we reached Key West because we stopped at Isla Mujeres and took a bus to visit the Mayan ruins at Chichen Itza. When we finally arrived, Captain Bob rode over on his new bicycle, picked up his chart, took us home to meet his wife, and treated us to dinner at a nice restaurant. He boasted that he had purchased a new pink Volvo for his wife, who had just completed expensive dental work. The couple had also acquired a new sailboat. We wondered if Captain Bob was making a better living from his boat deliveries than he ought to.

He entertained us with his stories. He had run off with a circus as a teenager. Once, he was "zapped" for sailing too close to Cuba, tied to a dock, and watched by an armed guard. He plotted an escape, but the Cubans let him go before he could execute it. We enjoyed his company and his wild stories, but we were suspicious. In those days, when somebody in Florida suddenly came into lots of money, rumor had it that drug-running was involved.

We worked our way from the Keys to Fort Lauderdale and, on May 20, hauled *Jacana* at Summerfield's boatyard, where we spent weeks painting and fixing her up. We hired Lydia, the boatyard's painter, to coach us on using some special boat paints. She and her husband John became our friends. The sheer amount of exhausting work kept me from dwelling upon why we were fixing up the boat.

Then, Captain Bob showed up at Summerfield's with a new motor sailor on which he was installing $10,000 worth of instruments. He paid our boys to sleep on the boat to keep thieves at bay while he and his wife stayed in an expensive hotel. He asked if I would be interested in sailing a boat back from the Bahamas for him. The job would pay well. The money was tempting, but I was afraid drugs might be involved, so I turned him down. We were just speculating about Bob's business. Maybe he simply enjoyed our company, and his attention to us had no ulterior motive.

One of the boats at the Summerfield Boatyard was the famous *Tzu Hang* that once belonged to Miles and Beryl Smeeton, authors of some of my favorite sailing books. The boat and its owners had survived pitchpoling and dismasting on two different occasions near Cape Horn. While we were in the boatyard, a workman rescued three abandoned kittens who had climbed through one of the boat's portlights and fallen into the water. We looked after them until we departed, then left them with Lydia. I felt a bit like an abandoned kitten myself. I was losing the boat and abandoning the dream I'd mistakenly thought we all shared.

We finished work on *Jacana* and took her to a yacht brokerage across the river. I could not bear to look back as we left. Despite my best efforts, our experiment in creating a new life had failed. We returned to Brookings in the late summer of 1985. The boat sold quickly, giving us enough cash to buy another house. I returned to teaching, and Jake to school with his football-playing friends. Andy rose to the top of his class in mathematics and remained there through high school. How sad that left unaddressed, a small problem like difficulty memorizing multiplication tables could keep a child from succeeding. His teachers did not have the time that we did to work with him. The school principals, who thought we were destroying the children's education by taking them out of school and had told us they would not let them back without a credential, never asked to see the Calvert School certificates the boys had completed.

Jake was surprised that some students he admired envied his sailing adventure. He realized that he and his family may have done something remarkable. Later in life, he regretted that he had not made the Atlantic crossing with us and was sorry we had cut short our time on the boat.

Pam resumed her interests in music, history, art, and literature. We bought another Victorian house, even older than the first one, and returned to life much as it had been before. I busied

Jake, Andy, and Pam at Summerfield Boatyard, Fort Lauderdale.

myself renovating and restoring the house during the summers and continued struggling to reach those disinterested students in the back row. It was good to see our friends again and take summer vacations at our Black Hills cabin.

Even though our experiment did not turn out as I had hoped, our family benefited. Jake joined the Peace Corps after graduating from college and served in Papua New Guinea, bringing home a wife and child. Andy spent a year backpacking through Canada, Latin America, Southeast Asia, and the Middle East. Pam and I were shocked at how seriously others took things that seemed trivial to us and lacked interest in things we considered important.

We all (so the boys now tell me) experienced enormous shifts of perspective.

Living on boats, traveling in foreign lands, relying on our wits, and living simply challenged us and helped us distinguish the real from the unreal and the important from the unimportant. We also learned about the danger of blindly following firmly held ideas, the need to be open and honest with those we love, and the strength of the bonds that hold two people together despite the stresses caused by their shortcomings.

I wrote:

Whether our experience leaves us capable of adjusting to life in the States again remains an open question. So far, we find it difficult, not because the United States is worse than other countries, but because this is *our* country, and the faults that we see are, consequently, *our* faults, and we should do something about them. We are like the escaped prisoner in Plato's allegory of the cave who, upon his return, could not convince his former cave-mates that what they saw and thought to be real was nothing but a shadow.

The discontent and frustration that led us to run away to sea continued to fester and grow, despite our efforts to settle down and enjoy our relatively easy, enviable, active life. Once Jake finished high school and started college, we would take off again. I have a degree in mathematics, but I was not prepared for the surprise that when Jake graduated from high school, his ten-year-old little brother had become fourteen! Rather than subject Andy to the same trauma as Jake, we postponed our search for an alternate way of life until Andy was in college.

In the meantime, we bought a fifteen-foot sailboat (a Chrysler Mutineer) and a boat trailer and practiced sailing on the small lakes near our South Dakota home. We learned to enjoy sailing. We missed the sights and sounds of the wind, the sky, and the waves. As our little boat plowed forward, it created in its wake a private yet unfinished road to an unknown, beckoning future. I lived for the day when we would take off again. Pam, too, was eager to escape, although she, not having lost her sense entirely, had some practical concerns such as how to make a living and be parents to our boys.

Kent working on Jacana in Fort Lauderdale, with Jake and Andy looking on

II
———

Grounded

1985–1994

Chapter 7

Between the Boats

It is not that life ashore is distasteful to me.
But life at sea is better. —SIR FRANCIS DRAKE

I taught and accumulated more retirement pay. Pam's memories of seasickness and anxiety faded, while those of beautiful sunsets, balmy air, lovely snorkeling, and the daring adventure of our life on the boat grew stronger. We wanted to get back to the cruising life again. We didn't know it would take ten years.

I took every opportunity to escape teaching. I finished writing a logic textbook during a sabbatical semester, presented a paper to my old department in Oregon, and checked out boats for sale in Washington. During the summers, I built a garage and renovated our Victorian house instead of writing and teaching. Pam, Andy, and I went to Kunming, China, during Andy's junior year in high school, where Pam and I taught at Yunan Normal University. I was no longer interested in furthering my academic career.

We got interested in a couple of steel boats. I found an intriguing Zeeland yawl in Anacortes, Washington, but when I called the marina for more information, I learned that the boat had sunk at the dock and was a complete loss. Months later, a Zeeland yawl appeared for sale in Alameda, California. When we flew out to look, I recognized that it was the same (supposedly sunk) boat I had seen in Anacortes. We were suspicious. The seller wanted to complete the transaction with a cash payment made five miles offshore. We backed out.

One weekend we made a marathon drive to Buffalo, New York, to see another steel boat. The evening before we left, the owner called and said we should know before we made such a long trip that the boat had sunk at the dock the previous year. He had raised it and repaired the leak. That explained why the listing did not include the usual radio and electronic equipment. We made the trip, anyway, but decided the boat would require too much of a commitment to make it seaworthy.

I had looked for a steel boat before we bought *Jacana*. Steel is the strongest material for a hull and is most likely to survive grounding on a reef. It's also heavy, and we wanted a strong boat with a heavy displacement hull that could hold lots of stores. A heavy boat would be slow and need lots of wind to make it go, but that was a tradeoff we were willing to make.

We had almost given up when we found *Coot*. We were running behind schedule while looking at boats in New England, so we called to cancel an appointment in Newburyport, Massachusetts, to see a boat that seemed a bit small to be a likely candidate. The broker convinced us that the showing would take just a few minutes. Besides, the owner had already gone out of his way for us.

When we arrived, we looked at the anchored boats, trying to pick out the one we would visit. We saw a rough, hard-chine steel boat and were not impressed. When the owner arrived in his dinghy to ferry us out, he headed toward the steel boat but stopped before getting to it and pulled up to what looked like a beautiful fiberglass or wood boat. I could not believe it was steel! The interior was as beautifully finished as the outside. It was small—

about the size of *Jacana* without the aft cabin. But convinced that the two of us could fit without the boys, we bought her.

I liked its simplicity, fool-proof tiller steering, and the absence of refrigeration or pressure water that would require repairs. The basic instruments were good quality: wind-vane steering (not quite as heavy-duty as it should have been) and a well-regarded three-cylinder Volvo diesel engine. Instead of an awkward vee-berth, there was a small double berth forward on the starboard with clothing lockers to port. Standing headroom was limited in the forward cabin because of a flush deck forward of the mast. But there was plenty of headspace under the coach house. A standing-height chart table was to port of the companionway ladder, and a small head was tucked into the aft port corner under the bridge deck. There was a so-called double berth in the starboard quarter, but a shoehorn would be required to get two people into

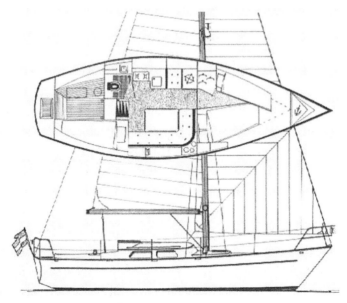

Coot Diagram, Breewijd 31.

it. The galley was to port and a settee that could be made into a double berth to starboard. It had an enormous amount of storage for a boat its size.

—

Pam wrote a letter to her godparents Bill and Marie Ray on September 15, 1992:

> We had been ambling along in our usual unproductive fashion with Kent, Andy, and Jake going to school and me trying to look busy but reading detective novels, when last August (1991), we found our dream boat in Newburyport, Massachusetts. [Pam was actually comparing British and American detective novels for her master's thesis in English.]
>
> For nearly two years, Kent and I had been combing the sailing periodicals and brokerage listings for a boat to replace our beloved *Jacana*. We had promised ourselves we would not buy one in 1991 because we were going to China on an exchange teaching program early in 1992.
>
> It would be absurd to buy a boat, ship it to our part of the country, sail it for a short time, haul it from the water, leave for China, and worry about the boat left abandoned in some cold midwestern boatyard. However, *Coot* turned out to be the boat of our dreams, or at least close enough to buy her.
>
> She is a 31-foot Dutch-built (Breewijd) steel sloop a little small but cozy and rather elegant all at the same time. We wrote a check and found a trucking company to drive her to Superior, Wisconsin, on Lake Superior, the closest big water to Brookings, South Dakota, with an outlet to the ocean. Then we leaped into our car to get back to Brookings, where we cut the grass, made sure Andy was still managing on his own and arranged for the marina in Superior to accept *Coot*.
>
> After we left Massachusetts late that summer, Hurricane

Bob tore right over the top of *Coot,* leaving her unscathed. Still, her parents were furious that the boatyard manager had not gotten her loaded onto the truck and out of hurricane country on schedule.

We managed to get her into the water and even did some sailing in the frigid fresh water of Lake Superior during September and early October. The boat was just as sweet and ladylike in the water as she'd promised to be. We didn't get our fill of sailing before we had to haul her out to be safe from the ice that promised to sock in the lake. It was just as well, as we had been driving up from Brookings on the weekends, and it was a seven-hour trip each way. Ah, the things that we'll do for those we love—and *Coot* has become as important a member of our family as a new infant—and just as expensive.

We got home to Brookings from China in the spring of 1992, said hello to Jake, cut the grass, cleaned the house, and left Andy in charge of the house and cat. Kent and I departed for Superior and *Coot.* In Superior, which must have the worst climate in the continental U.S., we scraped, painted, and organized *Coot* for launching. We got her in the water, did a little sailing, and made our way across the lake and through the Apostle Islands. We learned more about the boat and what we would need to do to make her a home rather than just a toy.

We expect to be here for at least another year. Kent is eager to move onto the boat as soon as possible, but that won't be until we have Andy settled in college and our house sold. We hope to go ocean voyaging on *Coot* if health and finances permit. But that is still in the future.

In a piece perhaps intended for publication, also written in the fall of 1992, Pam describes our preparations and captures our eagerness to return to life at sea:

There is a chill October rain falling on the eastern South
Dakota prairies, and although my daydreams have me
anchored off a warm, sunny Caribbean beach, I am about as
far geographically from that dream as it is possible to be.

I walk into the guest room to stow in its closet the
stainless-steel wire and sta-lock fittings that just arrived on
the UPS truck. My closet is probably the only one in South
Dakota that contains sea-going oilies, two sextants, rigging
tape, a Baja filter, a marine head, a life-sling, and other
assorted nautical paraphernalia. The most prominent feature
in the room is the bed; however, two gray, conical-shaped
tubes protrude from underneath its foot. My husband and
I have stored the new dinghy, partially inflated, beneath the
bed. My startled guests tell me it looks like the pale, flabby
remains of some unidentifiable monster.

After the mother ship herself, the dinghy, a lovely new
roll-up, is our largest purchase and represents much more
than a dollar value. Our future home, a 31-foot steel sloop
pulled ignominiously out of the water in Duluth, Minnesota,
is wrapped now in her winter cover. It would be a long seven-
hour drive through uncertain midwestern weather to assure
ourselves that our dream has some substance. But the dinghy
is here, living quietly like a friendly, elderly dog beneath the
bed. I sometimes think I can hear it sigh a little wistfully, just
as I do, for the time we'll both be at sea.

We put the dinghy in its unusual location simply because
we couldn't think of a better place. The garage is dusty, oily,
and cold. The attic is dusty, draughty, and cold. The basement
is dusty, dark, and damp. The owner's manual tells us that
all these environments are unhealthy for young dinghies.
We wanted only the best for the new dinghy, and in lieu of
putting it in the bed, we put it under it.

We are slowly outfitting a small sailing vessel for future voyages. Like many other high-latitude sailors, we spend the winter months studying boating catalogs, placing orders, waiting for the UPS truck, and longing for spring. Next summer, we will begin to move mother and son (for some inexplicable reason, this dinghy is definitely male) east through Lake Superior and Lake Huron. The summer after that, maybe we'll make it into salt water. It's a long and frustrating process to move from a landlocked South Dakota job and home to the sea. It's also a lonely process, for none of our friends share or even understand our dream. But the dinghy, peacefully resting beneath the bed, silently encourages us to keep dreaming.

Pam described our continued preparations and the beginning of our voyage through the Great Lakes in the summer of 1993 in another letter to Bill and Marie, written on January 7, 1994:

Kent continued to teach philosophy to reluctant South Dakota students. Andy started his senior year in high school, Jake his senior year in college, and I went on housewifing. However, Kent's and my hearts and dreams lived not in Brookings but with our boat, *Coot*, moored at Duluth, MN. The winter was employed dreaming up more plans, ordering more boating gear, and organizing our final escape from Brookings. By the summer of 1993, Jake had graduated from college, and Andy from high school. Both boys had summer jobs, and Kent was not teaching. We had shown and sold the house in May, or rather we had a purchase agreement to be completed by the 3rd of January, 1994.

We traveled to Duluth and prepared the boat for the water in one of the wettest, coldest, most miserable Springs on record. Then we beat our way out of that frigid southwest corner of Lake Superior. From the middle of June to the middle of August 1993, we sailed the south shore of Lake Superior, through the Sault Saint Marie locks, into the North Channel of Lake Huron, and finally into Georgian Bay.

We thought we would enjoy a leisurely cruise through some of the most beautiful waters of the GreatLakes. We were still getting used to the boat and had a lot to learn, so the two-month shakedown cruise during the summer of 1993 was good preparation. It would also give us a head start on our way to the Atlantic the following year. As we neared Lake Superior's notorious Whitefish Point (now home to the Great Lakes Shipwreck Museum), the winds picked up to 20–25 knots, the heaviest we'd yet experienced on *Coot*. Because we were sailing close to shore and the wind was coming from that direction, the waves were minimal. However, when we rounded the point, the full strength of the forces that had been building for miles hit us. Because the water was shallow, the waves were short and steep—not much longer than *Coot*— and the motion was like riding a hobbyhorse.

The Harbor of Refuge was tucked behind the point, so I started the engine and went forward to drop the sails while we pitched, then plunged straight down from the top of each wave. When I lowered the jib, I was buried to my waist in water before the bow rose, threw the water off, and pointed at the sky. I managed to lower the sails and tie them down by the time we reached the harbor entrance. Each wave picked us up and set us down ten feet, and I feared we would pound the bottom. We were pushed hard and fast between the narrow steel-lined corridor of the harbor entrance that bent sharply at the end to block the waves. I managed to make the turn without smashing against the walls. Inside the harbor, the water thankfully flattened, although the wind still whistled.

Relieved, I motored slowly in a circle while Pam got the docking lines and fenders arranged. Then, suddenly, inexplicably, the engine ran away, driving the boat at high speed. Moving the control lever and pulling the kill switch did nothing. I kicked the helm over to avoid crashing into the dock, yelled at Pam to take over, then rushed below to open the engine compartment and pull the throttle linkage by hand.

Pam, perplexed and not knowing what had happened, headed back toward the harbor entrance and the wild open water. Then I accidentally killed the engine by pulling the wrong linkage. The wind now blew us toward a collision with a solid granite outcrop. I rushed to the bow in desperation and dropped the anchor, hoping it would catch on something. It caught and pulled the bow into the wind, saving us from hitting the rocks.

The boat was okay, but I was a wreck. All that kept us from blowing onto the rocks was a poorly set anchor. I didn't know what caused the engine to run away. I tightened a set screw or two, fired it up again, and everything worked fine. We raised the anchor and moved the boat to the dock. The engine never ran away again, but it took a long time for me to be comfortable motoring in tight spaces.

From Whitefish Point,[1] we passed through the Soo Locks and gunk-holed through the North Channel of Lake Huron and Georgian Bay to Midland, Ontario. We met our friends Sue and

---

1. Years later, I told Linnea, who had grown up in the area, the story of facing those granite outcrops. She looked puzzled and asked if this had not happened somewhere farther west, where rocky cliffs line Lake Superior. "Whitefish Point is nothing but a spit of sand: there's no rock," she told me. The mystery was solved when we visited the area. I had to admit she was right. Whitefish Point is just a sand spit. The Harbor of Refuge was lined with large limestone rocks hauled from far away. In my panic, I saw granite cliffs. I would not have been so panicked if I'd realized that my anchor was set in a nice sand bottom rather than snagged on a nubbin of granite.

Jeff Grant and explored Georgian Bay with them. We left *Coot* in Midland for the winter and returned to Brookings for one last school year.

It would have made sense to continue teaching for two more years rather than one when I would be eligible for early retirement at age fifty-five. But we'd already postponed our return to

Coot *under sail*

sea longer than we'd anticipated. We felt time was running out. We needed to make the break now if we were ever going to do it. Thoughts of future financial repercussions went by the wayside.

Pam's January 7, 1994 letter to Bill and Marie Ray concludes:

Mid-August, 1993, regretfully, found us back in Brookings after a reasonably successful first voyage on *Coot*. We learned a lot about how to sail her, how not to sail her, what we would need to do to make her more comfortable, and what we could expect a boat of her type to do. We learned that we could live on her, even if she was not the most luxurious of vessels, and we'd be like starving graduate students again.

During our final year in Brookings, we needed to settle down, stop thinking about boats and sailing, and work on freeing ourselves of the impediments we'd accumulated since we were last at sea. Jake moved back home after graduating from college in the spring of 1993, and that fall entered the Peace Corps, while Andy started his first year at college.

I corralled the boys, gave them each an old steamer trunk, and told them they had to fit their childhoods into their respective trunks. They did this without much grief. Then, I stuffed the rest of the family treasures into the fewest possible boxes. We pared our material goods down significantly, but I secretly hoped the house would burn down, and I would be spared deciding what to keep, what to throw away, and what to sell.

The boat is now hauled out in Midland, Ontario, Canada, at the southern end of Georgian Bay. As soon as Kent turns his grades in this spring, we'll take a few last possessions to the cabin in the Black Hills, then head for Ontario and *Coot*. We hope to get into the Atlantic and far enough down the East Coast to be in warm weather by November. Right now, we're drooling over the different ways to get south.

From Midland, we'll probably go through the Trent-Severn
Waterway (a canal, lake, and lock system that connects
Georgian Bay to Lake Ontario). We have no desire to see
Detroit by water or sail Lake Erie, so this shortcut looks good.

We'll then start up the St. Lawrence Seaway. At Montreal,
we'll decide whether to leave the Great Lakes by the seaway
and the Canadian Maritime Provinces or travel via the
Richelieu River to Lake Champlain and the Hudson. Kent
is legislating for the Maritime Provinces, as we'll probably
never be this way again. I worry about the cold and fog. We'll
see what works. It's a long way around if we go the northern
route, and we may not have time if we have a lot of work to do
on *Coot* after her winter out of the water.

We toyed with heading straight across to Ireland from
the mouth of the St. Lawrence. We worry about the summer
hurricane season on the East Coast. There's no way to
avoid it other than going across to Europe and sailing south
down its west coast, but it's possibly foolish to begin with
such ambitious plans our first year out. We're not going to
be retired folks with a steady income; we're going to have
to stop and work as we travel, and finding work abroad is
difficult. South Carolina or Florida will be closer than the
Mediterranean, and I'll be more accessible for Jake and Andy.

We moved out of the house in January and moved in with our
neighbor and good friend Signe Stuart[2] during our last semester.
After turning in my final set of grades that spring, we left our few
remaining family heirlooms at Pam's family cabin, returned to

---

2. Signe Stuart is a longtime friend, artist, and professor of art at South
   Dakota State University. Since retiring to New Mexico, she continues to
   be active as an artist, and her ever-evolving work is found in many collec-
   tions and galleries. Wikipedia, "Signe Margaret Stuart." Last modified
   2 June 2022.

Brookings, and loaded our van with all we needed for life on the boat. Sue and Jeff Grant threw a lovely farewell party. On May fourteenth, ten years after we had set out in search of *Jacana*, we climbed into our overloaded van and headed for *Coot*, who was anxiously waiting for us in Midland, Ontario.

Gleefully telling each other, "It's just you and me, kid!" we left Brookings behind for what would surely be the last time. Maybe we'd sail to Ireland and Scotland through the North Atlantic and see places in Europe we missed before. From there, we could cross the Atlantic to the Caribbean, the Panama Canal, and the Pacific. We could meet Jake in Papua New Guinea when he finished the Peace Corps. The world was our oyster.

III

Coot

1994–2006

Chapter 8

Hope Springs Eternal

May–June 1994

Man never is, but always to be blest.
—ALEXANDER POPE, *Essay on Man*

It's a long story, and I'll begin the whole gruesome tale from the beginning when we left Brookings. By May 14 [1994], we loaded all our remaining possessions into our dilapidated van and took off for Midland, Ontario, and *Coot*. Life seemed sweet. Our van was behaving, and we moved toward Ontario with great dispatch.

We made it to Midland late on the sixteenth, checked into a motel, and drove through gloom and rain to the boatyard to see *Coot*. Although she was a bit grubby from her winter storage, she wasn't in the shape I had pessimistically imagined during the long Brookings winter. The morning dawned sunny and cheerful, and we began to unload the van and set up some semblance of living aboard, even though she was high on dry land. *Coot* looked much smaller than she had the previous summer, and the contents of the van seemed to require the space of Mount Rushmore. However, we managed to stow most of our stuff, including Kent's massive miter box, a huge vise, assorted tools, clothes for all seasons, pots, pans,

Unloading the van in Midland

food for a month, some books, two sextants, and the nautical charts for the East Coast of the United States. What didn't fit, we sold, gave away, or pitched in the dumpster.

We spent three weeks on carpentry, painting, wiring, sandblasting, and recoating the bottom. We lived on board, going up and down a twelve-foot ladder for every little errand and project. Each pound I had put on during the winter was associated with an ache. We became relatively comfortable and began to think this was boating until it was time to go in the water. The travel lift arrived, hauled us over the liquid stuff, and dropped us in.

Then came the moment I had been dreading. I am pessimistic about anything I don't understand, and I don't understand diesel engines. I had nightmares about our engine all winter and feared it wouldn't start in the spring. Kent encourages my worrying because the things I worry about seldom happen. Only those I don't worry about do. He had great confidence that the engine would start. It didn't. So we

squirted some ether down its throat, and it took off with a
roar. We smiled, provisioned *Coot* with food and fuel, and
headed for the Trent-Severn Waterway.

However, when we stopped, I noticed the motor wasn't
making a characteristic gurgling sound as it died. We had
been warned that this sound should be heard, but the prior
owner had not said why. Kent thought we didn't hear it
because of the stuff we'd packed around the vent. *(Pam's letter
to friends written from Clayton, New York, July 27, 1994)*

How I wish I had paid more attention to Pam and the lack of
the gurgling sound! The early part of our adventure would have
been quite different had I done so. I also wish I'd paid more attention to her misgivings and hesitation. The van was sold, *Coot*
was fully provisioned, the water and fuel tanks were full, and it
was time to go. I was at the helm with the engine running, waiting
for Pam to cast off the lines and come aboard.

Then she said, "We don't have to go. We got out of Brookings."

I felt as though I had jumped out of a plane, only to discover
my ripcord was stuck.

"I can't stop now!"

She stepped aboard, and the ripcord slipped free. I breathed a
sigh of relief, and we were off. We never talked about that moment
of hesitation, but we should have.

We motored into the Trent-Severn waterway. Because our
mast was down to fit under the low bridges that cross the
waterway, we were essentially a motorboat. Two days into the
waterway, we could not start the engine. We bled it, changed
its fuel and oil filters, cursed, and scratched our heads. Finally,
Kent said he needed help. We called a mechanic.

Robin, a lean, handsome man, came to the boat. He
looked and talked like an English country vicar. He bled the

engine, asked if we had changed the filter, scratched his head, and squirted ether down its throat. It started! He charged little for the visit but recommended we have the engine looked at because it made some untoward sounds. He was not drumming up business, and we thought we should get to an area with big marinas and sailboats before having work done.

Then we realized we could get stuck in a much worse place than Bobcaygeon—perhaps in the middle of a cow pasture. We had four more days of motoring through the waterway, and we were impressed with Robin's soft-spoken expertise. We asked if his marina had enough depth to accommodate *Coot's* draft, if he was equipped to do some major work on the engine, and if he had the time to do it. He answered yes to all three questions, so we decided to have him do the work.

It turned out that the absence of the gurgling sound was of utmost importance. It meant that the anti-siphon vent on the water exhaust was not working, and we now had an engine full of water that would need a complete rebuild. We dubbed it the "sucking sound," taking all our money south á la Ross Perot.

We spent three weeks at Bobcaygeon, Ontario, taking the engine apart, hauling it out of the boat, waiting for parts, and putting it back together. We scraped and painted under the engine, touched up the varnish, and caught up on laundry. Bobcaygeon was a friendly place to go through an unpleasant procedure. We got to know other boaters, who gently commiserated with us. Robin and his French wife invited us to their home for a lovely dinner. So did the marina owner. We got to know their children and grandchildren. The lockkeeper waved when we took our daily walk and asked

THE TRENT-SEVERN WATERWAY

The waterway is an historic Canadian river, canal, lake, and lock system, 386 km in length, that links Lake Huron to Lake Ontario. For more information, visit the Trent-Severn Website.

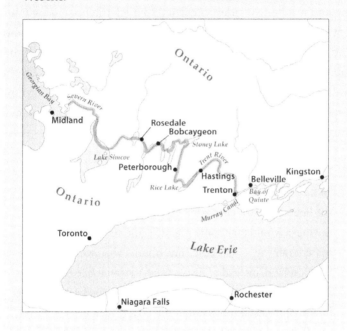

when we planned to immigrate. Finally, we departed and babied the engine through the remaining thirty-two locks.

The Trent-Severn Waterway is fascinating, even though sailors usually abhor places where they cannot sail. I dreaded the passage because I dislike docking, and each lock required us to dock. While we still had the van, we drove to Port Severn to view the first lock. The entrance was surrounded by rapids tumbling over vicious rocks. I trembled, but Kent said, "A piece of cake." As it happened, we navigated the rapids easily, only to ram the mast, stored flat on crutches and extending a bit beyond the bow, into the end gate of the lock.

Even though we had sailed across the Atlantic, I was not an expert at maneuvering a boat. We seldom docked *Jacana*. By reading and watching a video, I learned to dock the boat using lines, not the motor. It was hard to judge *Coot's* speed and momentum, and I went into the first lock too fast because I was worried that my slowness was holding others up. In the first lock, we hit the wall hard and bounced before Pam could get her line around anything. The boat stopped when it rammed the foot of the mast into the closed gate.

We didn't damage either the gate or the mast and gave the lock keepers a laugh. Kent learned he would have to stop the boat a bit sooner. We realized that maneuvering into the locks would take some practice. The second lock was a marine railway, a marvelous invention. I wish we could have been on land, instead of inside *Coot*, to watch her go over the mountain. We motored over a submerged railed carriage; the lockmaster raised slings under the boat (much like the travel lifts that move boats in boatyards), then the whole kit and caboodle was hauled up one side of a hill and down the other. The slings were lowered, and we motored off.

We increased our elevation for the first ten locks. Uplocking was difficult. I used the boat hook to catch the cable hanging down from the wall, looped my line around it, and tried to stop the boat by holding tight. The only immovable objects were the lifelines against which my thighs were pressed.

I didn't realize how much damage I'd done to my thighs until it was warm enough to take off my jeans. I was grateful

Kent in a Trent-Severn lock

that the extended pause for engine repair in Bobcaygeon gave them time to heal. Kent realized he should stop the boat by reversing the engine harder. Down-locking, in contrast, was as smooth as pulling the plug from a bathtub because we didn't have to fight the inrush of water to the locks.

The Trent-Severn also had a remarkable hydraulic lift

lock, essentially a pair of huge tubs that could be filled with up to ten boats each. One side dropped as the other lifted. A few inches of extra water on the upper side added enough weight to hoist the lighter side. We rose forty-eight feet one time and dropped fifty feet another. The experience was somewhat like a quick trip on an elevator.

We enjoyed the variety of people we met in Canada and the mélange of accents ranging from Scots, English, and German to Greek, West Indian, and Chinese. Canada is truly a melting-pot country but is not problem-free. Residents of Toronto told us they are beginning to suffer from the kind of crime that New York and Chicago have experienced for decades. However, we found Toronto a vital, safe, and delightful city.

The American side of the St. Lawrence is grimmer and grimier than the Canadian side. I don't know how to account for this since all the Canadians we have met bemoan the recession and say that the United States must be prosperous in comparison. However, appearances belie this. The Canadian towns are bustling and exceptionally clean, the gardens lush and well-cared for, and the houses painted and obviously loved. The marina washrooms are as tidy and clean as those we have at home. People are better educated and informed about U.S. geography and political events than Americans. Even the dogs, of which every boater in Canadian waters has at least one, are young and friendly.

On the American side, the towns are litter-blown and seedy. Empty storefronts line main streets. The houses are peeling with weed-grown, junk-strewn lawns. We hate to enter the restrooms at the marinas and never step into them without our shower shoes. No one here knows where South Dakota is. The dogs are old, lame, and ill-tempered. We wonder whether the go-getters went north with the Loyalists after the Revolutionary War and left the ne'er-do-wells behind.

While we were anchored in Kingston, Ontario, we met a Canadian couple on a lovely vessel they had built themselves. I had done some work on *Coot*, of which I was overly proud. I made some small brass castings and designed and constructed latches for the drawers and drop boards. We invited the Canadians over and showed them my work. The husband nodded and said, "Very nice," and they invited us over to see his work. He had made substantial bronze castings for hatches, portlights, rigging screws, and latches. I was thoroughly impressed.

The following day I suggested to Pam that we invite them over for a drink. She was reading in the cockpit, looked over at their boat, and said that their dinghy was gone, so most likely nobody was home. I stuck my head up the companionway hatch and saw a man sitting in their cockpit. As I waved, I told Pam, "I see somebody in their cockpit."

He waved back.

Pam said, "I don't see anybody."

"Right there, don't you see him waving?"

I called over, "Would you like to come over for a drink?"

He responded, "That sounds nice, but we don't have a dinghy."

That was odd because they most certainly had a dinghy when they came over yesterday, but I said, "That's okay, I'll come over and get you."

Pam was puzzled. She turned and saw that I was talking to somebody on a boat we had never seen before. She laughed. Our acquaintances had a white, rounded, fiberglass boat rigged as a ketch. I was talking to a person on a green, hard-chine, metal boat rigged as a sloop. The wind had shifted, and we had turned, so the green boat had moved to our port side, roughly where the white boat had been. Even so, a green boat does not look much like a white one, and a sloop doesn't look like a ketch. I certainly had not developed an eye for boats, and I had invited complete strangers over for a drink!

After we exited the Trent-Severn, we realized we were still burning excessive oil, so we called Robin. He suggested various remedies, ranging from changing oil weight to rechecking the injectors, all of which we tried while cruising around the Thousand Islands. We also had a costly, loquacious Scottish mechanic come to the boat to feel for blow-by and various exotic diesel things.

As you may have guessed, as much as we liked Robin, he didn't fix the engine. We visited a few islands and spent days quietly at anchor, reading, and swimming. We planned to go to Montreal and follow the Richelieu River/Canal System to Lake Champlain and the Hudson River (which would be our last passage with the mast still down). Yet, by the time we reached the first St. Lawrence Seaway lock (an easy, non-bruising transit), I began to get nervous about the engine.

Instead of visiting French-speaking Canada, I talked Kent into turning back to the United States to find another mechanic; sooner rather than later. Quebec probably has good mechanics, too, but I was afraid we would need to speak French or that we'd reach the Richelieu and get stuck in a place with no services.

Thus, we are now in Clayton, NY, with an authorized Volvo mechanic and a coordinated Volvo distribution system. This morning a forklift snatched the engine away. We will stay here to write letters, catch up on laundry, and paint those inaccessible spots under the engine we missed last time. It looks as though we are in for another complete rebuild. Robin had used some non-Volvo parts, and the oil rings had not seated correctly. Consequentially, we have been burning excessive amounts of oil and producing quantities of blue smoke. I cannot believe I can speak with such fluency of oil rings, anti-siphon valves, and head gaskets. I'm learning more about diesel engines than I ever wanted to know.

This brings us to the present. After we escape from Clayton (if we manage to), we will cross Lake Ontario to reach the Erie Canal at Oswego, New York. From there, we'll connect with the Hudson and eventually Chesapeake Bay. I hesitate to say anything more for fear we'll jinx our plans. We are keeping a modicum of cool, wondering how far we'll get before we need to go to work to feed the engine and its mechanics. *(Conclusion of Pam's letter to friends written from Clayton, New York, July 27, 1994.)*

Fortunately, Pam had insisted on buying costly boat insurance. Without it, we would have been in deep trouble with these engine repairs. Once we left the States, we couldn't afford boat insurance, so we lived the rest of our years afloat without it.

Chapter 9

The Ninth Circle of Hell

July–August 1994

Abandon hope, all ye who enter here.
—DANTE, *The Divine Comedy*

After three weeks in Clayton, Pam was ready to give up the boat.
I was upset, but Pam was close to a nervous breakdown. This was
not the boating life we'd envisioned. She described our ordeal in
a lengthy letter to friends, written from St. Michaels, Maryland,
September 27, 1994, weeks after the events described:

> I had intended to begin this lengthy epistle before now,
> but the trouble we ran into in Clayton, New York, so
> disheartened me that I couldn't write. I am finally prepared
> to put the whole mess down on paper to rid myself of the
> devils that plagued us. I've always believed writing could be
> cathartic and therapeutic, and now I'll have the chance to
> find out. However, you will have to suffer with me. You might
> want to put this letter down and read no further.
>
> When we had the engine yanked out in Clayton for the
> second time in less than a month, we had no idea that we
> had walked through a gate with "Abandon all hope, ye who
> enter here" printed above it. We had fallen into the Ninth

Circle of Hell. During the first week, when we still expected to be moving soon, we took long walks around Clayton. Kent wanted to watch Frank, the mechanic, work so he could become more familiar with the engine. But Frank, a young man in his twenties and the marina owner's son, obviously couldn't deal with that. He struck me as immature and defensive. He'd work incredibly slowly when Kent was around, then come back at night and not tell Kent.

We began varnishing during the second week, confident that the mechanic would arrive with our engine dangling from the forklift as soon as we started a messy project. During the third week, I paced, fumed, and kvetched to the other boaters. I had a spooky feeling about Clayton, especially after seeing a worker wearing a cap that said, "God, Guts, and Guns made America free. Let's keep all three!"

Frank told Kent that people who lived on boats must be rich. It was clear that we existed to be taken advantage of, and we should be grateful that he was there to do it. We felt we had dropped into the middle of the movie *Deliverance*. We kept quiet and walked humbly.

Near the end of the third week, the engine was re-installed. We took a test run with Frank, and the engine sounded good. There was one minor oil leak that he said could be fixed with a slight tightening. Then he noticed the gear lever wasn't functioning correctly, and when he tried to readjust it, he couldn't. He concluded that the transmission was failing. And guess what? His father (the marina owner) had two Volvo transmissions that would fit our engine. Furthermore, they told us these were the only two 2003 Volvo transmissions available anywhere. Kent noticed that neither of these transmissions had the same gear ratio as ours, but Frank said not to worry. All we'd need was a new propeller to match the new transmission. Transmissions go for about $2500 and new props $2000.

By now, we were beginning to wise up. Kent called the boatyard we'd initially contacted, whose owner had honestly told us he couldn't start work for a week. He said he could get a Volvo transmission with the proper gear ratio in two days, and he'd give us a discount. He remembered our call three weeks earlier and asked why we were still in Clayton.

With great hopes of finally escaping, we prepared to leave the next morning. We would move out of the St. Lawrence River and into the eastern end of Lake Ontario to Sackett's Harbor, where we could deal with a new mechanic and transmission. However, one half-hour out of Clayton, Kent checked the engine compartment and saw oil floating in the bilge. We returned to the marina demanding, "It's on warranty, fix it!"

When we returned to the dock, Frank discovered that the bolts on one side of the engine were only finger-tight. He had forgotten to tighten them. I noticed one bolt was missing. He tightened the bolts on the engine, replaced the missing one, and assured us this would take care of the leak. I was skeptical but didn't question him.

We set out again the next day. Half an hour later, we had another puddle of oil in the bilge. We returned to the marina, and this time Frank found the dipstick loose. I didn't think that was the problem, either, but I chose not to argue. We stayed at the dock and ran the engine, and within half an hour, had another puddle of oil. To find the leak, Frank had to pull the engine again.

We motored back to the wall (boy, were we ever against the wall!) so the forklift could lift the engine and dig into our fresh varnish a second time. Frank had intended our job to be the last before he left for his new position in Norfolk, Virginia. Volvo was hiring this guy to train mechanics. Now he, too, was up against the wall. His brother was getting married, and our fourth week in Clayton was filled with wedding festivities that kept him from repairing his repairs expediently. The only good thing to come of the delay was that Kent had time to pick up the new transmission in Sackett's Harbor and bolt it onto the engine himself, avoiding a more complicated installation once the engine was back in the boat.

When Frank came to take the engine, I suggested that since we were stuck there again, he should clean up the mess he had made in the fuel tank. We had already paid him twice to filter the fuel, so it should have been clean. I pointed out that the sediment bowl was full of dirt after just a couple of hours. When he said he could do this for another hundred dollars, I blew up.

"What the hell, Frank! We already paid you twice for what you should have done once! And it still isn't done! You made it dirtier than ever! Get the hell off the boat!"

I immediately realized my mistake. Frank had my engine, and we could not leave without it. I walked into the shop to make amends. Frank was whining to his father about the mean things I had said. They both turned and shouted at me.

I tried to explain to the father about the dirty fuel, but he said, "I'm calling the sheriff to put you off my dock!"

Now I had done it! As I walked back, I wondered how I could move the boat. The mast was down, and Frank had our engine. Then one of our navigational radios caught fire. I discovered a burned ground wire. Frank had left the hot battery cable from the engine loose against the steel hull.

The radio was a Loran (an acronym for long-range naviga-tion) which was superseded by GPS, so I was not too concerned about its loss. However, running electricity through a steel hull when a boat is in the water invites serious electrolysis problems that could corrode and weaken the hull. We'd have to have the boat hauled and surveyed to make sure no harm had been done. I waited for the sheriff to arrive and kick us off the dock, fearing he'd be Frank's relative.

The sheriff, much to my relief, took one look at our boat and said, "You're not seaworthy, are you?"

We obviously were not.

"I don't see how I can kick you off the dock, then."

When I mentioned what had happened to the Loran, he came aboard with his camera, recorded everything, and wrote an affidavit. Instead of kicking us off the dock, he was an excellent witness to Frank's latest folly.

Frank dismantled the engine yet again, found a misplaced O-Ring, and ran the engine to make sure it wasn't leaking. A workman informed me that when Frank came to install the engine, I was to stay fifty feet away from the boat. When we heard the forklift coming, Pam and I departed to sit on a log the required distance away. A workman stayed with us to make sure I did not cross the fifty-foot mark and amused us by telling unflattering stories about Frank and his father. When Frank had a question, he sent another workman to talk to me. Had I not been so out of sorts, the situation would have been funny.

Once the engine was installed, Frank wanted to take the boat out to ensure that everything was working. I didn't want him to take it out without me, so he agreed that we could go together if I did not lose my temper and speak harshly to him. By the time we returned to the dock, we were on speaking terms. His parting words were, "Kent, your problem is you don't have enough money to be in boating. Boating is a rich man's sport."

Because the summer was almost gone (it was now August 24th), our only option was to head south through the Erie Canal and the Hudson River to New York City and the Atlantic. We'd follow the Intracoastal Waterway south and then decide where to jump off for the Bahamas, Puerto Rico, or the Virgin Islands. We would see places we had missed in *Jacana*, learn to handle the boat, and settle into the cruising life while contemplating the big leap into the Pacific through the Panama Canal.

Chapter 10

Free at Last!

August–October 1994

The luck of the third adventure is proverbial.
—ELIZABETH BARRETT BROWNING

We motored directly to a neighboring yard and lifted *Coot*
from the water. The surveyor from Syracuse, who made
the adjustment for the insurance company when we first
arrived in Clayton, came at once, examined the boat, and
pronounced her sound. He was a lawyer and a certified
marine surveyor. You can imagine our relief. We returned
Coot to the water and motored gleefully toward Lake Ontario
and the entrance to the Eric Canal.

I felt confident for the first time since we'd begun our trip.
I've become terribly superstitious since coming on the boat.
It may be my Scottish grandmother's sayings rolling around
in my head, like "bad things happen in threes" and "the third
time's a charm." Now the threes were coming up. I'd had no
faith that the engine's second rebuild would be the last of
our problems. I knew there would be a third problem of at
least comparable magnitude. It was almost a relief when we
had to replace the transmission—that made a third disaster.
When we finally left Clayton, it was for the third time. The

engine had been out of the boat three times. We'd had three beginnings to our trip—Midland, Bobcaygeon, and Clayton. What could go wrong now?

Well, nothing too much did. We came near to sinking, but Kent, with great courage staved that off. We were fiddling with the head's seacock in preparation for opening it when we reached the open sea and could pump our sewage overboard, when the fitting cracked, and water began to leak in. Kent dived over the side, drove a wooden plug into the hole, and saved us from that disaster. We found a new fitting and now have several extra seacocks. I am counting this as our "sinking" and don't expect to have another.

I warned you at the beginning of this letter that I was writing not for your enlightenment but as a release for me. I needed some way to put our whole dreadful Clayton experience to rest. I hope it works, but I also hope you will read on about the good times.

We waited at Cape Vincent for the weather to clear for the Lake Ontario crossing. A sailboat with the mast down is unstable, and we were hoping for calm weather. After several days of waiting, we decided to make a run for it on a day that looked a bit iffy. We lucked out, making it across the lake on the only day possible for a week.

We had heard that the Erie Canal was dirty, with locks in pitiful shape, surly lockkeepers, unsafe towns, and dangerous commercial traffic. We had also heard that it was clean, with new locks, helpful lockkeepers, interesting towns, and little commercial traffic. To our delight, the second description was accurate. The New York Department of Transportation now charges for recreational use of the canal, and those funds are used to improve its facilities. Many towns are run-down and sad because of the recession, but they are still historically interesting.

We entered the Hudson River at Troy, where we experienced our first tides. It seems incredible that a place so far from the sea can have a four-foot fresh-water tide, but it does, so we used the tide and current tables to our advantage, remembering to anchor in enough water to account for the tidal range.

At Castleton-on-Hudson, New York, we stepped the mast. Kent had always wanted to try the wishbone, line, and winch method of raising our mast, but I had been fearfully reluctant and insisted that we use a crane to lift the unwieldy length of aluminum. Now I gave in. The signs were propitious, and if we were ever going to justify carrying that awkward wishbone, this was the time. The do-it-yourself boat club at Castleton had a crane in case we got in trouble.

While waiting in St. Vincent, we met Lew and Ann Tucker,[1] a charming couple who offered to be our forwarding address and help step the mast. We got up early, before traffic, wind, and waves picked up, and got the stick up with Lew's help. Lew helped step seven masts for people coming out of the canal that day. He also drove Kent to find a replacement seacock.

We have discovered that as tedious, uncomfortable, and expensive as boating can be, it's balanced by the generosity and kindness of boaters like the Tuckers who take us grocery shopping and invite us to their homes for dinner on the slightest acquaintance. We create a family in nearly every anchorage or dock, and because we might not meet again, we make friends fast. The one obligation for all the kindness that has been shown us is to pass it on by helping someone else. Would that we were able.

---

1. Our paths will cross with the Tuckers again over the next twenty years.

We passed Hyde Park, West Point, Sing Sing, Nyack (where we were treated to free showers at the yacht club), and Washington Irving's home before reaching the Big Apple. When we were in Clayton, a tall, good-looking guy with a French accent walked by *Coot* and said, "You're not really from Brookings, South Dakota, are you?" We said yes, and Christian proceeded to tell us that he'd graduated from the University of South Dakota at Vermillion and that his wife Mary had been raised in Elk Point. Although they now lived in Canton, New York, they had just returned from a year of cruising along the East Coast and in the Bahamas with their two teenaged daughters. They were eager to share their experiences, and we were keen to learn.

I had been worried about New York City. I'm a country girl, and big cities terrify me. Christian and Mary calmed our fears and told us we must stop at the 79th Street Boat Basin, where we could pick up a mooring for five dollars a night and have a safe place to leave the dinghy. We had spoken to other people we'd met along the canal and the Hudson, and most said they either wanted to whiz by New York without stopping or go into one of the more well-known, very expensive marinas.

Because of Christian and Mary, we stopped at 79th Street and now wish we'd spent a week there, not just one night. I was reminded of the live-aboard marinas in Sausalito from twenty years ago. People at the basin, both the residents and the workers, seemed more like laid-back Californians than hopped-up New Yorkers. Some of the boats apparently hadn't moved in years. They were strung about with extension cords, rusting bits of nautical junk, and giant flowerpots filled with dying sunflowers. It was like being back in our old hippie days.

After finding someone to take our five dollars and direct us to an empty mooring, we put the outboard on the dinghy

and motored to shore in search of a couple of charts of the
New Jersey coast that we'd been unable to locate. The people
at the boat basin were most helpful. They gave us a subway
schedule and clear directions to New York Nautical. We set
off with great trepidation, sure that we would be mugged on
the subway. But much to our surprise, we had a pleasant ride,
found the chart shop without trouble, and returned safely to
the boat basin. The basin was three blocks from the Museum
of Natural History and the Hayden Planetarium, so we
walked over to see the outside and the grounds.

Beyond that was Central Park. Of course, I had to sit on a
bench and smoke a cigarette. We wandered around, looking at
the snazzy apartment buildings with signs on their doorways
saying, "No Menus," and found what we are always looking
for—a hardware store. It was buried beneath an elegant
brownstone, and after twenty minutes of minutely describing
our requirements, we were presented with something we'd long
been looking for, an 18-inch length of ¼-inch copper tubing.

Mary and Christian had also told us to stop at Zabar's,
a grocery to please the most critical gourmet. I could have
spent a week there. I didn't recognize half of the meats or
cheeses and wished they had written explanations. A guided
tour would have been great.

The following day, we rose early to catch the tide. We sped
through the mouth of the Hudson, past the skyscrapers, the
Staten Island Ferries, the Statue of Liberty, Ellis Island, and
the freighters entering New York harbor under the Verrazano
Narrows Bridge. We had reached the Atlantic! Wow! We'd
really done it. We had a boat with the mast up and were
finally in saltwater.

We sailed from New York to Cape May, New Jersey, in
one rather tiring hop, spent the next day catching up on sleep,
and left on the first convenient tide to scoot up Delaware Bay

New York City Sunrise

to the Chesapeake and Delaware Canal. Because we could not find a decent place to anchor, we traversed the C and D Canal at night. It was spooky moving in constrained waters in the dark, but the shore of the canal was well-lighted, so we managed almost without mishap.

We had two close calls during our night in the Chesapeake and Delaware Canal. At two in the morning, just after I radioed a bridge to open, a speeding Coast Guard cutter burst toward us out of the darkness on our side of the canal, forcing me toward a bridge support. I saw the pilot's eyes as big as saucers as he turned hard to avoid us, creating a huge wave that soaked us to the skin and poured through our wide-open forehatch onto our berth. A bed soaked in saltwater is miserable, but we could have been sunk. I grabbed the radio to tell the pilot what I thought about his "seamanship," but Pam stopped me. She thought I might not be tactful and would get in trouble with the Coast Guard.

That same night, guided only by the lights alongside the canal, we approached Chesapeake City, where we planned to anchor to dry out. I was about to turn into the harbor entrance when the lights of the town and the entrance markers vanished. I saw nothing and heard nothing. I started to turn to port, assuming I'd see something when we got closer. Then, I sensed something moving beside us. The hair rose on the back of my neck. The lights had not gone out! There was a large ship moving beside us, just yards away, its lights so far above us, its hull so high that there was only a dark wall of steel sliding past. Thankfully, I delayed the turn, the lights returned, and I clearly saw the harbor entrance.

Once, we despaired of ever making it out of the Great Lakes, but we have reached the tidal waters of Chesapeake Bay. We winkled *Coot* into Baltimore's inner harbor, where we found a prime spot between a World War II submarine on display near the aquarium and the last sail-rigged U.S. battleship, the Constellation. Kent refuses to be as circumspect as I am and will get us into the tiniest and most interesting spots.

We found a crazy hardware store run by a ninety-five-year-old woman bent to the size of a paper clip. She had drawers of fittings, with no idea of their use, but she unlocked the door and let us rummage to our hearts' content, all the while keeping up a running commentary on the state of the world. I wish I had this old lady as a neighbor—she made more sense than McNeil/Lehrer.

Kent and I took a sun shower in the cockpit, right under the windows of the World Trade Center in the heart of Baltimore, while tourists strolled on the shore. I told Kent I never thought I'd sink so low as to have to bathe in public, and he responded that he never thought he'd be so exalted as not to care.

We endured our first gale in Annapolis and spent much of the night watching to be sure our anchor held, calling one boat that threatened to drag down on us. We had gusts to fifty knots, even in our protected spot, and steady winds near thirty-five. The night must have been wild out in the bay and on the ocean. On the radio, we heard about searches for missing windsurfers, a sunk tug, and boats taking on water and calling for help. I suppose we had to go through a gale sometime, and sitting relatively comfortably at anchor is the way to do it, although I'd just as soon have given it a miss.

We shopped for boating gear because Annapolis may have the best boating supplies in the country. My former sister-in-law Corkie Kirkham and her mother brought mail and luxurious goodies and took us on a ride into the country that rounded out our time in Annapolis.

Many other boaters suggest that we give the Virgin Islands and the whole northern part of the Caribbean a miss because it's become expensive, crowded, and unfriendly. Everyone has raved about the Bahamas, so we are thinking of going there. We won't decide until we reach our proposed jumping-off place of Moorhead City, North Carolina, but don't be surprised if my next letter comes from Florida instead of St. Thomas. (Conclusion of Pam's letter to friends, written from St. Michaels, Maryland, September 27, 1994)

Pam's next letter to friends came from Elizabeth City, North Carolina, near Albemarle Sound, on October 12, 1994:

We're sitting up the creek, waiting for a heavy northeaster to pass over Albemarle Sound so we can cross in relative comfort. This is our third day hanging on the anchor, hoping the weatherman will give the go-ahead to continue our way south. It's starting to get cold, and the leaves have begun to turn, so we want to move to a lower latitude soon. It's been a couple of weeks since the wind and outside temperatures have let us use the sun shower, and both Kent and I are getting pretty rank. We take wee scrubs at the galley sink, but this doesn't satisfy my desire for an all-over wash. I'm so dirty

that my crevices could support intelligent life. But let me
catch you up on how we got here.

From St. Michaels, we made a day sail to hidden,
untenanted Mill Creek, a place the cruising guide calls
"the-Bay-As-It-Used-To-Be." It was a lovely spot once we
found our way in, but we almost got stuck on a shoal when
we refused to believe our compass and GPS and followed
the wrong markers to the entrance of the creek. The depth
sounder, which had been on its usual strike, sent out a weak
beep as we approached shallow water, warning that we were
almost aground. Kent immediately put the engine in neutral,
and we bobbed about, wondering how to get ourselves back
in deep water.

I use the term deep loosely, as the depth of the
Chesapeake averages only twenty-one feet. The shipping
channels run about forty feet, which means that the edges are
remarkably shallow. We crept in one direction, then another,
hoping to find our way, when two dolphins leaped from the
water and swam to the left. Kent had not been expecting
dolphins, and when they surfaced, he thought for a moment
that they were rocks. The dolphins swam back to the boat,
surfaced, smiled in their dolphinny way, and swam off to the
left. Kent said, "What the hell," and followed them. Yes, the
Flipper stories are true. We got back into adequate depths,
saw the proper marks, and made our way into Mill Creek
without further incident. These were the only dolphins we
saw in the Chesapeake, and other boaters we talked with had
not seen any. We have now decided to ignore the GPS, the
depth sounder, and the compass and navigate entirely by the
"dolphin method."

We decided to whiz through the large city of Norfolk,
which was to be our last stop in the Chesapeake. We
anchored for the night at the north end of the city and
started through the massive harbor at first light. We passed

an array of Navy vessels, including destroyers, troop carriers, submarines, and aircraft carriers. The harbor was filled with the traffic of enormous sea-going freighters, tugs, and barges. We were small, but the way was clear, and we managed to avoid collisions. By the time we'd made it to the beginning of the Intracoastal Waterway (ICW), we'd fallen into a line of a dozen or more cruising boats. Someone called that they had sailed on *Coot* in the Bahamas with her previous owner. He wanted to buy our boat! We had just one last bridge before turning off to the Dismal Swamp.

I was listening on channel 13 (the channel for communicating with bridges) when I heard that a tug pushing a large barge was coming from the other direction, entirely out of sight of those waiting with us. The bridge opened, and the lead catamaran started through. A laconic, slow-speaking Southerner on the bridge channel warned the tug captain that the catamaran was coming through.

In a calm melodic drawl, the tug captain responded, "It will be to her advantage if she doesn't."

Then a voice over a loudspeaker ordered the cat to stay put, and she did. The tug and the barge came through; then, the bridge closed to allow long lines of cars to cross. Now twelve boats were milling around between the barge and the low bridge, trying to avoid the shallows. My tongue was out, and I dropped another two pounds, but we didn't bump anyone. [Pam pressed her tongue against the back of her upper front teeth, a dead giveaway that she was nervous.]

The Intracoastal Waterway (ICW) divides after the bridge. The deeper channel is used by larger cruising boats and barges. The Great Dismal Swamp Canal is the shallower, and only *Coot* took that route. In our usual well-prepared fashion, we had spoken to one other boater who told us that the Coast Guard had informed them that the Great Dismal Swamp Canal was open. We did not bother checking further.

The cruising guide noted that there would be a sign where
the channels divided, telling us whether the route was open
or closed. When water levels are low, the canal is sometimes
closed at either end to preserve the lake that feeds it. At the
turning point, we saw a sign so small and insignificant that we
had to get close before I could read it, even with binoculars. It
said merely, "Dismal Swamp Canal." I guess I had expected a
flashing neon sign—DISMAL SWAMP—OPEN (or closed).

Kent, of course, said, "Let's go in and see." We did. We
saw no one and felt as though we had left the planet. It was
hard to believe that less than a mile back lay Norfolk, the navy
base, the shipyards, and the marinas. We wound through
reeds and stumps (the depth sounder was not working) until
we came to the first lock, where, to our relief, three sailboats
waited to lock through. It was a truly pleasant motor through
the swamp, although it was more like gliding through a
forest along this oldest, still-in-use canal in the United States.
George Washington surveyed the area as a young man and
had timber interests on its banks. How would the swamp have
looked had George and his buddies not gone into the logging
business? Maybe the giant ancient cedars would still be here.
It is lovely as it is, but it must once have been spectacular.

We spent the night at a highway rest stop between the
locks at each end of the canal. The highway came close to the
canal here, with a rest stop for cars on one side and a dock
for boats on the other. Motorists came down to the dock and
asked, "How did you get here? Did you have the boat on a
trailer?"

The friendly staffers gave us brochures about North
Carolina and insisted we watch a video that described the
creatures that inhabit the swamp—bears, water moccasins,
deer, and mosquitos. We learned it's a beautiful place to
hike if you have good gumboots and that the water from

Lake Drummond is healthful (although it is the color of weak coffee). Commodore Perry took barrels of it on his expeditions. The pictures of the lake, with its magnificently grotesque cypress trees and contorted roots, made us want to dinghy to it. The lake's perfectly round shape is said to have been formed by a meteor, but I like the Indian legend that claims it was a firebird's nest.

We reached Elizabeth City, North Carolina, after navigating our seventy-sixth and final lock of the summer and leaving the Dismal Swamp. This is a town on the Pasquotank River that welcomes cruising sailors and gives them two nights of free dockage. The Rose Buddies present roses to the women and hold wine and cheese parties on the dock. The town has preserved its Victorian houses, and we enjoyed walking through the tree-shaded neighborhoods.

On the morning we planned to leave, high winds closed the Alligator Bridge. So we went back up the river to anchor in a sheltered spot until the weather looked better and the bridge opened. Kent pulled his back but got us into the river even in his pain, where we anchored a few miles up. He's been quite immobile for the last couple of days, so it was good to have this rest. The weatherman is also forecasting a gale for tomorrow, so we may be here for some time, although we'll have to move around another curve to get shelter from easterly winds.

It's very peaceful right now. At sunset, the water goes perfectly calm and reflects the red and golden leaves. We are out of sight of all civilization and feel like we are cruising. I dread motoring down to Beaufort with the barges, motorboats, and currents, but we hope to go offshore from Beaufort, maybe to Charleston, South Carolina, and see some real sailing soon.

Chapter 11

Going South

October–November 1994

Take the adventure, heed the call, now ere the
irrevocable moment passes! —KENNETH GRAHAME,
Wind in the Willows, Chapter 9, Wayfarers All

The following letter to friends covers several chapters and took
Pam several months to finish. By the time it was ready to mail
on February 4, 1995, we'd arrived at Hawksnest Bay in the Virgin
Islands, having completed our passage of the Intracoastal Waterway and sailing to Florida, the Bahamas, and the Virgin Islands:

> After Elizabeth City, we kept up our lemming-like motoring
> down the Intracoastal Waterway. We made it through the
> Alligator Bridge along with 200 other boats that had been
> held up by the bad weather. I knew that many people made
> this watery trek each year, moving north in the spring and
> south in the fall along the ICW, but I had no idea that there
> were this many. We felt like we were a part of a Wally Byam[1]

---

1. Wallace Merle "Wally" Byam (1896–1962) founded the Airstream travel
   trailer company and promoted traveling and camping worldwide in the
   streamlined aluminum trailers. Wikipedia, "Wally Byam." Last modified
   31 August 2021.

caravan of Airstreams. Our next big stop was Beaufort, North Carolina.

In Beaufort, we decided to get rid of all the paper charts we had used so far. We had so many piles of charts on our little boat that we could hardly move. So, we packaged them in a box and, using all our strength, lugged them to the Post Office to send to Pam's brother. We struggled to lift the box onto the Post Office scale, only to be told it exceeded the 75-pound per package limit. We could not tell by how much because the scale only went to 75 pounds. So, we lugged the box back to the boat, divided it between two boxes, returned to the post office, and discovered that we had used 85 pounds of charts to sail from Duluth, Minnesota, to Beaufort, North Carolina.

Why did we have so many charts? Today people often sail with nothing but electronic versions, but printed nautical charts were essential before GPS (Global Positioning System) and electronic

GLOBAL POSITIONING SYSTEM (GPS)

In the years between the two boats (1985–1994), GPS was developed by the United States for the military and released for civilian use shortly before we left on *Coot*. The signal was purposely degraded, and sometimes we had to wait for three satellites to pass before we could receive a reading of our latitude and longitude. We then transferred those numbers to a paper chart to see where we were. Today GPS instruments, phones, and computers let us see where we are, where we've been and where we are going almost instantly. Even in its primitive state, GPS was easier and more accurate than navigating with a sextant and compass. See the National Geographic Education Resources website for an excellent explanation of GPS and its history.

charts took over wayfinding. We had acquired these charts in an unusual manner.

South Dakota is about as far away from an ocean as any place in North America. However, between the main course and dessert at a Christmas dinner with our friends Sue and Jeff, a guest asked, "Do you know anyone who needs nautical charts? We have some that we're going to throw away." Had Sue and Jeff invited this person on purpose?

Pam responded, "Why yes, maybe we do. Which charts do you have?"

"All of them. Or just about all of them. A few were sent back."

"All of the NOAA charts?" asked Pam incredulously. "There are thousands!"

It turned out that NOAA (National Oceanographic and Atmospheric Administration), which publishes the nautical charts for domestic waters, had contracted with a small cartography firm in Brookings to check the place name accuracy. With the task completed, they now had a roomful of charts. At that time, one chart cost $14, and we would need hundreds of them.

So, of course, we took them. We sorted the charts into piles and spent a week flattening, folding, and arranging them. The East Coast went in the living room, the west coast and the Pacific in the family room, and Alaska had the spare bedroom to itself. The Great Lakes and inland rivers went in another pile. The only ones missing were a few with mistakes that had been returned to NOAA. We had with us the charts (of every scale) covering the Great Lakes and the East Coast. They were so detailed that we used five for a sail of a few hours from Chesapeake Bay to Baltimore's inner harbor. One or two small-scale charts would have sufficed, but we felt compelled to use the large ones because we had them. They added an element of mystery to our travels because when the cartographers completed their comparisons, they crossed off the names with felt-tipped markers. We joked that we could get anywhere with our charts, but we would not always know where we were.

Beaufort has the largest concentration of foreign yachts on the East Coast outside of Ft. Lauderdale. It's also a town that welcomes boaters and provides dinghy dockage, courtesy cars to the grocery store, and hot showers for a small fee. All in all, it's a great place to get the lowdown on what's down the road. We renewed acquaintances we'd made previously, especially with two English boats, *Viking* and *Lady of Spain*, crewed by two young English couples.

Kent and I do not have a lot in common with most boaters our age. First, *Coot* is tiny compared to most of the over-fifties' boats, and secondly, we haven't all the bells and whistles that most of them have, such as wind generators, freezers, refrigerators, radar, single-side-band radios, sun awnings, roller-furling, powerful engines, electronic self-steering devices, and large spaces to stow edible and drinkable goodies. We are to the floating condos as a pup tent is to a Winnebago.

As you know, we have had our share of mechanical problems, but can you imagine the difficulties these affluent folks have? They have them, and they talk about them. We bored ourselves and those around us silly by talking about our engine problems, and we were not going to be as kind as people were to us by listening to a litany of woes about failing equipment of a kind that we don't have. Thus, we find ourselves drawn to young sailors with radically limited means and small, old, simple sailboats like *Viking* and *Lady of Spain*. These younger people talked about things other than their boats and the weather, and they had books to trade that weren't covered in lurid foil.

We first met *Viking* when we headed down the river from St. Michaels at the end of September. We noticed a little boat ahead of us turn out into Chesapeake Bay. A few minutes later, it came back and sailed into a protected cove. We thought maybe it was blowing a hooley around the corner, and sure enough, when we made the turn, we did not want to beat our way into those waves, either. So, we, too, turned back and anchored. *Viking* was a small, old-fashioned wooden boat that flew the British ensign. I rowed over to have a look.

Ned and Kate were puttering about, and I called out, "I like your boat."

Ned called back, "Yes, it's a nice little boat. It was built for an Englishman in Germany in 1945."

When I told Pam, she immediately asked, "How did an Englishman have a boat built in Germany during World War II?"

The winds continued through the night, and both boats remained in the cove for a second day. So, we invited Ned and Kate for tea, and heard *Viking*'s extraordinary story.

A Royal Air Force quartermaster, who was also an avid sailor, served in one of the forces that occupied Germany at the end of the Second World War. His troops liberated a small fishing and boat-building village on the north coast of Germany. The people were destitute and needed almost everything. beds, blankets, clothing, and food. However, they had plenty of well-aged oak, teak, and spruce, since the war had kept them from building boats.

The quartermaster had access to many things that the villagers needed, and the villagers had all that was necessary to build him a fine little boat. He made some deals, and may have bent some rules, because he was later court-martialed for consorting with the enemy. He managed to beat the rap, and when his hitch was over, he sailed his little boat back to England.

Over the years, *Viking* had several owners. When Ned and Kate bought her, they investigated her history and contacted the son of the quartermaster. The son had emigrated to Nova Scotia, so Ned and Kate sailed *Viking* across the Atlantic via the northern route, partly to visit him. When they arrived, they found that the old quartermaster was also visiting, so they took him for a sail on his old boat.

> We continued to bump into Ned and Kate, who had taken two years off from their work in a London architect's office. They were waiting to connect with another young English couple, Ben and Beth Munro of *Lady of Spain,* who had spent the summer in Maine. All three boats met in Elizabeth City and traveled to Beaufort together.
>
> *Lady of Spain* was a wooden Vertue,[2] even more modest in size and appointments than *Viking.* Built in 1952 and lengthened from a miserly twenty-five feet to a princely twenty-seven by the addition of an elegant but very narrow stern, *Lady of Spain* is only seven feet in the beam and five-and-a-half feet in draft. She is a bit like a sheet of plywood pushed vertically in the water with only a foot or so sticking out. She is the only boat we have met that has been to sea, or has pretensions of going to sea, with less freeboard than *Coot,* and she gave me great faith that we could contemplate a successful sea voyage.

Friendships were formed among the steady stream of boaters along the waterway. Some had pets onboard, and one day the VHF radio was filled with queries about a dog that was in difficulty because there was no dry ground where he could relieve himself. Much advice was forthcoming as to how to teach poor

---

2. Vertue yachts were renowned long-distance small cruising boats designed by British boat designer Laurent Giles beginning in 1936. Wikipedia, "John Laurent Giles." Last modified 1 June 2022.

Fifi to defecate on a newspaper or in a box. Because the VHF radio is supposed to be used only for emergencies and serious boating business, the Brits,[3] Ben and Beth and Ned and Kate, were a bit flabbergasted.

One evening in a pub, we amused ourselves by imagining how we might turn the radio chatter to a more serious matter. What would happen if I called either *Lady of Spain* or *Viking* after we had been underway for a couple of hours and asked to speak to Kevin. Ben would reply, "Isn't he with you? I haven't seen him. Maybe he is on *Viking*."

I would then call *Viking* who would tell me he was not with them, either. We would discuss where we had seen him last, and reveal that Kevin was a ten-year-old child ("What's that dear? . . . Oh, I guess he is only eight—but he is big for his age. . .").

I played the blasé father who resisted going back to look for him. "He knows we are heading for Beaufort. He's a smart kid. I bet he'll find his own way there. . . ." Other boaters would hear these conversations through the radio that is kept on at all times while underway. What advice might we get, and how we would respond? We never actually did this, of course, although once I called *Lady of Spain* and jokingly asked if Kevin was there, and Ben replied, "No but his shoes are here." It became a joke among us to ask about Kevin. Indeed, over the years we received Kevin's postcards from various parts of the world.

---

3. We met many British sailors, including Ned and Kate Phillips and Ben and Beth Munro. Today Ned designs dioramas for museums, and Kate is a teacher. They still sail. Ben and Beth and their daughters live in the village of Downderry, overlooking the sea near the Southwest Coast Path. Ben is an engineer and naval architect, and Beth is a printmaker. See Beth's webpage, "Beth Munro Printmaker." In 2013, Linnea and I departed from their home on our multi-day walk to Falmouth.

Ben is a wooden boat builder, and Beth is one of the freest and most generous spirits I've ever met. We all planned to go our separate ways after a few blow-outs at Beaufort's Back Street Pub and a thorough raid on the canned-goods section of the local Food Lion. *Viking* intended to sail from Beaufort to Miami before going to Cuba. *Lady of Spain* intended to sail to the British Virgin Islands and then down to Grenada. *Coot* planned to sail from Beaufort to northern Florida, hoping to finally get a taste of ocean travel. After Kent and I arrived in Florida, we would make our way to Ft. Lauderdale, where we hoped to get whatever nautical junk we still needed. We would meet Andy in the Bahamas over Christmas. All three boats planned to leave on the same day, but only *Coot* managed to keep to her itinerary.

We left Beaufort after a hectic night at anchor off the town dock. In much of the ICW, two anchors are required— one up- and one down-current. A boat swings with the direction of the current and changes her heading with the in-going or out-going tide. But, if someone anchors with only one anchor and a strong wind comes in a direction opposite to the current, and if moorings are scattered among the anchored boats, or the anchorage is exceptionally crowded, the wind and currents can play merry hell, as they did that night in Beaufort. All the ingredients for disaster were present. People dragged. People danced and sailed around their anchors, and everyone sat in their cockpits, waiting to fend off the next wayward boat. One boat near us had been rear-ended by a single-anchored boat. The captain was in his dinghy checking out the damage to his stern when an enormous catamaran sailed around her mooring at about four knots and creamed her bow. Somehow, we managed to escape the mayhem of the night, only to have a nightmare retrieving our anchors the next day, which we were able to do when that infamous fellow on one anchor used his dinghy to push his boat out of our way. What an inauspicious prelude to the first major hop of our trip!

But it may have been a blessing that we'd had a sleepless night before starting a longer passage. When our off-watch turns came, we went right to sleep. We are usually keyed up during a first night at sea and wear ourselves to exhaustion. I dreaded seasickness. Kent, of course, was eager to get the sails up and go. We left in little wind, but in a horrendous slop left over from the night before.

Even with my scopolamine patches, I got green. We had several bail-out points programmed into our GPS in case we wanted to get out of the ocean and back into the ICW, but in the end, we rather enjoyed the freedom of the open water and kept outside until we turned back into the coast at Fernandina Beach, Florida—a trip of three and a half days. Hundreds of dolphins kept pace with us for nearly two hours—the most we'd ever seen of these charming creatures.

To our surprise, we liked northern Florida. We were sorry to have missed storied Charleston, South Carolina, and the swamps of Georgia with their nine-foot tides and meandering waterways (where almost everyone ran aground), but we were grateful to be a couple of weeks ahead of schedule after spending too much time in the fleshpots and marine stores of Beaufort. The miles of uninhabited marsh called to mind the long grass prairies of South Dakota. The birds seemed to be on a winter vacation from Oakwood Lakes. We recognized pelicans, great blue herons, cormorants, and night herons. The palm trees and our first and only alligator did not remind us of South Dakota, however, and we were grateful. We anchored in a sea of grasses entirely by ourselves. We had left the post-gale bulge of boats in Beaufort and now enjoyed our leisurely meandering through the ICW, which felt like taking a back road rather than fighting rush hour on I-90.

We intended to treat ourselves to a pleasant stay at St. Augustine, but while we were enjoying lunch onshore with a South Dakota friend, the wind came up, and I began to twitch. I always twitch when the wind comes up, whether I'm on shore or on the boat. First, I become distracted, and then I get irritable. With accelerating irritation, I insisted we go back to the waterfront.

The wind always blows ten knots higher near the shore, and when we arrived, the boats in the anchorage, *Coot* included, were rearing at their rodes. We had anchored *Coot* upwind of the other boats, thinking that no boats would drag down on us if the predicted winds materialized. However, that meant we were far from the dinghy dock. We flung ourselves into our dinghy and, taking green water at every wave, beat our wet way back to *Coot*. We were not able to leave the boat for three days.

Late one afternoon, during the gale, we overheard a call to the Coast Guard from a boat named *Serenity*:

Coast Guard, Coast Guard. This is the sailing boat, *Serenity*. We are approaching marker number 3 at the St. Augustine inlet. Is there deep water there? We've lost our engine, our mainsail blew out, and our chart washed overboard.

Coast Guard: Do you request our assistance?

Serenity: We want to know how much water we have around marker number 3—we have lost our chart and have no engine.

Coast Guard: How many people do you have onboard? Do you have your life vests on?

Serenity: Yes, we have our life jackets on. There are four of us. Oh, my God, we just bumped the bottom! Can you tell us which way to go to find deep water?

Coast Guard: Please confirm that you have your life vests on.

About this time, a local fisherman interrupted: *Serenity*, turn around—get the hell out of there!

Coast Guard: Whoever interrupted, do not interfere. *Serenity*, did you say there were four people on board? Do you have your life vests on? Do you want us to take you off your boat?"

Fisherman: *Serenity*, can you maintain a heading of 120 degrees?

Coast Guard: Who is that interrupting? Stay off this frequency!

Serenity: Almost. I can just make 100 degrees. Will that get me into trouble?

Fisherman: That will be enough. Head out two miles or so. I will guide you down the coast. Do not try to come in this inlet.

Coast Guard: Stop interrupting! *Serenity*, do you want to be taken off your boat?

Serenity: No, we are sailing now.

The Coast Guard then dropped out. Tow Boat, a commercial outfit, offered to take them fuel, but was unable to make it through the inlet and came back with one engine knocked out. We listened to the fisherman direct *Serenity* down the coast until we lost contact. Who was *Serenity*, and why was she trying to cross the notorious St. Augustine bar during a gale? Over the years, whenever we saw a boat named *Serenity*, we wanted to ask if she was the one, but we never did. Perhaps *Serenity* is not a suitable name for a boat.

After this excitement, and after the wind dropped, I begged Kent to go into a marina, our first since Clayton, since more wind was expected, and we hadn't yet seen any of St. Augustine beyond its shoreline. He acquiesced on the condition that we find a spot on the south side of the dock. He'd watched the boats on the north side bang themselves senseless during the gale and decided, rightly, that it was better to be at anchor. When I called the marina, the desperation in my voice must have been obvious. They gave us the only available slip on the south side of the dock—one big enough for a sixty-foot boat. I would have taken anything, even a more dangerous berth, because if the boat decided to bounce, I could walk off.

We pulled in, put out all our mooring line, which was a lot with the 200 additional feet we'd purchased in Beaufort, and I relaxed until the next weather report. I'd been tracking hurricanes on a handy chart we'd been given at the rest stop in the Great Dismal Swamp. I saw Florence whirl her way into the northeast Atlantic far away from us, and just as I erased her tracks, we began to get reports of Gordon. Dear little Gordon! I'd watched and plotted him before he had a name, when he was merely a tropical trough in the western Caribbean. Then he became a tropical depression, grew into a tropical storm, and got his name.

I didn't think Gordon would affect us. Storms starting in the western Caribbean usually go ashore in Nicaragua, Belize, or Mexico. But Gordon moved north and east. He came through the Caymans, savaged Jamaica, and raged along the southern side of Cuba. He didn't hit a big enough landmass to stop him but veered and gathered enough strength over the sea to keep him coming. He banged hard into the Bahamas and southern Florida, spawned some destructive tornadoes, and went overland into the Gulf of Mexico. The jaunt across Florida should have killed him, but everyone, including me, thought that if it didn't, he'd at least blow himself out in the northern Gulf.

We and others at the marina were getting ready to move south when we heard that Gordon was once more crossing Florida and entering the Atlantic. I was enormously glad not to be on the north side of the dock when the boats snapped their mooring lines, and the people sat in the marina lounge all night rather than in their pitching boats. We lay in a perfectly calm slick provided by the dock in front of us. Because we were in such a long slip, we were well back from the waves breaking over the dock. Gordon became an official hurricane heading toward Cape Hatteras with a vengeance. All of us at St. Augustine pitied those further north, but we were relieved. We had thought about Gordon long enough.

We liked St. Augustine, a funky blend of faux history and the real thing. The old city is full of secret streets and walled gardens filled with exotic blooms that I'd seen only in the glossy, tropical gardening books I used to check out from the Brookings Public Library. We enjoyed seeing Spanish Colonial buildings next to turn-of-the-century imitations. In Canada, at the beginning of the summer, we'd visited British forts, and now in St. Augustine, we saw our first Spanish fort.

After the winds dropped, we motored down the ICW to the Cape Canaveral inlet, the first one recommended for accessing the ocean. We thought we were done with locks when we left the Great Dismal Swamp, but there was one last lock on the Cape Canaveral Barge Canal, and it was our worst. We nearly crashed and burned in the currents, but fortunately, no one else was locking through with us, and our uncontrolled spinning caused no damage.

Once in the ocean, we intended to go straight down to Ft. Lauderdale, missing the bridges and traffic in central and southern Florida. But near the Lake Worth entrance, we realized that we'd been traveling far faster than we'd anticipated, and we'd arrive at Ft. Lauderdale at midnight instead of at dawn. It was getting bumpy with a nasty northeast swell, and my stomach said it would be nice to stop swaying. So, we anchored just inside the entrance to Lake Worth and went below for a peaceful lunch, thinking we could leave at dusk and finish our trip to Ft. Lauderdale.

Then we heard someone call, "*Coot, Coot, Coot.*" Many sailors travel with buddy boats. Boats with dogs usually travel with other boats with dogs. Boats with children, pair with other boats with children. French Canadian boats travel together. We've never fallen into this habit. We enjoy the company of other boaters and occasionally get together for cocktails, but we are seldom going in the same direction. Nor do we want to spend the same amount of time at various stops. Often this is because we are looking for some bit of gear. Other boats may be more sensibly provisioned, and their owners don't spend their free time walking to hardware stores.

So, it was odd to hear someone call our name at a stop we hadn't intended to make. The caller was, to our amazement, *Viking*, whom we'd never expected to see again. Ned and Kate were supposed to have gone to Cuba and then sailed back to England.

Viking hadn't left Beaufort when we did but decided to enjoy a last night on the town. Then, shortly out of Beaufort, one of the pre-Gordon gales drove *Viking* into the Gulf Stream. After three days of hard sailing, they were broken,

weary, and grateful to have survived. Ned, an experienced
North Sea sailor, said he'd never seen such seas, and
although *Viking* stood up well, the dinghy broke loose, the
wind generator nearly tore itself free, and the glassware and
everything below shattered and scattered.

Kate and Ned were now heading to Ft. Lauderdale for
repairs before sailing to Cuba. They hadn't heard from *Lady of
Spain*, and we all worried because we knew that she must have
faced rough weather, too. In Ft. Lauderdale, we shared with
Viking some of the craziness of "The Capital of U.S. Sailing."

We also saw Lydia and John again. Ten years ago, when we
had hauled *Jacana* at Summerfield's boatyard, Lydia taught us
how to paint and varnish and helped us in innumerable ways.
I hadn't been in touch with her for nine of those ten years,
but the old phone number still worked. The people and the
yard were nearly the same. The travel lift stood in the same
spot, and Lydia was still using the same paints and varnishes.
John and Lydia took us shopping, and we reminisced for long
hours.

We had our first serious lessons in carless city travel
and learned the bus routes to the marine supply houses.
We bought a second folding bicycle and became adept at
dodging traffic while loaded down with sacks of laundry.
Kent discovered that when we replaced the transmission,
we should have replaced a toothed flange connecting the
flywheel to the starter. He spent two days crouched behind
the engine pulling the transmission and the flywheel. Then
he loaded the fifty-pound flywheel into a sack into the dinghy
and biked it to a Volvo mechanic who turned its teeth around.
Then he hauled it back, and reinstalled it.

Now that we have given up having much to do with
mechanics, life is better. We continue to have problems: the
starter in Fernandina, a broken throttle cable in St. Augustine,

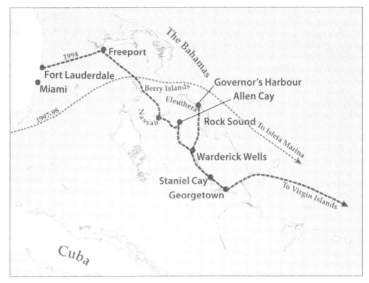

Coot's passage through the Bahamas (1994–95) and around the islands (1997–98)

the flywheel in Ft. Lauderdale, a fuel pump in the Bahamas, and an unlocatable air leak in the fuel system. But at least these problems are ours, and the resulting mess is entirely our fault.

As you can see from my heading, we have finally made it into the Caribbean after many unexpected twists and turns. I have no good excuse for my lengthy silence except that somehow the gestalt for writing never seemed right. I thank you for your much-appreciated letters, even though your news and comments have made me terribly lonely for my friends and have made it even more difficult to write.

Chapter 12

Going Foreign

December 1994–January 1995

And you, you will come too, young brother;
for the days pass, and never return, and the
South still waits for you. —KENNETH GRAHAME,
Wind in the Willows, *Chapter 9, Wayfarers All*

By now [December], the date of Andy's arrival in Nassau was
getting perilously close, so we stowed everything and waited
for the first weather window that would allow us to cross the
dreaded Gulf Stream and leave the United States. On a day
with a light southerly wind, we motored out of Ft. Lauderdale
into a nasty swell left over from the last northeaster. It was late
afternoon, and we planned to arrive at first light in Freeport,
Grand Bahama. I anticipated a terrible night. We pitched and
lunged through the waves, and I wanted to turn back. I feared
it would be worse when we entered the Stream.

Kent said, "Hold on; let's at least see what it's like: we
can always turn back later." Amazingly, it calmed down once
we entered that fabled river. We made an easy Gulf Stream
crossing, arrived on schedule at Freeport, and cleared
customs easily before we slept the day away. The hurdle of

crossing the Stream that everyone on the ICW had been talking about since Norfolk was over.

From Freeport, we took another overnighter to a remote anchorage in the Berry Islands (one of the several groups of islands that make up the Bahamas), where we spent two nights waiting for favorable winds to move us down to Nassau. However, they didn't come, and if we ever expected to see our son, we were going to have to—horrors—beat. The English say that a gentleman never beats to windward, but as we had no gentlemen on board, we decided that we'd have to. It turned out to be a remarkably pleasant sail, albeit hard on the wind, with only a couple of tacks and calm seas. Andy arrived on time on December 14, and we spent an extra day in Nassau so he could see a bit of the city.

When we asked how to get to the airport in Nassau, we learned that there were no alternatives to outrageously expensive taxis. Surely the local people did not pay those rates! We kept asking until a lad told us that a bus to Adelaide passed close to the airport.

We found the Adelaide bus, and I told the driver that I wanted to get off close to the airport. He looked a bit puzzled but said, "Okay."

When he let us off, he pointed us toward the airport—two miles away. That was farther than we expected, but even with the long walk, we were happy to avoid the rip-off price for a taxi. We later learned we could have taken another bus to Adelaide that went closer.

We did not want to walk all the way to the bus with Andy's luggage, but I noticed vans from posh hotels waiting for passengers. One driver agreed to take us when the next plane arrived.

We joyously greeted Andy, waited for an hour after his arrival, then slipped into the line of passengers. I was pleased to be beating the taxi cartel coming and going. The driver dropped passengers at the hotel, then asked where we wanted to go. I thought we'd get off with everybody else and then catch an inexpensive city bus to the boat. But this was going to be even better! The driver took us right to our dock, just as a taxi would have. When I asked how much he wanted for the ride, the price was the same outrageous amount as a taxi! Pam wrote, "If you ever dreamed about being a powerful union boss, you couldn't do better than lead the Bahamian Taxi Driver's Union."

We were delighted to see Andy. He was half-way through his second year of college, and we realized he had ideas of his own, just as we hoped and dreaded he would. He had let his beard and mustache grow. Pam thought he was beginning to look like Rasputin.

"How about a haircut, Andy?"

"No thanks!"

We sailed the Bahama Banks for the first time. The banks are shallow and coral strewn, a major reason not to come here. Thin water makes us nervous, and we are not experienced in negotiating its dangers. The cruising guides post pictures, supposedly making it clear how one "reads" water depth by sight, but when I climb up on the bow pulpit, I can't tell whether the water is fifty, ten, or a keel-stopping four-feet deep. I don't know whether I'm seeing a coral head or a harmless patch of weeds. The guides advise traveling between the hours of 10 am and 2 pm, with the sun high over one's shoulder. However, it is impossible to leave with the sun behind and arrive with the sun high and behind within four hours. Fortunately, we finally got the knot-meter and the depth-sounder working when we dived under the boat in clear Berry Islands water. We had traveled the length of the shallow ICW with both instruments disabled by encrusted growth.

On our crossing of the banks from Nassau to the Exumas, we followed a couple who had made the trip four times before. They had a six-foot draft, and we have only five, so we felt safe. We stuck to their stern like a new foal to its dam. It took the sting out of our first banks crossing and put me in a much better and less nervous frame of mind.

The water was spectacular clear turquoise that shaded into sugar-white beaches. The islands were mostly small, uninhabited, scrub-covered green jewels. Our first stop, Allen Cay, was tucked between other cays and protected from winds in all directions with a nice reef to snorkel. A nearby cay was known for its iguanas. Kent was enamored of these protected creatures.

He watched a dinghy land. The iguanas advanced toward the visitors expecting treats. The newcomers gazed at the fearsome, prehistoric faces, then beat a hasty retreat. The confused iguanas then milled about on the beach, switching their tails in disappointment. Kent was reminded of the beginning of every semester when the students, eager to begin a new adventure, arrived, and the philosophy professors eagerly came forth from the scrub to meet them, only to gaze in confusion as the students, horrified at what they faced, hurriedly withdrew.

We moved down the island chain until we reached Warderick Wells, the center of the Exuma Islands Trust, a new national park. We hoped to put Andy on a plane to Nassau from Georgetown, the largest town in the Exumas at 800 souls, but the connections were impossible. However, we managed to get him a ticket from Governor's Harbor, Eleuthera, to Nassau. We planned to spend a few days at Warderick Wells, move down the chain to Georgetown, then take a mighty leap to Governor's Harbor before returning to Georgetown and its great congregation of wintering boats.

We spent three days at Warderick, walking the paths, visiting the ruins of failed plantations, and getting gnawed by no-see-ums. Just when we were hoping to leave, the weather turned sour. The storm had hurricane intensity, but for some reason, it never received a proper name. Afterwards, boaters asked each other, "Where were you during the pre-Christmas no-name storm?" We were in what may have been the best and safest spot in the Bahamas.

Warderick forbids anchoring to prevent damage to the surrounding coral and weed beds and provides excellent moorings. There were plenty of boaters to look out for each other. We didn't keep anchor watch but merely doubled our lines, put out lots of chaffing gear, and went to sleep. We could not get off the boat for a couple of days, but we were comfortable. Andy helped Kent jerry-rig the fuel pump into working order with tiny screws tapped into its innards and valves held down by plumber's strapping. It was probably more substantial and reliable than the genuine Volvo replacement we ordered.

When the storm ended on Christmas Eve, we were invited to bring munchies and drinks to the park headquarters building. A congenial Jewish harmonica player led a Christmas carol sing-along, and the park director fired up a generator to provide twinkling lights on an evergreen tree.

Andy hadn't had the vacation we'd envisioned for him, but I don't think he had high expectations of his parents' plans. He was driven nearly mad by the no-see-ums and broke out in a rash that rivaled any pre-vaccine case of measles. He had done little swimming, and two days below, fixing bits and pieces of the engine did little to improve the tan I'd hoped to send him back with. We spent Christmas Day sailing to Eleuthera, a place we knew nothing about and that none of the other boaters recommended.

At Cape Eleuthera, we found a nearly defunct marina. It was a spooky place. About ten years ago, it had been a thriving resort with a modern marina surrounded by luxury vacation condos. There were dozens of bungalows, a golf course, swimming pools, miles of paved roads, and artificial harbors. Apart from a few boats stored in the marina, the entire resort was deserted. The bungalows were windowless hulks, their gardens reverting to jungle. Golf carts sat abandoned on the fairways, and the roads led nowhere.

We found interesting flotsam kicked up by the storm. Andy made a Christmas tree and decorations from a nicely shaped branch, some bits of sea fan, a pretty shell or two, some attractive coral, and hibiscus flowers swiped from an abandoned bungalow garden. The surroundings made for a quiet and strangely sad Christmas. We've seen many lovely private homes and resorts shut up and going to seed. Apparently, junk-bond salesmen who made and lost their wads in the eighties had built and lost posh houses in the islands.

From the Cape, we went to Rock Sound, Eleuthera, one of the first real towns we'd come to. There were only two other yachts in the harbor, and there were no tourists and T-shirt sellers. There was a grocery, a hardware store, and a filling station in a newly built little strip mall, and the houses looked as though they'd been there longer than twenty years. We wanted to stay longer, but we had to be within striking distance of Andy's airplane.

So, we plugged on to Governor's Harbor, which we discovered must have been paved. We tried. We tried in about ten different spots to get the anchor to hold, but it wouldn't. The harbor floor was either well-troweled concrete or solid, smooth rock. Finally, we threw out a lot of chain and hoped the wind wouldn't drag us away before we could get Andy on the plane. Kent was up all-night checking to see if we were still in the same spot.

It's awful to say, but we were relieved to put Andy on the plane. Meeting a deadline is always traumatic. He, of course, was delighted to be shot of his parents after seeing far too much of them for seventeen days. His one unforgivable act

Andy on Coot *in the Bahamas*

was to leave his shoes behind. Andy has only one pair of shoes, and we think that given their importance in Minnesota in the wintertime, they ought to have been uppermost in his mind. We had to get up at five in the morning to deliver Andy to the shore by six. There was no place to tie up, so we landed the dinghy through the surf and dragged it up on shore, an operation always done barefoot. He did have flip-flops to get him on the plane. His shoes mocked me every time I caught sight of them until we mailed them back to Minnesota at great expense. How prophetic Ben's quip had been about Kevin leaving his shoes behind!

After we'd dumped shoeless Andy by his Cadillac taxi, we fled the paved harbor and went back to Cape Eleuthera. We hoped to sail directly to Georgetown from there on an overnighter. The forecast of light southeasterly winds was not favorable, but we'd had such good luck previously that we weren't worried.

We set out at dusk, clearing the reef just before the sunset. We got all the big sails up and the wind vane steering. It looked like a comfortable night of easy close-hauled sailing until the wind picked up. It kept picking up, but we assumed it was a minor local disturbance that would pass quickly. We didn't think we'd need to reduce the sail. I was so confident this would be a piece of cake that I hadn't even put on my scopolamine patch. Then, I began to get seasick. The genoa blew a seam, and Kent put up the working jib and a reef in the main, followed by a second reef in the main and the storm jib. By now, all I could do was alternately barf over the side and winch in the sheets when Kent made the sail changes.

I'd go below, leaving him dripping wet from tossing on the bow to keep the boat on track. We hove-to, trying figure things out without bashing into the head seas. I was useless,

and Kent got no rest. About three in the morning, we looked
at the chart and saw that if we maintained two knots, we
could be at Warderick Wells at sun-up, go through the cut,
hang on a nice safe mooring, and get some sleep.

We stayed there for two days, mending sails and drying
water from the leaking forehatch. We didn't even go ashore.
Then, rather than go through the deep water of Exuma Sound
to Georgetown, we took the inside passage along the banks
and stopped at a few places along the way.

I found my tropical home on Little Farmer's Cay. It
was an old drop-sided frame cabin perched on stilts on
the only hill, painted the gayest yellow with brilliant green
hurricane shutters. This is where I want to retire. Kent calls it
a Dogpatch shack, and I believe he's right. It only needs Daisy
Mae lounging or Pappy Yokum spitting on the porch to make
it complete. I'll need a dog to lie under the porch at noon
when the sun gets hot, so if anyone can find a thirty-pound
yellow dog, keep it for me.

We stopped to watch a couple of men from a large power yacht
filleting a dozen large dorados at the dock at Staniel Cay. Those
guys knew what they were doing. They cut the fillets off with just
a few strokes of the knife and then threw the offal into the water,
where large stingrays circled. Rays and men looked like they were
performing a dance. I watched for a while, but I was eager to see
the rest of the island.

"C'mon, let's go," I said. But Pam remained fascinated by the
guys at work.

She looked at me and mouthed the words, "Just another
minute."

I don't know how she knew, but she did.

One of the guys looked at her and asked, "Would you like a

fillet?" Pam acted pleasantly surprised. She accepted just half of one—enough for two days' worth of meals.

We called this "fishing for fillet." When we were anchored in rich fishing waters, we sometimes heard a wife call out to her spear-fishing husband, "Don't you dare bring another fish back with you!" What would the poor guy do if he could not kill something? Then, Pam would call him over to our boat. "How about a nice grouper—not too large."

When he came back with a nice, medium-sized grouper and handed it to Pam, she'd say, "Oh, thank you very much. Should I fillet it?"

She'd take a couple of pokes at it with her knife.

"No, no, not like that—here, let me show you."

The man would come aboard and have it ready for the pan in minutes.

When Pam was on a "fishing" expedition, I stayed below reading. I was embarrassed to watch someone else do the "man's work." Although I enjoyed eating fish, I preferred swimming with them to killing them.

Pam was disgusted with me for not fishing. She bought a spool of 200-pound test line, a few hooks, a lure, and a steel leader. She tied the line to a deck cleat and towed the lure behind us. I think we moved too slowly to have much luck. We may have caught more fish than we realized, but because we dragged them through the water until we remembered to check the line, the fish probably became shark bait. The steel leader would be nipped off, and the lure and hook missing.

We looked forward to Georgetown, a fabled place in the annals of sailing. Boaters have wintered here for years, traveling from Florida, the Chesapeake, and Maine in a seasonal rotation so profound there must be a groove in the ocean to mark the passage. In April, before everyone heads back home, Georgetown holds a regatta with upwards of 400 cruising boats anchored in its huge harbor.

As we approached the Georgetown harbor, we heard someone call *Lady of Spain* on the radio. We tried to call after they finished but were out of range and got no response. So, we asked the intermediate boat to call again and ask, "Can we speak to Kevin?" Ben's reply, passed to us was, "Kevin is in trouble because he played with Gordon and that was a terrible idea. Where are those guys?"

We were surprised and delighted to encounter *Lady of Spain* in Georgetown. We knew there had been trouble and that *Viking* had been right to worry. After leaving Beaufort, Ben and Beth realized they were right in the path of Hurricane Gordon. They tied down everything on deck, put up the storm shutters, took the sails down, and lay a-hull waiting. Gordon came and went, and they survived. But they were so shaken, and the boat was leaking so badly, that they decided not to continue to the Virgins. The Bahamas were reasonably close, and they ended up in Georgetown. They were enormously grateful to have survived.

Beth admitted she probably hadn't properly secured the dinghy, which floated away with their outboard. They arrived in Georgetown with no way to get to shore, but when they announced their plight on the VHF, they received a loaner until Ben could build a plywood rowing dink. We were delighted to see these two and learn that they were safe. They already knew Georgetown and told us about the best pubs and when the ship brought the fresh fruit. Ben and Beth were always fonts of information about telecommunications, shopping, bars, and boatyards, plus Beth made the best curry I've ever eaten.

Boaters and local businesses held a Koffee Klatch each morning via the VHF, when they exchanged weather information, made announcements, replayed U.S. news programs, and shared Dave Barry quotations. The daily volleyball schedule, restaurant luncheon specials, and the arrivals of mail, faxes, and packages at the local grocery store were also announced. The elementary school invited boaters to a cookout to support a trip to Nassau, and a long-time sailor encouraged boaters to get their bread and sticky buns at Mom's Bakery Van, where the hugs were free. (I had one of Mom's hugs, and it was even more comforting than her excellent banana bread.)

We got up at five each day to listen to the National Weather Service, and the Bahamas always had the most complicated report in the western North Atlantic. It went something like: "A low-pressure center located at 32N and 75W is trailing a low front from the center to south Florida. It will move to 28N and 65W to east Cuba by Saturday and following it will be a high-pressure ridge running along 32N. Today N of 25N and W of 75W, the winds will be NW at 25 knots, and the seas will be 10 feet."

Ugh! Yech!

I had a terrible time getting it down as a computer-generated voice read it at high speed over our staticky reception. I longed for a television with pictures. At 5:30 am, Kent and I got out a chart and plotted the features we managed to copy. We located ourselves and tried to figure out which way the winds would come. The harbor in Georgetown was so big that we had to move to be protected when the wind changed direction, and we didn't want to move at night when we couldn't see the coral heads. The fronts moved through at a rate of two a week, and the wind could clock around the compass as the front approached and passed.

I desperately wanted a place where we could put the hook down and survive a hurricane coming from all directions at once.

When we were in the Caribbean on *Jacana*, we never bothered to listen to the weather. Right before the portion of the forecast that included us was the Caribbean forecast, which inevitably began by saying, "no significant features," with winds E to SE or E to NE at 15 knots with four-foot seas today, tonight, and tomorrow. It sounded like heaven.

We bought a book in Beaufort called *The Gentleman's Guide to Passages South or, The Thornless Path*. It promoted a route against the prevailing trade winds from Georgetown to the Caribbean, a route it claimed was painless enough that the amateur geriatric set with fragile engines could make it without fear. It promised that we would always be snugged up for the night in time for a leisurely sundowner and that if we were very dutiful in following the gentleman's advice, we would never write whining letters to the Seven Seas Cruising Association.

It sounded perfect. It described slow, short passages from Georgetown through the Outer Out-Islands of the Bahamas and down along the north coast of the Dominican Republic, along the southern coast of Puerto Rico to the Virgins, and then to Venezuela. According to this plan, sailing from Georgetown to the U. S. Virgin Islands could take three months if one waited for the proper weather windows and the right kinds of fronts. Along the coasts of the Dominican Republic and Puerto Rico, it could be necessary to motor sail at night to get the land breezes. It sounded tedious, but it was what we had opted for when we decided to go to the Bahamas rather than straight to the Virgins from Beaufort.

We left Georgetown, following our guru gentleman's advice to the letter, even moving the boat closer to the cut the evening before to enable a quick start through the reef in the morning. Unexpectedly, we had a lovely calm westerly wind, the vane was steering, I wasn't too seasick, and we had waypoints in the GPS to lead us to half-a-dozen islands if we needed to seek shelter. Kent was looking forward to snorkeling near Conception Island on reefs that are said to be the best in the Bahamas. But the westerlies held, and Conception is no place to be in a westerly, so we kept going.

We passed San Salvador and thought we'd keep moving so long as the wind was favorable, ignoring our guru's advice because we were already well on the way to St. Thomas. By our third morning, we were over a hundred miles east of San Salvador and a bit south when the wind turned on our nose softly and comfortably. We took a couple of long tacks, not making much headway but telling ourselves that if the sea got the least bit heavy, we would run toward Mayaguana or a place where we could easily take up the thornless path. However, the wind went SW and continued to clock around the compass gently. We had an easterly on our nose on the seventh day, but by then, we were just a few miles from St. Thomas. It was time to turn south, go into port, and clear customs.

During our unexpectedly easy passage from the Bahamas to the Virgin Islands, we encountered big ships. I had read accounts by single-handed sailors who could not always keep watch in shipping lanes. Since the stories were those of sailors who survived, I underestimated the danger, and we had some close calls.

We radioed any ship we thought might be a danger and discovered that in large seas, we were invisible. We carried a radar reflector on the mast and thought a steel boat made a good radar target. That gave us a false sense of security about our visibility. We did not realize that even our high-in-the-rigging radar reflector was often below the height of the ocean waves and thus masked by wave clutter on radar screens. At night in large seas, ships might not even see our masthead light.

During one daytime watch, Pam noticed a ship approaching from astern. When it was within reach of our radio, she called, asking if the captain saw us. He did not. She gave our coordinates and said we were directly off his bow. The captain sent someone forward to look. "I've got you lined up!" he chuckled a few minutes later. Then we heard, "I'll leave you to port." Minutes later, the ship rushed past at tremendous speed. Had our radio not worked, and had we needed to maneuver to avoid a collision, we would not have known which way to turn or had much time to do so.

Another time, just north of Puerto Rico, I was keeping watch at dawn when I spotted a large, brightly lit, round object in the mist. After a while, I realized it was a cruise ship pointing right at us. We were near the end of our passage, and I was tired and not thinking clearly. Suddenly, I was wide awake. The ship responded to my call, but the captain could not see us, even when I told him the ship was bearing down on us. I gave him our coordinates, and although he still could not see us, he knew I was right in his path. "I will leave you to port," he radioed. Then a moment later, "No, too late! I see you now! I will leave you to starboard!" People on deck looked down on us and waved as the ship passed. I was grateful for the VHF radio.

During another passage on one very dark night, I watched the lights of a ship remain on the same bearing for a long time. It was difficult to know how to address the vessel we were trying to reach, so this time, trying to sound desperate, I called, "Big ship, big ship, this is little sailing vessel *Coot* at 23 degrees, 25.7 minutes north and 78 degrees, 25.8 minutes west. Will we pass safely?"

A voice with a German accent came back, "This is Big Ship. What is your speed and course?"

I told him my speed and heading, and he called back, "I will pass your bow by 1.3 miles. This is Big Ship out." He seemed pleased to be called Big Ship.

We're here in the Virgin Islands, and even though we did not follow the *Gentleman's Guide* but made a straight shot, we'll not write any whining letters to the Seven Seas Cruising Association. I love getting up at eight in the morning, turning on the radio, and hearing on the weather report that there are no significant features, that there won't be any within the foreseeable future, and that although it might rain, briefly, this afternoon, even that will pass quietly.

Unfortunately, now our work begins. That painting we didn't get done in Beaufort is turning poor *Coot* into an unsightly rust bucket. Out of ignorance, we applied a boot stripe of bottom paint over our regular topside paint when we raised our waterline in Ontario this spring. The paints turned out to be incompatible, and the boot stripe is peeling off, along with the topside paint underneath, making *Coot* look like she's got a bad case of eczema at the waterline. We are hauling her at a yard on St. Thomas on Monday, and we'll work hard for a week. Our friend Hugh Randall, unemployed and going nuts in Brookings this winter, is coming. He has even been so foolish as to want to visit while *Coot* is out of the water and help us scrape and paint. (*Conclusion of Pam's letter to friends, written from Hawksnest Bay, St. John, Virgin Islands, February 4, 1995*)

Chapter 13

Dreams and Realities

February–March 1995

If you can't repair it, maybe it shouldn't be on board.
—*LIN AND LARRY PARDEY*

Pam's estimate that we would complete work on *Coot* in a week was wildly optimistic. Hugh Randall arrived as scheduled, and we spent two weeks working on the boat. Pam wrote to Sue and Jeff Grant, our longtime Brookings friends, from Leinster Bay, St. John, on March 6, 1995:

> We hope the winter was kind to you and that 1995 is shaping up as a winner. As you can see, it's taken me a bit of time to get the original fifteen single-spaced pages off, and it will be a couple of days until I can get this one mailed, as we are now sitting comfortably in an isolated bay on St. John with not even a telephone pole in sight, much less a post box. I'll consign the whole shebang to the U.S. Postal Service when we return to St. Thomas to get our mail, which should contain all the stuff we'll need for IRS for 1994.
>
> We think the engine may be healed—at least for the moment—and we're celebrating by doing very little. Your

letters made me so homesick that I hated to write because I'd
sound like such a dithering whiner, and I know how pissed
you'd be to get whining letters from paradise. Now I'm in the
mood to write about the stuff of dreams and disasters.

First, the disasters, namely, the hell of working on a
boat hauled out of water. We had some peeling paint at the
waterline and were concerned it could be serious. I had
visions of the boat opening like a canned ham, leaving us with
two un-joined halves—top sides and bottom sides. We made
an appointment to be hauled on a Monday morning, and by
Monday afternoon, Kent had all the peeling parts ground
down and all the wood removed from the coach house.

He'd made an appointment with the welder (who was
to come and weld studs to which we would then attach the
wooden bits) and started tabs with the yard, the marine
supply store, the carpentry shop, and a sign painter. I was
about to collapse as the thermometer read in the nineties.

There was little air movement, we were near a mangrove
swamp, and the mosquitoes and no-see-ums were thick. I
didn't realize how debilitated I was from our week-long trip
from the Bahamas. I'd been seasick the whole time and had
only been able to hold down a daily ration of saltines. We
now realize that we need at least twice as long to recuperate as
to make a passage.

I got up at five to catch a bus to the airport to pick up
Hugh Randall. Poor Hugh! After two days of traveling and
sleeping in airports, he walked into a torn-up boat simmering
on a toxic dumpsite. I do not kid about that. A Japanese
company wanted to buy the land to build condominiums, but
the EPA wouldn't allow it. Hugh has had trouble with skin
cancer, and his feet swell if they get hot. He'd been sitting in
Brookings all winter drinking beer, and he's gotten quite hefty,

so hauling his 200 pounds up and down a twelve-foot ladder
on swollen feet surely wasn't what he had in mind when he
opted for the Caribbean in February.

Even though we told him not to come until after we were
out of the yard, there was no way to warn him how awful
living on our boat in a boatyard would be. Kent thought it
would take a week to get all our jobs done. Then we could
sail to where the swaying palms and sugar beaches kiss the
turquoise waters. Well, of course, that didn't happen. One
week lengthened to two, one job led to another, and then
rain interfered with the final painting for three days. Hugh
toughed it out, sleeping on deck, swatting bugs, and jumping
below when the nightly rain soaked his sheet. The quarter
berth would have been one step down on the torture scale
from an oubliette in a tenth-century castle.

When we finally left the yard, Hugh got his first dunk
in the Caribbean. But, of course, that reprieve didn't last
long. We had not done laundry since the Bahamas, and we
desperately needed supplies, so we had to return to Charlotte
Amalie and provision. I know you guys in the frozen north
envision us cavorting in our string bikinis, sailing across the
sparkling blue ocean with the breeze streaming our long,
golden tresses back from our handsomely bronzed faces, but
you are wrong.

Cruising sailors are eighty percent of the time found in
hardware stores, laundromats, grocery stores, or on the streets
hauling their purchases. Twenty percent of the time, we
are in the boatyard or buried under engine parts. The other
ten percent of the time, we are perfect sybarites, drinking
rum punches and running naked on moonlit beaches. My
arithmetic is wrong, you say. Guess which percentage is
inaccurate? Hugh got to spend a few days on and in the water,

but he left last Thursday, and Kent and I went back to the grocery store.

Pam's humorous exaggeration had a basis in fact. Boatyard work is grueling and hot, climbing up and down a ladder is tiring, and shopping and carrying bags of stuff home is mundane anywhere. I liked manual labor and found the work interesting. Unlike me, Pam was stuck in limbo. She helped with difficult and tedious tasks to get them done and return to the fun parts of cruising. For her, the haul-outs were interruptions in the cruising life she enjoyed, whereas for me, they were part of the experience.

The Virgins may be the final resting place of marginal people from the upper 48. We had just set *Coot* safely down from the travel lift when we saw the next boat to be hauled, a steel boat that was rustier than *Coot*. Captain Ken, the owner of *Anne Marie*, was inordinately proud of her. He'd lived aboard for sixteen years, bringing her from the Great Lakes with hopes of a circumnavigation. Ken made it as far as the U.S. Virgins, went back to work to feed the cruising kitty, and never made it any farther. She'd cost him his wife and any normal kind of life, but he wouldn't say a thing against her. She'd originally had teak decks, but one day as he and his wife quietly sailed along, the whole cabin shifted to port. The cabin had rusted free from the deck, and since the mast was stepped on the cabin top, this was a serious occurrence.

Anne Marie was a Zeeland yawl, like the one we considered buying in San Francisco. Ken tapped about the boat's underbody with a mountain climber's pick, finding a hole with almost every tap.

Then he'd smile and say, "Just a quick patch, and she'll be better than new."

The hull was rusting from the inside out from lime leaching from its concrete ballast. His chainplates were also rusting through. Even though he was in a rush to get out of the yard, he had them refastened by the welder, who muttered to us that there wasn't enough metal to weld anything to.

Ken didn't hold much with sanding. He watched us sand, prime, epoxy, paint, and then sand the last coat and begin again. He didn't need to do all that. He just painted. We watched rust bleed through the new paint before he even left the yard. He charters out of Red Hook, and we last saw him anchored with a couple from Massachusetts in one of the British Virgins. They looked looped to me, but how would you respond if you'd come from Massachusetts for your dream vacation and found Ken's boat waiting for you? At least they were still afloat. His paint must be better than we thought.

We also met Brett, a Kiwi boat builder, repairer, and mooch extraordinaire. He was employed by the yard to do whatever needed doing, which was a lot. He had spent his life in love with boats, and his latest passion was his newly acquired 65-foot Herreshoff ketch. The boat was wrecked in Hurricane Hugo five years ago, and Brett had watched her all that time. When she was pulled from the water in a sinking state, he began to think that she might be his someday. He checked the jack stands to make sure they supported her properly and pumped water from her bilges when rain filled her up.

Others tried to buy her. Finally, the owner had to get rid of her at a fire sale price, and Brett got her for a song. He also got a project which would daze even Kent. He re-planked most of her bottom and remade all 75 feet of her main mast. He lives in her stripped interior with his handsaw, planer, and other tools. The engine works, so he can dodge the authorities when they come to collect his registration fee.

We're now at Leinster Bay, St. John, part of the national park Laurance Rockefeller gave the government. It's an especially lovely anchorage as there is a reef on which to snorkel, a beach to walk on, and an old plantation site to visit. There is splendid swimming with lots of starfish and rays, and because it's in the park, we can tell any boater who wants to run his engine or generator to can it after 10 pm, as it's against the rules.

We're trying very hard to get into "island time," and maybe we're beginning to manage it. After we'd purchased vegetables and a bottle of rum and filled up with water in Charlotte Amalie, we sailed for Leinster Bay—a fabulous journey of twenty miles. After ten miles of vigorous beating, we passed Christmas Cove around noon. I asked Kent what he thought about stopping. He said if I wanted to, he wouldn't complain. So, we did.

We invited a couple we'd met in Charlotte Amalie for coffee and then went to their boat for drinks. I had been reluctant to get in the water because I saw several five-foot sharks lurking underneath the boarding ladder. One smiled lovingly at me as I peered into the water, but Kay said Caribbean sharks are quite shy and usually disappear the moment a body splashes into the water. She looked over the side of the boat and said, "Remora, not sharks. They're curious but harmless."

We've met a sister ship to *Coot*. I got up early in the morning in Leinster Bay and gazed out of the companionway at a boat we didn't see on our arrival. It looked remarkably familiar. I got out the binoculars, went over each nautical feature, then woke up Kent. We could barely wait until it was late enough to go over to meet the people who had the excellent taste to sail such a vessel. *Styx* is a 1980 Breewijd, *Coot* is a 1985. *Styx* is from Amsterdam and was designed and built in the same yard as *Coot*, but she was finished by her owners and is much different inside. We like a lot of what they've done and can see some new possibilities to improve *Coot*. Sake and Agat are former teachers in their early thirties. They have recently completed a six-year circumnavigation aboard *Styx* and have nothing but praise for the design and strength of the boat, which makes us feel smug. They support themselves by making jewelry, selling it to charter boats, and doing quite well.

Leinster Bay has no settlements, but each morning and evening feral donkeys bray at one another. There are also mongooses on St. John, imported to help control the rats. They have become a problem. If they are poisoned, other species will be affected. Someone suggested that the best way to eliminate them is to spread a rumor in Cruz Bay that mongoose fur is hallucinogenic when smoked.

Fifty kinds of small lizards flit around the palms, bougainvillea, and sea grape. We see brown pelicans, brown boobies, and my favorite, the magnificent frigate bird. The pelicans entertain us morning and evening, skimming near the anchorages. When they see something tasty, they make a graceless splat into the water and then float smugly while they swallow their catch. The frigates sail like prehistoric pterodactyls above the hoi-polloi.

The boats in the Virgins are some of the nicest and raunchiest anywhere. Because of the magnificent sailing, diving, and interesting towns, there are lots of tourists who pay to ride on gaff-rigged schooners and old wooden boats maintained in Bristol fashion. There are also spectacular motor yachts with helicopters on the afterdeck, staffed by uniformed crews. We scorn those palaces of conspicuous consumption. There are also floating derelicts held together by chewing gum and string, with piles of rum bottles underneath. Whatever one's taste in things that float, it can be satisfied here.

I'll end on the best note of all. For the first time since Midland, Ontario, the engine has started, just as it should, without any coaxing, bleeding, swearing, battery shifts, kicks, or anguished moans from me. Kent replaced the fuel hoses at the boatyard, so maybe, just maybe, it's fixed.

Pam continued writing letters during our relaxing time in Leinster Bay, including this one (written on March 7) to my brother Doug's wife Phyllis,[1] that revealed her understanding of me was still growing:

I have discovered, rather chagrinned, that it's taken me nearly thirty years to realize that Kent is extraordinarily goal oriented. He becomes a blinkered mule with the strength and endurance to shoulder all obstacles aside. In his forward-looking stance, his peripheral vision is lost, and he fails to see that I, rather than being at his side pushing onward, am lagging farther and farther behind. He feels resentful that he's out there alone, working hard for what he thought was a previously agreed-upon goal, and I'm exhausted, defensive, and feeling guilty. Guilt always makes me irritable, combative, and bitchy, and keeps me from supporting him.

---

1. My brother Doug Kedl and his wife Phyllis provided much support to us during our sailing years. They handled our mail when we were on *Coot* and helped Andy find summer jobs and gave him a place to stay at their home in St. Paul, Minnesota. Later, Jake confided in them about his problems. Phyllis was an excellent writer, and we wish she were still here to critique and proofread our writing. She died in 2015.

I'd give anything to have his strength and single-
mindedness, but I don't. I'm beginning to see some
advantages in not finishing what we set out to do. One of
my tactics is to refuse to set any goal at all. This is difficult
because I'm always saying things like, "Wouldn't it be fun to
put the bikes together, dinghy them ashore and ride into Cruz
Bay?" Then, Kent jumps on the idea and wants to get going.

There is a nice deli near Coral Harbor, a town across the
island. When we visited, I saw a trail sign that said 1.5 miles
to Leinster Bay. Foolishly, I mentioned hiking across the
hilly island to pick up some ingredients for supper. Kent asks
each morning if we're going to Coral Harbor today. I calmly
respond, "Let's wait and see." I'm learning. Kent's learning,
but it's taking a while.

The letter concludes:

Kent is outside doing more sanding to the varnish. We have
discussed this thoroughly, and he says it is perfectly fine for
me to sit in the cool inside the boat and finish letters that
I need to get written while he sweats miserably in the sun.
Indeed, Kent wouldn't characterize our jobs this way, but our
Calvinistic heritage seems to drive us to assume nothing is
worthwhile unless it hurts. We're working at not making the
pleasure painful.

We both wanted to see as much of the Caribbean as we could.
Pam was the one who read the guidebooks and knew what there
was to see and do. I was happy she did this research and wrote
letters to our friends back home and the people we met while
cruising. I began to realize that our approaches to life were quite
different. Like the houses I remodeled, the boat was an enjoyable
project for me. For Pam, the boat was a means to travel and a

place to live. As we lay on our berth, I looked at the front end of the boat.

"We could move the chain locker further aft and make it deeper and self-stowing. That would reduce the weight on the bow and make better storage space in the forepeak."

"How much work would that be?"

"Pretty straightforward. We'd move the windless aft about a foot, move the haws pipe and make the chain locker vertical and deeper. I could do that in a couple of days. We'd need to find a welder. We could also turn the quarter berth into a cockpit locker and build an aft-facing chart table like we had on *Jacana*!"

"Hold on! Let's not get carried away."

Trinidad was now the place to go for boat work, and it was right on our way to South America. I wanted to take Pam to Colombia and show her the places I'd known during my Peace Corps Days. She, too, wanted to do that. We'd make the circle of the Leeward and Windward Islands on our way to Trinidad, where we'd stop briefly to make improvements to the boat. We'd visit Trinidad, Colombia, and then, I fervently hoped, Panama and the Pacific! We were on our way!

Chapter 14

The Dutch, the French, and the British

March 1995

*Every sign, every person, and every dog spoke
perfect English.* —PAMELA T. KEDL

After lolling around Leinster Bay, we returned to Charlotte
Amalie on St. Thomas, re-provisioned, did laundry, and got
our final batch of mail with all our IRS tax forms. We filled
out our 1040, posted it, cleared customs, and left for the
British Virgins, sailing first to an island that had charmed
us ten years ago—Jost Van Dyke. Like everything else, ten
years had changed it   for the worse. There were more T-shirt
sellers, more snack bars, more boats, and it was noisier. Our
favorite bar from 1985, Rudy's, was bigger and more modern,
but it had no customers. Now Foxy's is the place to go if one
is on a big-budget holiday.

We walked around but decided we would be happier
farther south, so we went to Road Town, Tortola, to see
what ten years had done to that sleepy Caribbean capital. It,
too, had grown, but since we hadn't spent much time there
ten years ago, we walked through some parts we hadn't seen
before that still had some old West Indies style.

We'd dinghied a couple of miles from our anchorage
into one of the marinas near town, and as we were leaving,
I spotted a boat with the same name as Walter Cronkite's.[1]
I told Kent that might be Walter's boat.

Kent looked over and said, "Well, there's Walter Cronkite!"

Walter was standing on the dock, getting ready to board.
Kent regrets that we didn't stop and introduce ourselves. He
wanted to tell Walter his potato joke, which is famous for
eliciting groans. The repeated telling of this joke was one of
the major reasons Brookings was glad to be shot of us. I'll
repeat it here for those who have not been privileged to hear
it before. Although, I can't think of anyone we know who has
been spared. *(Pam's letter to friends, from Rodney Bay, St. Lucia,
April 24, 1995)*

Sorry to interrupt, but I want to tell this joke myself:

Little Sweet Pea Potato from Idaho went east to Wellesley
College. In her letters home, she mentioned that she'd met a
friend she liked very much. His name was Walter Cronkite. Before Christmas break, she wrote asking her parents if it would
be okay if she invited Walter to visit Idaho for Christmas. At the
Christmas dinner, between the main course and dessert, Sweet
Pea could no longer contain herself.

"Mom, Dad, Walter has asked me to marry him, and I said
'yes.' Isn't that wonderful?"

Her parents' reaction was more subdued than she expected.
"What's the matter? Don't you like Walter?"

Her father responded, "No, no . . . it's not that. Walter seems
like a fine man. But you must understand, Sweet Pea, your mother

---

1. Walter Cronkite was an American broadcast journalist who served as
   anchorman for the CBS Evening News for 19 years (1962–1981). Wikipedia, "Walter Cronkite." Last modified October 23, 2022.

is a pure-bred russet potato, and I'm a pure Idaho potato, whereas Walter, well, he is just a common tater."

We cleared out of the British Virgins at Road Town. We had seen some of the famous beauty spots, such as the Baths, ten years before, and we knew we would have trouble finding anchoring space now. We were also anxious to get into some new territory. Late March was approaching, and if we were to make it to Trinidad by mid-June, we would have to get some southing on the compass.

At noon, we left Road Town to sail the Anegada Passage overnight [March 20] and arrive in Sint Maarten after dawn. In this passage, one gets the full force of the Atlantic. Sint Maarten is often dead to windward and beating against waves that have had a chance to build since Africa is no treat.

This crossing should weed out the faint-hearted and fragile, so we hoped to see hardier sailors farther south. We'd made this passage three times ten years ago, and we ended up motoring the whole way each time because the winds were so light. Our luck held, with gentle winds, just slightly forward of the beam, so we put up our spinnaker for the first time and kept it there all night. So much for reputations.

Sint [Dutch version] Maarten/Saint Martin is divided almost in half, the northern part French and the southern part Dutch. I'm always startled by how carefully Europeans have maintained their national characteristics in the West Indies. With two countries occupying the same island, the differences were stark. In Sint Maarten, the houses were narrow with steep roofs and a stepped gabled end, as in Holland. In Saint Martin, the houses had wide, gingerbread-trimmed verandas encircling the first and second floors. Sadly, the homes of the native islanders (most of them descendants of slaves) are much the same on all the islands.

They're mostly shacks on stilts with corrugated metal roofs. New apartment buildings, condos, and private villas are mostly built of plastered concrete blocks. We dislike the concrete boxes, but they are more hurricane and termite-proof and easier to make, so even poorer people can have sturdy homes with running water and electricity.

Both sides of the island are free ports, with an emphasis on shopping. Emerald stores are as common as 7-Elevens in the U.S., and four T-shirts for $10 can be purchased on any corner. On the Dutch side, electronic gadgets, cameras, stereos, tape recorders, watches, and emeralds are sold from cut-rate discount shops inevitably run by East Indian families, while cheese and chocolate come from Chinese-owned groceries. On the French side, not just T-shirts but snazzy outfits from Paris are sold, and the shop assistants are stunning young women. The emerald stores on the French side aren't hidden on side streets, with wares arranged under hanging signs saying $100–$500 or over $1000. They are marble-floored, discreetly lit, and staffed by stylish men and women.

The French spoke English with reluctance, but the Dutch made no show of preserving their language. Every sign, every person, and every dog spoke perfect English. The women in Sint Maarten were dumpy and wore serviceable polyester, and although the storefronts were a little shabby, the sewers functioned perfectly. In Saint Martin, the women were stylishly svelte, but as we passed the elegant shops, we had to dodge backed-up sewage on the sidewalk.

We're not sure whether to giggle or be ashamed of one thing we did in Sint Maarten. When we stopped to get maps at one of the many information booths that line the main street of Philipsburg, we didn't realize they were owned by dive shops, sailboat charter companies, and time-share condos and were set up to lure people into their enterprises.

The attendants receive commissions for each person they sign up. Almost without realizing it, we signed up to tour a time-share condo with the enticement of $60 in cash, a boat trip to Saba, or $60 worth of chips in the resort's casino. We were promised that this excursion would take just 90 minutes, including a taxi ride to the resort and hard cash at the end. We were cautioned not to let anyone know we lived on a boat.

When we arrived at the Pelican Cay Condos, we were whisked into a large room filled with tables and chairs, each occupied by one browned hyper-salesperson and a pallid middle-aged couple from Detroit or Amsterdam. The salespeople talked furiously, illustrating their lectures with lavish photographs and four-color charts, while the couples looked at each other in confusion. We were even browner than the salespeople, who repeatedly asked if we lived on a boat. Feeling foolish loyalty to the young girl who had suckered us in, we denied this. Philipsburg harbor is filled with marginal boat people eking out a living, who would love an extra $60, so I'm sure the shill who lured us into this trap was instructed not to invite boat people. In the end, we got a tour of the complex, lunch, and not $60 in cash, but in scrip, which we spent at the resort's expensive grocery store. Our curiosity was satisfied, but we turned down offers from other "information booths."

Several islands later, we met a couple who had done five such tours in Sint Maarten and came away with $50 cash, a boat trip to Saba, a new watch, casino chips, and a gold bracelet. We don't know whether we should feel ashamed or stupid for not taking greater advantage of these opportunities. Quite a few people would have benefitted if we had—the struggling shill, the taxi drivers, the salesmen. Only the developer littering the Caribbean with high-rise condos would be out-of-pocket, but despite the many people who attend but don't buy, they seem to be making out okay.

It was a quick sail from St. Martin to Île Fourche (Île Fourchue, March 24), a tiny desert island between St. Martin and St. Barts. We'd visited there with the boys and loved it because it was inhabited only by goats, hermit crabs, and inedible cacti. It looked the same, although more desolate since the goats had eaten more of the vegetation. Ten years ago, we were the only boat. Now there were twenty. So much for thinking we'd be away from crowds once we'd crossed the Anegada Passage.

The anchorage was thick with brown pelicans and brown boobies, all congregating in one area. We snorkeled and discovered huge schools of fish swirling in the water. I got the courage to join Kent, diving among them and losing my sense of direction in their silver eddies. I found my way to the surface only because the pressure on my ears decreased when I went up.

At Île Fourche, I saw the green flash again. I've seen it four times now. Kent still can't see it and claims it's just an invention of spaced-out hippies. I think it's genetic, like rolling up one's tongue, and Kent can't do that either.

For you northerners who have never experienced this phenomenon, the green flash comes at sundown. There can't be any clouds or land between you and the setting sun, although a little haze is okay. The moment the upper limb of the sun dips beneath the horizon, there is a little blip of fluorescent green that lasts less than a second. Kent and I have often peered at the setting sun, and I can see it, but he can't. We'd hoped to have Hugh Randall settle the argument, but he's red/green color blind, so we couldn't rely on his judgment. Most sailors have seen it, and there is a color photograph in our cruising guide.

We sailed to Saba [March 27], an island we missed the last time around. I'd been afraid to go there because it's very steep-sided, and the anchorages are deep and unprotected.

The island is one round, dormant volcano rising directly from the bottom of the sea, so the swells from the Atlantic creep all around its un-indented perimeter. Cruising guides advise sailors to leave their boats in St. Martin and visit Saba by air. If the coast looked too rough for us, we'd skip it.

When we arrived at a tiny artificial harbor where we could leave the dinghy safely and easily, we saw an empty mooring buoy. We called the harbormaster on the VHF, who said it was used by a small cruise ship that wouldn't be in until Wednesday. It was Monday, and if we were gone by 10 am Wednesday, it was ours for free.

We grabbed it gleefully, and I felt secure enough to go ashore immediately. I usually sit in the cockpit for an hour after anchoring to make sure we won't slide away to Central America or into another boat. However, it was a dreadful anchorage. The swells were so bad that we nearly rolled the gunnels under, and at night we had to sleep with the lee cloths up—something we still haven't had to do at sea

Saba has no beaches or condos, and the charterers don't go there. Day-trippers come, so there are T-shirt sellers, but not in the numbers found on Saint Martin. However, we knew the age of tourism had arrived when the women ran from their houses to invite us in to look at lace. Someone brought lacemaking to Saba sixty or seventy years ago, and it became a profitable hobby for women to pursue while their husbands were at sea. It's indifferent stuff, and I wasn't tempted. But Saba is a remarkable island, different from others we have seen and was worth the queasy anchorage.

It looks like a Swiss landscape set amidst tropical greenery. The mountain angles steeply up from the sea, and the major settlements, The Bottom and Windwardside, are located on a bench of land halfway to the summit of the volcano. We landed our dinghy at the little harbor at Fort Baie and walked up to The Bottom.

In the old days, just twenty years ago, we would have had to ride a wave to a stone staircase cut into the mountainside, grab a rope hanging down from above, and haul ourselves and the dinghy out, all in the space of one wave. That was the procedure on a calm day. Many days would pass when no one could land. Now, with the little harbor, it's a piece of cake.

The walk to The Bottom, however, wasn't. It was 45 minutes of strenuous walking on the "road that couldn't be built." This road has an incline that I thought was 45 degrees, but Kent said was closer to 30. Whatever the angle, it was a killer in the mid-afternoon sun. The next day we were about to hire a cab when someone told us that most people hitch-hike. But we *must* catch our ride either at the bottom of the hill or at the top because no one could or would stop mid-hill. For years, engineers told the Dutch that a road could not be built from the sea to The Bottom. But a local man sent away for a mail-order road-building course and started building the road the following year.

Another road goes from The Bottom to a bit of the west coast, and the local cab drivers call it "the road that shouldn't have been built." We didn't attempt it. There are not, nor have there ever been, any trains on Saba. Someone once intended to import donkeys to haul goods from the sea up to The Bottom, but there was a strike among the men who made their living hauling on foot, and nothing came of it. The airport on the northeast corner of the island has the shortest runway in the world.

Maybe only the diligent, tidy Dutch could have made anything of Saba. It was never a center for trading, agriculture, or piracy. It hasn't the beaches or the emerald stores that

attract modern-day pirates. The forest was cut down for
plantation-type farming, and some slaves were imported,
but that worked even less well on Saba than on other islands.
When the plantations failed, the Dutch of Saba, unlike
colonists on other islands, didn't abandon the place. They
stayed and became fishermen, cobblers, and lace makers.
Whites and Blacks worked side-by-side in the small fields.

The villages of The Bottom and Windwardside cling to
their narrow bench. The houses are small, white-walled, and
red-roofed. Stones from the tiny terraces are used to build
walls for gardens and the kitchens of the houses. The hip
roofs have fringes of gingerbread and gutters to direct the rain
into well-maintained cisterns. Most of the islands we visited
before Saba didn't have enough water, but people collected
and used rainwater here. Because Saba is relatively high, its
single mountain catches some rain, and the peak is almost
always hidden in clouds.

The catchment systems were in disrepair on other islands,
and people paid a great deal for desalinated or imported
water. Sabans grew vegetables in tiny garden plots near their
houses. We did not see that on the other islands. Sabans gave
garden space to trees, flowering bushes, and the tombs of
their relatives.

One of the attractive houses was for sale, and I asked
the museum director about the price. I was enamored by
the possibility of living in such a house, although I was a
little intimidated at the thought of caring for the grave of
someone's ancestor. The asking price was $250,000. The
director then went on a little huffily, saying that she couldn't
understand why it was so expensive because the owner
had paid only $59,000 a few years ago and had done only
a bit of repair on the roof. Kent thought this inflation was
unfortunate. Yuppiedom had come even to Saba, and young,

Pam on Saba.

newly married Sabans would never have a chance to own
something so graceful.

Our next stop was St. Eustatius [March 29], which we
reached in a little over three hours of sailing close-hauled in a
nice breeze. We made our first foray into nude sailing on this
leg and arrived pink in places that hadn't seen sunlight since
we were nippers.

Today Statia's wealth has sunk into the sea along with
most of the buildings of the earlier period. It is a sad contrast
to Saba. Plantations destroyed the land, the British destroyed
the commerce, and Statia never recovered. Some local
people are trying to attract the tourist trade by promoting

Statia's good diving and peaceful life. They've improved the area around the waterfront and restored the few remaining buildings of historical interest, but the rest of the island is strewn with garbage. The poverty is too apparent to be tolerated by tourists, the harbor too rolley for cruisers, and the beaches less lovely than those on neighboring islands.

Statia has two extinct volcanos; a smaller one at the northern end and a big one with a crater at the southern end near Oranje Baie, where we were anchored. We got up at first light to beat the heat and, carrying sandwiches and water, began a two-hour hike into the crater of the large volcano. It was gorgeous inside—truly a jungle, with giant trees, ferns, and mammoth split-leaf philodendrons twining around the trunks of trees to reach the sun.

There were volcanic boulders the size of houses. Kent thought he saw a dinosaur lurking in the green-filtered sunlight. There was a small snake that the tourist bureau had assured us was non-poisonous. He hung from a branch, licked his chops with a little pointed tongue, and followed in the trees above us for some distance. He was not timid. We also walked to the windward side and south end of the island, where we saw the ruins of gun batteries on every point of land.

We have been struck by the ruthlessness of the white occupation of the islands. Europeans came, imported slaves, stripped the rain forests, and built plantations on poor volcanic slopes. When the plantations failed because of poor soil or changing world economic conditions, the Europeans returned home in droves, abandoning their slaves to a raped environment. Now the Europeans are returning in droves to build or buy condos, retire, and drive jet skis around the shores, while the Blacks still live in poverty, enslaved once more by the outsiders' greed and ambition.

Pam in the Volcanic Crater on Statia

As we hopped down the chain of islands, Pam was enjoying herself and writing long letters to family and friends. I worried less about her happiness. I, too, was enjoying myself. I was compiling lists of projects we could work on in Trinidad.

"If we move the deck-fills for water and diesel onto the bridge deck, we could put them on the centerline and cut out most of the hoses that run to the tanks."

I was inspired. "It would mean changing the decking, but Trinidad is a great source of teak."

"Sounds fine. But let me finish this letter so we can get it in the mail."

Chapter 15

Cruising As We Thought It Would Be

April–May 1995

On a whee of a broad reach. —PAMELA T. KEDL

We left Statia [April 2] in the late afternoon to make the 70-mile journey to Montserrat as an overnighter. We expected a beam wind, but we had a rough beat in sloppy seas. In the end, we didn't arrive in Montserrat until ten in the morning. My new seasick remedy (Gravol) was better than the old scopolamine patches, and I had hopes that my suffering would be at an end.

As was typical of British bureaucracy, we were required to visit three offices to clear in and out of customs, immigration, and the port authority, plus a fourth to get a cruising permit. This was not the efficient Dutch system. We had to travel several extra miles to the south for a cruising permit, then return north to anchor. Upon leaving, we were required to reverse the procedure and visit four offices in different parts of the town.

Our comfortable, though rolling anchorage was near a lush hibiscus, oleander, and palm-studded golf course overlooking the blue sea. Streams ran through it, and the sand traps were black volcanic sand. Hazards included cattle egrets, iguanas, and milk cows staked near some streams. It could have been a country-club-estate development in the United States. I woke up to the sound of lawnmowers, not goats or roosters. The landscaped lawns of lovely villas sloped down to the golf course and beach. The black volcanic sand beach provided a backdrop for novice water skiers and windsurfers who toppled from their boards and were rescued by a resident Adonis who patiently picked them up and set them to rights.

Plymouth had narrow streets, small, ill-stocked shops, and high prices. The government buildings were painted pink and white, like in the Bahamas. I like the idea of a government that paints buildings pink. The chickens and goats didn't run loose. Perhaps because the goats are tethered, this island is still lush and green. In fact, it's called the Emerald Isle of the Caribbean, not only because it's green but because early settlers were Irish, fleeing from religious oppression.

Names are Irish, March 17th is a holiday, the harp and shamrock are national symbols, and people still speak with an Irish brogue. Goat water (a goat meat stew) is the national dish. There are no boom boxes and no Rastafarians. Montserrat claims the lowest crime rate in the world and many rich retirees. We felt completely out of place.

The anchorage got bouncy, so I talked Kent into making a night sail to Deshaies, Guadeloupe, instead of hanging onto the bed all night. Kent doesn't like night sails because we don't sleep well and spend the next day catching up. I figure we're either going to be sailing or catching up, so it doesn't much matter whether we sail at night or in the daytime. We set sail under a double-reefed main and working jib at close to six knots, hard into the wind and seas. *Coot*'s theoretical hull speed is only about six knots, so this was moving at a rapid

MONSERRAT VOLCANO ERUPTIONS

Between 1995 and 1997, beginning just months after our visit, volcanic eruptions destroyed the capital city of Plymouth and much of the arable land on the island. Volcanic activity continues, and hurricanes have also impacted the island. Two-thirds of the population was evacuated in 1997, and only some have returned. Tourists now come to view the volcano and its damage, but the southern two-thirds of the island is now an exclusion zone. Mudslides completely covered the golf course and nearby homes. *Wikipedia, "Montserrat." Last modified 22 October 2022.*

pace. It may have been our bumpiest ride so far. We had to heave-to for about three hours so we wouldn't arrive in the dark. The pause made us sag so far to leeward that we gave ourselves a hell of a beat to Deshaies [April 7]. We finally turned on the engine and powered in.

We felt we'd truly gone foreign. No one spoke English in this little seaside village, and I was reduced to asking directions and ordering things in my non-existent 30-year-old French. The town was pleasant, if a bit tacky, the prices were much higher than we'd anticipated, and we spent too much for lunch at a restaurant on the beach. However, the food was the best I've had on the whole trip (*poisson en brochette et salade* for me and steak and *frites* for Kent). Since the anchorage was so pleasant, we stayed for a few days. On Palm Sunday morning, we had espresso and *pain au chocolat* at the *boulangerie* and watched the villagers march to church carrying palm fronds.

The next day, we rock-hopped up the Deshaies River; and since we had the place to ourselves, we splashed nude in the fresh water. It was a treat and totally out of character with our modest Calvinist natures. I'd made sandwiches of chewy French bread, Spanish aioli, sharp English white cheddar (from Montserrat), and Italian pepperoni. If only we'd had a bottle of wine rather than a jug of water! The river was just a large creek, but it ran through a tropical forest, and we felt as though we were intrepid explorers.

We'd hoped to fill our lockers with fine French goodies here, but the dollar isn't performing well against European currencies right now, and we found that we would have to hold down on provisioning. Bread and wine are affordable, so we didn't suffer too terribly. Guadeloupe differs from the English or Dutch islands or even from St. Martin and St. Barts. The customs man is never at the shed, so he puts the entry forms in a cardboard box in front of the office. We fill them out, keep a copy, leave a copy, and don't worry. There is no charge and no hassle. It's harder for those going north, as they must have a properly signed and stamped clearance to show the next officious Brits. It's hard to get properness from the French.

On Maundy Thursday, we roared into Les Saintes[April 13] on a whee of a broad reach. Les Saintes is a group of islands south of Guadeloupe. It was the only place I saw people wearing holiday clothes and pareos rather than old shorts and T-shirts. The women, especially the young ones, have splendid figures and look extremely feminine, even when grinding a winch or hauling up an anchor. Nude bathing is *interdit* on the beaches, meaning bottoms are required, but the rules don't apply to the boats. Kent and I are so modest that we even shower in the cockpit in our swimming suits, but the French have no such inhibitions. I bought a bright red French bikini so I can burn some new bits of fish-belly-white flesh.

We enjoyed a brisk sail under main and working jib, a little more on the wind than we'd like, but with just one tack before the wind died entirely in Dominica's massive lee. I'd been looking forward to Dominica, touted as the most environmentally unspoiled of all the Caribbean islands, and I'd saved money for some inland travel here. From the sea, the mountainous, heavily forested island looked as primeval as the interior of the crater on St. Eustatius.

To winkle the last dollar out of the few visitors at the Portsmouth anchorage, young men in fast, hard dinghies have taken to meeting cruising sailors nearly a mile out to sea, offering them river tours, help buying fruits ("fruit" always has an 's' after it in Dominica), arranging ice and bread delivery, and guide and ferry services. We were surrounded by boats and young boys on surfboards, all vying to offer their services before we got the anchor off the bow roller.

We worried we'd conk one of them on the head when we dropped the anchor. If anything could have driven us away from Dominica, it would have been their persistence. From first light to sunset, people banged into the boat, wanting to sell us something.

When we moved on to Roseau [April 20] one young man sidled up to us when we were half a mile from shore, so we agreed to have him help us and gave him the amount for his services recommended by our cruising guide. We followed Oscar so close to shore that I (driving because Kent was handling the anchor) thought I'd be able to touch a palm frond from my position in the cockpit. I steered the boat perpendicularly away from the mean, rocky shore before Oscar told Kent to drop the anchor. Then, I backed the boat toward the rocks and passed Oscar a long line he took to shore and tied onto a palm tree growing in someone's backyard. It went smoothly, as do many of these nautical procedures that I worry about. The water was so clear that we saw the coral and sea fans lick hungrily at our keel.

We'd been warned to be careful here. Fishermen are tempted by all the nice line strung from boats to palm trees and have been known to cut it. A few years ago, a couple of cruisers were murdered here. We were advised to lock ourselves in at night. We don't have any internal locks; plus, closing everything would make our berth a sweat box. As usual, I was nervous, and as usual, nothing happened, but I was awfully tempted to leave immediately for Martinique and forego my inland tour.

There is an ongoing discussion among boaters about whether to carry a firearm. The arguments in favor of carrying a gun are stronger for boaters than for the average American homeowner. We often anchored and sailed alone with no policemen or telephone nearby. In a foreign country, especially a poor one, even a modest boat can appear to be an ostentatious display of wealth to residents, who don't always feel neighborly toward visitors. Anchorages are often located near the poorest and roughest parts of towns. But we never carried a gun.

At our anchorage in Dominica, Pam tied a string to a pan on the counter and stretched it across the companionway ladder. The falling pan would awaken us if someone attempted to enter—but then what? She set a spray bottle of Windex beside her berth.

"What are you going to do if an intruder comes?" I teased her. "Wash his glasses?"

As it turned out, the pan stayed put, and Pam never had to defend herself with Windex. We later purchased some pepper spray but never used it.

Kent has given up reasoning with me about my nervousness. I've finally convinced him that talking me into something

I'm timid about doesn't allow me to overcome the fear on my own, and consequently, I don't get over it. If he teases me to do something I'm cowardly about, I get little pleasure while we are doing it. I wanted to see Dominica badly enough that I was willing to risk my safety and the boat's.

We hired Roy and his aged Mazda to take us to some of Dominica's famous beauty spots. He lived on the shore near our boat and had a hand-lettered sign advertising his services. He was also recommended in our cruising guide. Before our tour, he took us shopping for vegetables and fruits and drove us to the customs and immigration office to get our clearance for Martinique.

Dominica is all that it's cracked up to be. We got to see the Emerald Pool, Trafalgar Falls, and some sulphur springs, although we didn't make it to the boiling lake or the Carib Indian Reservation. Before the Europeans showed up in the Caribbean, many islands were settled by peaceful Arawak Indian farmers who were originally from South America. The fierce Caribs were said to have killed or eaten most of them before Europeans or Africans arrived. The jury seems to still be out on whether the Caribs were cannibals.[1] Recent archaeological research suggests they were not.

Dominica may be our favorite island. It is lush, steep, and a riot of greenery and lavish color. On one 20-foot fern tree, I counted eight varieties of plants, including mosses and ferns. We sucked on the lemongrass that grew along the road, and Roy picked bananas (the best in the world, he claimed), grapefruit and coconuts along the way. It was as though we had walked into a massive nursery where all the house

1. Articles in *Newsweek* and *The Guardian* published in 2018 suggest that European colonizers were the source of myths that claimed the early inhabitants of the Caribbean were cannibals. An update in Newsweek in 2020 presents yet another view.

plants in South Dakota had grown to tree height. People are desperate for more outside development. The locals we spoke to want marinas, cruise ship docks, and free port status, but Kent and I think much will be lost when it comes. We're glad we made it here when we did.

We left Dominica for Martinique [April 22], sailing under reefed main and working jib, hard on the 25-knot wind. The seas rolling in from the Atlantic were green and breaking. This was our roughest ride, but *Coot* behaved well and even scooted up to seven knots. I was my usual queasy self and spent most of the time hanging on until the wind vane broke, and I had to take my turn steering. We went through storms with crazy wind shifts and lulls, followed by a stiff wind and wind-driven rain. We expect more of this as we near the time of spring storms. When we finally got to St. Pierre, Martinique, we were so wet and pooped that we didn't even pump up the dinghy until the next day.

We are now in Rodney Bay, St. Lucia. The mail is here, and I'm going to close. We're in a perfect hurricane hole, a lagoon accessed from the bay by a constructed channel. We are surrounded by boats, a marina, luxury condos, and a mini mall. We're not rocking and rolling, and we can respond to your letters and get some boat work done. The engine's still performing well; the wind vane's mended, and—touch wood—everything looks good. We're looking forward to seeing the Grenadines next. *(Pam's letter to friends concludes, from Rodney Bay, St. Lucia, April 24, 1995)*

We sailed to the Grenadines and, after a brief stop in Bequia, moved to the uninhabited Tobago Cays, which were set in the middle of a huge coral reef. To the east, there was nothing between us and Africa. Because there was nothing to block the wind, we funneled it through the boat and stayed comfortable despite the heat. There were no waves in the shelter of the reef, so when we got warm, we rolled off the side of the boat and snorkeled. It was idyllic. One of the nearby boats was home to an accomplished swimmer. She departed at ten doing a wonderful crawl stroke, and when she returned one-and-a-half hours later, she was still swimming strongly, with no mask, snorkel, and no swimming suit.

North of Grenada, we stopped at the tiny island of Carriacou and watched workers building a 70-foot boat on the beach. They did not work from plans. The frames had natural bends and crooks from tree limbs, and with a bit of shaving and some wedges here and there, they bent the planking to make the graceful curves of the hull.

We decided to eat at a little cafe nearby. I ordered a sandwich, and Pam ordered fish from the menu, but it would be two hours before we got our food. We were the only customers. We sipped our beers and watched the sun sink into the sea.

"You will be fed in a while again!" the woman in charge assured us from time to time.

Boat construction on Carriacou

The food was good when it finally came, but we had to search the anchorage to find our blue-hulled boat in the dark. We had not set an anchor light when we left in mid-afternoon.

In Grenada, we met Jack. We noticed a small racy boat with a Swiss ensign and a little bubble on top that we thought was an inside steering station. We guessed such a boat would belong to a young single-handed sailor. Then we saw an elderly man row a tiny inflatable dinghy to the boat. Jack wore a beret, smoked a pipe, and had a nose to rival Charles De Gaulle's. He was a retired physicist who read mathematics for amusement and wrote about physics. When he learned that I had taught philosophy, he was eager to chat.

He had taken two months to cross the Atlantic, which was more than twice the time most sailors take. He dropped his sails every night when he went to sleep. Most boats in Grenada were heading to Trinidad, but with his small boat and sailing style, he didn't think he could beat the currents in the Bocas. He would follow the winds westward.

"From a scientific perspective," he said, "there is no such thing as right and wrong and good and bad. It's all relative."

"Absolutely," I replied. "Oops. Didn't we just contradict ourselves?"

He had spent his working life in armaments.

"I'd be willing to build any kind of weapon for anyone."

He'd built weapons for Muammar Gaddafi.

"I could build a bomb that would blow him up but not hurt anyone around him."

Despite these statements, he was a pleasant man, clearly intelligent, polite, and gracious. Yet, I think he was dangerous. His profession may have required him to ignore questions of right and wrong for the sake of his conscience. He had a lifetime invested in his beliefs, and he was not going to change them now.

We ran into him again a year later at Susana's Laguna on the

Rio Dulce in Guatemala. Pam and I had taken *Coot* into the lagoon to get protection from the weather. I had taken the engine apart, and while we were waiting for some tools and parts to arrive, we assembled our second dinghy with a sailing rig for our amusement. One afternoon we sailed to Susana's for a bite to eat, and there was Jack, waiting for us on the dock.

"That's quite a dinghy you've got there!"

Dinghy outfitted for sailing

He had puttered his way downwind as far as he could, stopping at Cuba and even getting into Guantanamo Bay.

"How did you manage that? We can't even get charts for it."

"Ah-ha!" he said. "I just sailed back and forth around the entrance for a few days until the U.S. military grew suspicious and hauled me in for questioning. Just as I planned." He was very pleased with himself.

Chapter 16

Trinidad and Tribulations

June–September 1995

*Cruising is sailing from one exotic port to another to
work on your boat.* —COMMON EXPRESSION

I had ambitious plans for working on the boat in Trinidad, and I
figured we could get it all done in a week. But, knowing that things
always take longer than anticipated, I allowed two weeks. Well, we
ended up staying in Trinidad from June 7 to September 22—three
and a half months! It didn't seem too bad at first, as Pam wrote in
her letter to Sue and Jeff Grant on July 3, 1995:

> We've been here in Trinidad for three weeks already, and
> we still haven't decided where to haul the boat and what
> work we'll do. We have interviewed and received estimates
> from three welders, two carpenters, and a canvas maker. We
> took our dodger to the canvas maker to use as a pattern for
> a replacement, but we don't know if he intends to do the
> job. He has been expected at his workshop "within the next
> hour" for three days running. Organizing appointments,
> scheduling visits to the boat, and getting estimates has taxed
> our patience.

Trinidad is becoming *the* place to have boat work done.
Skilled labor is cheaper than farther north. Trinidad has
teak plantations, and the price of lumber is a quarter of
that in the U.S. But the workers are overwhelmed by the
influx of yachties. Boats have sailed across the Atlantic to be
refurbished here. The Trinis are being rushed off their feet.
Some laborers work seven days a week. It's not a dull place.

But almost two months later her tune had changed, as she
poured out her frustration to our son Jake, still in Papua New
Guinea in the Peace Corps, on August 22. I should have let the
boat work go:

Our lives are on an expensive hold since we are hauled
out of the water and paying for lay days whether we are
accomplishing anything or not. With the rain, incompetent
or irresponsible workmen, daily water and electrical outages,
lack of proper materials, and our own inability, we may not be
back in the water by the time you get out of the Peace Corps.
We try to be patient, but there are times when the delays
seem intolerable.

We're supposed to relax and take it easy—after all, we're
in Trinidad. But, of course, we came here because we were
told that everything was available, not particularly expensive,
and the workmen were skilled and hardworking. All of this
was an outrageous lie. We sit with the boat torn entirely apart,
except for the corner of the dinette table where I am typing. It
is the only place on the boat where one lucky person can sit,
and Kent and I take turns.

We finally decided to do the work ourselves because we
could wait till doomsday for the workmen to show up. Six
weeks after we finally got things organized, we were going

Coot *on the hard in Trinidad*

great guns. Kent rebuilt the forepeak for better storage, and I
painted all the new shelves and bulkheads under a cunningly
contrived shelter. Then, I got an infection in my finger. It
started the day after we came into the yard, but I let it go until
I began to feel as though I was walking about with leaden
boots with one tenth of my usual energy.

I went to the doctor, waited about five hours, and he
barely looked at my finger. Instead, he peered under my lower
eyelid, looked at the bottom of my tongue, and said, "You
are seriously anemic." I felt an utter fool. No wonder I have
been dragging myself around, forcing myself to get up every
morning with the disposition of an irritable sloth. Now I'm
eating red meat, taking iron injections in the nether regions,
and downing antibiotics, hoping that I will have the strength
to go dancing in a few days. Kent is inside and, for once,
not doing very much because it's pouring buckets, and even

our clever shelter is no match for an honest-to-God tropical downpour.

During the months in the Trinidad boatyard, Eric, an elderly Swede, making a second attempt to single-handedly sail around the world, dropped by to give advice. He had been a professional troubleshooter, hired to analyze problems and come up with solutions. He wanted facts, but only those he discovered himself, making him a curmudgeon of the first order. He and Pam enjoyed arguing with each other.

We had trouble with one of our paints, and Eric insisted we should require the company to replace and professionally apply the paint. He knew the big wigs at the International Paints headquarters and would take Pam with him on his next visit, so she could set them straight. Some of the other Swedes were embarrassed by Eric. He was stooped and half-shaven with uncombed hair, and he slopped around in shabby shorts with large strides and a peculiar gait. I doubt he owned a mirror. We heard he was extremely wealthy, although he was a penny-pincher.

One day Eric and Pam took the bus to the International Paints headquarters in Port-of-Spain. The woman behind the desk turned pale when they entered, looked at Pam when Eric's back was turned, and held up her fingers in the form of a cross. Eric demanded the two of them see the president. Pam presented her case, but the president interrupted.

"What bottom paint did you use over our barrier coat?"

"Petit soft paint."

"Sorry, there is nothing I can do since that's not our brand."

Case closed. Then Eric presented his.

He insisted they had sold him the wrong paint thinner, but the president assured him it was what professionals used. Undaunted, Eric pulled out several technical data sheets and began talking about the chemical properties of two thinners. Baffled by all the chemical jargon, the president promised to special-order the single quart Eric wanted. He'd have it in a week.

When we returned to Trinidad years later, we found Eric's boat at anchor, now dirty and tattered. Paint, no doubt thinned by the proper thinner, had spilled on the deck and run down the topsides. We were busy in the sandblast yard and didn't see much of him, but one evening he danced with Pam in a little bar while criticizing the other dancers and insisting she follow his awkward lead. We later heard he'd lost his boat while sailing to Grenada. He was rescued and returned to his wife and family in Sweden.

We finished work on *Coot* and put her in the water, but we could not leave Trinidad. Because we were a U.S. Coast Guard documented vessel, we were required to renew our boat's document by mail each year. I checked the mail daily and even took a bus to the main post office in Port-of-Spain. When the envelope finally arrived, several weeks late, it was stamped "Missent to Bangkok." Somebody in the post office did not know the East Indies from the West Indies.

While we waited for the document, we anchored in the deep Chaguaramas harbor that had formerly been a U.S. military base. We had to put out a lot of rode, and the bottom was fouled with junk. The chain snagged, keeping the boat from swinging completely around when the current changed, so we were never sure where our anchor was.

A boat anchored uncomfortably close to us. The couple on board looked like they belonged in a yacht club, not the Chaguaramas anchorage. He was nattily dressed in a blue blazer, white pants, and a yachtsman's cap. She was dolled up in a pink outfit and tottered forward in high-heeled shoes to push the button to release the anchor. Careful of her long pink fingernails, she set up an enormous amount of canvas over and around their cockpit. He took the wheel off the binnacle to get it out of the way, assembled a little table, and donned his smoking jacket. Then they sat down for cocktails. They headed to shore a little later in their elegant clothes. Concerned about the boat's proximity, we decided to stay on board.

Shortly after they returned, we went to bed, but Pam, always the worrier, could not sleep. She climbed into the cockpit and saw their boat just a few inches from the sharp metal edges of the Danforth anchor that was stowed outboard on our quarter. She sat on the rail, stuck her feet out to hold their boat away, and called, "Kent, I think their boat may be a little close."

Not wanting to be disturbed, I rolled over, mumbling, "I'm sure it's okay."

"Really, Kent, I think you should come."

I could see I was not going to get any sleep until I looked.

Pam grinned up at me, her feet pressed against the other boat. Without a word, I sat beside her, stuck my feet out, too, and rapped on their deck.

Nothing. I rapped again.

We heard some rustling. Several minutes later, the husband appeared in his silk pajamas, bathrobe, and slippers, surprised to see us with our feet pressed against his gunnels.

He stared for a moment, then said, "I suppose I should move."

"Uh-huh," we said in unison.

They dismantled their cocktail lounge, put their wheel back on, and departed, probably to a marina's dock. We never saw them again.

It was the end of September when we finally received our boat document and were free to sail to the Venezuelan islet of Chacachacare, the site of an intact abandoned leper colony. Paper records remained in file drawers and vials of medication on the shelves. A forlorn small cemetery contained the graves of some of the Catholic nuns who had operated the clinic. Because the Venezuelan army later used the area for military exercises, there is likely nothing left today.

We filled our tanks with fresh water from a stream emptying into uninhabited San Francisco Bay on Venezuela's north coast. Then we set out after dark for the small island group Los Testigos. We'd arrive in the morning when we could see into the water and navigate through the coral reefs.

When Pam turned on the GPS after we departed, it refused to start. Unfortunately, our compass was no longer accurate because of our two months on the hard in Trinidad. When a steel boat faces one direction for a long time, the earth's magnetism induces a severe error in its magnetic compass. We were now without either a working GPS or an accurate compass. It was too dark to return to the unlit anchorage.

There was no moon or stars to get a fix on our position on this cloudy night, and we were in danger of running into the coast that jutted out between Los Testigos and us. I would not be able to take a sun-sight with the sextant until morning, and making accurate calculations would be difficult because I was out of practice and had not reduced a sight in years.

Pam turned the GPS switch on and off several times, hoping its little light might diminish the humidity that could keep it from working. To our relief, it finally came on, and we sailed to Los Testigos without further difficulty.

The first thing we did that morning was work up a new deviation card. The compass was off more than 20 degrees, and I realized how dependent we had become on the GPS and how out-of-practice we were with traditional navigation tools. We were never again so lax about correcting the compass, knowing that the GPS could fail at any moment. We eventually bought a small hand-held backup GPS instead of relying solely on the sextant, ephemeris, and tables.

Before we set out in *Coot*, I was determined to navigate just as I had on *Jacana*. I vowed to use the GPS only as a check, but its ease of use quickly ended that resolution. The only time we had the sextant out of its box on *Coot* was to observe an eclipse of the sun using its filters.

In 1984, when we crossed the Atlantic, there was no GPS, we had no long-distance radio to call for help, and no way to receive signals to verify the accuracy of our wristwatches for celestial navigation. In ten years, GPS had changed everything.

We were not sailing purists, although we tried to keep our reliance on technology to a minimum. We met a few people with boats stripped down more than ours, and although we admired them, we never envied them. We were not good enough sailors to forego our engine, and we would have been hesitant to go into strange harbors without it.

Once, when we were motoring directly against the wind to the island of Margarita off the coast of Venezuela, we watched a boat ahead of us tack back and forth. It was a beautiful sight, like a needle in the water. We were not gaining, so she may have been making better time than we were.

We anchored nearby. *Emerald* was a small wooden racing sloop, longer than *Coot* but much narrower. She had been designed as a club racer by Laurent Giles before World War II in Lymington, England. Her precise age was unknown because the builder's records were destroyed during the war. Like us, the owners were probably in their fifties and had been living on the boat a long time. *Emerald* had little freeboard—they could do dishes in the cockpit and rinse them in the sea without leaving their seats. They had no engine or electricity.

There was no standing room below decks, and *Emerald* had little room inside because of her narrowness. The boat was always wet from seawater that washed the deck. We admired this couple's stamina and ability to get along with so little. When we invited them over, they looked at our dry, cozy little boat with what could have been envy. They may have been living as simply as they did from necessity rather than from a romantic notion of simplifying their lives. *Emerald* was the only boat we encountered that was simpler than *Coot* and not sailed by younger kids who were out for an adventure for a year or two.

The last we heard of them was from another boater who had given *Emerald* a tow against the wind to Trinidad. *Emerald* was a beautiful little boat that would have been great fun to sail, but we did not want to trade places. *Coot* pushed the minimalist boundary for cruising about as far as we wanted to go.

From Los Testigos, we island-hopped along the north coast of Venezuela to the mainland city of Puerto La Cruz, a handy place with doctors, hardware stores, and nearby small islands to visit. Over the next six weeks, from the end of October to mid-December 1995, we sailed in and out of Puerto la Cruz.

One hot steamy night, while we were at anchor, we were rudely awakened by a cigarette boat circling at high speed and focusing a spotlight on our cockpit. It was the *Guardia Costera* (the Venezuelan *Coast Guard*). On hot nights I often slept naked in the fresh air, so Pam threw me a pair of shorts. Our quick movements may have caught the eye of the lieutenant, who directed his boat alongside. Three military men with heavy, black-soled boots and sub-machineguns clambered aboard. The lieutenant, who seemed to enjoy practicing his English, ordered us to the bow of the boat and told us not to touch anything. Because his boat was banging into my un-fendered topsides, I put my foot out to hold it away, ignoring his admonitions.

They poked and felt everything that could contain drugs. When the lieutenant started down the companionway ladder, Pam followed him. She was not going to let anyone rummage down there alone. He repeatedly told her to remain on deck, but she refused to be ordered about on her own boat. Once it was clear that Pam was not going to leave, the lieutenant practiced his English by naming things as he searched: "closet," "skillet," "bed," and so on. Pam nodded and corrected his pronunciation.

He was young, and Pam began to feel rather motherly toward him. She put her hands on her hips and told him, "It's frightening to have you come aboard our boat fully armed and search it without our permission and with no provocation. This is our home. It's where we live, and everything we own in the world is here. Surely you would not do this to a Venezuelan family in town."

The lieutenant smiled and patted her on the back, "This is for your own protection." She was struck dumb. Afterwards, she thought of things she wished she had said, such as, "Protection from what—you?"

Chapter 17

Illness and Exile

October 1995–March 1996

I do not like thee, Dr. Fell, the reason why—I cannot tell.
But this I know, and know full well; I do not like thee,
Dr. Fell. —TRADITIONAL NURSERY RHYME

During our months on the hard in Trinidad, Pam ate greasy chicken with fries practically every day, and I ate lasagna. We rarely tasted fresh vegetables or fruit. The weather was hot, and we worked from dawn to dusk seven days a week. The one place to eat in our boatyard had a limited menu.

As she mentioned in her letter to Jake, Pam began to feel weak and tired. The doctor in Trinidad prescribed iron. Once we launched the boat, we cooked for ourselves but still failed to eat many fresh fruits and vegetables. When we left the boatyard, we relaxed in nearby Scotland Bay, but Pam's energy did not return.

By the time we reached Puerto la Cruz, she had grown dark green-black fuzz on her tongue and lost her sense of taste. Most foods made her gag, and she lost weight. Other boaters recommended she see a children's orthopedist.

"Why him?" we asked.

"He speaks English."

The doctor prescribed some medicine for menopausal

problems that Pam took religiously. When she did not improve, he offered to set up an appointment at his office with a female doctor. We arrived early and amused ourselves, watching people come and go. A woman dressed in a short skirt with tights, a close-fitting, half unbuttoned blouse, dark glasses, and a beehive hairdo disappeared down the hall. We thought she was a prostitute coming for her checkup.

Shortly afterwards, the orthopedist opened the door and announced, "She's here!" He seemed as excited as a schoolboy on the last day of school. The woman we had taken for a prostitute was the doctor! She did not say a word to Pam but listened to her chest and talked to the orthopedist. She seconded the orthopedist's diagnosis and left the treatment the same.

Pam grew so weak she could barely cross the street. So, we found another doctor. This new doctor listened to Pam and gave her a list of tests to be performed. She did not attempt to make a diagnosis but laughed when she saw the medicine Pam had been taking.

"Do you know what this is? It's a male hormone—an old-fashioned remedy for menopause. Throw it away."

Apparently, being female *was* the problem. For the first time, Pam had some confidence in her doctor. But by this time, we were nearing the Christmas holidays, and everything in Venezuela was closing, including the labs and doctors' offices. Because we had already been in the country so long, we had to leave for three months to avoid paying import duty on the boat. We decided to return to the Virgin Islands, where we thought medical care would be more accessible and familiar. Pam liked her new Venezuelan doctor, but we could not stay longer.

We decided to refresh our medical kit before leaving Puerto la Cruz. We had several broad-spectrum antibiotics and other prescription medicines we purchased before leaving home. Because they had been stored in the heat for more than a year, we thought we should replace them. We were hesitant because they had cost us about $200, but we took everything to a pharmacy to see what the cost would be. The pharmacist took the same brands with the same names off his shelf. He replaced all of them and gave us change for the equivalent of a $10 bill. We did not need a prescription. We wondered why the same medicines from the same pharmaceutical companies cost us twenty times more in the States.

> We had recently traded most of our Virgin Island charts and cruising guides for charts and guides to the South Pacific. Then we made a typical Cootish decision to leave Puerto La Cruz for St. Thomas. I don't know how many times we have done this, but it seems that if we get the charts for some new place, it's almost certain we won't go, and if we get rid of charts for the places we've already visited, it's tantamount to saying we will return. We left with a weather forecast for light south-easterlies but had moderate north-easterlies. *Coot* spent four days reefed down, rail down, hard on a wind of 20 to 25 knots with short, steep Caribbean seas crashing over the dodger into the cockpit. We found every leak we didn't know we had and got reacquainted with old friends. Now we are in the Virgins repainting the port side, which peeled down to the fairing material in a fit of pique at being submerged for so long. *(from a letter to Ian and Maggie Staples,[1] boating friends now living in Chile)*

---

1. Ian and Maggie Staples were boating friends who settled near Valdivia, Chile, where they operated a farm and a well-reviewed bed and breakfast and wrote a guidebook to sailing the southern tip of South America.

The doctor in Charlotte Amalie ran several blood tests and decided Pam had a severe thyroid problem. He directed her to go immediately to San Juan, Puerto Rico, to see a particular radiation therapist. He told us there was no time to waste. We called for an appointment but were told the doctor was unavailable for a month because he was on a golfing vacation. We informed the St. Thomas doctor, thinking he would recommend somebody else because of the urgency, but he said, "You mustn't interfere with his vacation. You will just have to wait until he returns."

So much for the urgency. Woe to the patient who gets between a doctor and his golf! While we marked time in Charlotte Amalie, we discovered Wendy's salad bar and started eating salads. For $1.99, we could pile a little plate high with green stuff. That was the start of Pam's recovery.

While we were waiting to see the doctor in San Juan, Andy met us in St. Thomas for his post-Christmas visit. His friends always enviously asked what exotic place he was off to this time. We revisited our favorite islands in both the American and British Virgins. Pam's holiday plans for Andy were not too ambitious in her weak condition, but we enjoyed quiet times, short sails between the islands, and no boat repairs. After Andy departed, we sailed to San Juan, Puerto Rico, for Pam's appointment with the radiation specialist. He didn't think she had a thyroid problem and ordered more tests—the same ones that Pam's Venezuelan doctor had recommended. Because the tests would cost a fraction of the U.S. price in Venezuela, we decided to sail back there.

Because of the regulations, we had to wait another month to return. Fortunately, Pam was feeling better, so we didn't need to hurry. We sailed east to St. Croix, hoping to catch better winds to Puerto La Cruz. Pam wrote to Andy from Christiansted Harbor, St. Croix, U.S. Virgin Islands, on March 12, 1996:

We are now in St. Croix. We went to Vieques, but the
anchorages were too rolley. So, we went to Christmas Cove,
where after a few days of swimming and lazing, we decided
the winds would allow us to sail here.

I'll give you a quick rundown of our general plans, so if
you don't have word from us in three or four months, you'll
know where to start the search. We will sail to Blanquilla,
then toward Puerto La Cruz, possibly stopping at Coche,
Cubagua, Margarita, Las Caracas, Chimana Grande, and
mainland bays such as Mochima, Manare, and Tigrillo. We
plan to be in Puerto La Cruz around the 20th to 24th of
March and will try to get my doctor's appointment and the
tests done then.

The harbor here is clean enough for swimming, and
there's always a cooling breeze with a few little waves. We
haven't yet been to Buck Island, a National Park with an
underwater snorkel trail.

Pam also wrote to Sue and Jeff Grant on that same date:

We like St. Croix, maybe better than any other U.S. Virgin
Islands. It doesn't get St. Thomas's cruise ship traffic, so the
streets aren't packed with frantic, pasty-legged shoppers
trying to buy the last Colombian emerald. The old Danish
buildings are remarkably well-preserved despite all the
hurricanes. We like dumpy Danish forts, and St. Croix has
two in perfect shape, one bright yellow and the other brick
red. They are in excellent condition because whenever
anyone threatened to fire on them, the Danes promptly
surrendered. Blood has been spilled in great quantities, but
the causes were natural, such as hurricanes and tidal waves,
or social, such as slave revolts and race riots. The island is
considered the most crime-ridden of the U.S. Virgins, which

keeps the yuppie factor small. But we have not been robbed or threatened and find the people kind and friendly.

The anchorage tends to rock rather than roll. It doesn't sound right, but rocking is more comfortable than rolling. St. Croix has a tradition of jazz, so we can sit in the cockpit, drink our own super-cheap Cruzan rum, and enjoy wonderful music from the pubs lining the shore at our stern.

Floatplanes tie up nearby. They used to wend their way through the anchored boats, but one day a fellow repairing his boat decided the pilot had come too close. He sprayed the plane with a hose, the pilot gave him the bird, and the sailor dinghied ashore and took a swipe at him. The pilot filed a complaint, and the sailor was charged with terrorism and interfering with aviation. We hear he's lost his case and will soon be carted off to jail, but in the meantime, each evening, as the last plane comes in for the night, he loads his two dogs into his tiny dinghy and rows into the plane's path. The plane screams to a halt and waits until dogs, dinghy, and master leisurely make their way toward the nearest fire hydrant. We enjoy this performance immensely.

We think that Andy made it home with everything, including his shoes. We wish he had more to return to—like the three jobs that Jeremy has acquired. We'd be happy if he had ONE. I *am* sorry that Jeremy isn't with the Christian Broadcasters anymore. We planned to use him as an ace in the hole if we thought prayer would be efficacious in dealing with our problems.

My taste is back. Only when I am especially tired or hungry do certain things briefly take on an odd flavor. I am putting on weight. The problem with getting my taste back is that I now know how awful the food on *Coot* is.

Now that you know Austen is so funny, you've got to read Trollope. I wish I could find more of him in the boater book swaps, but as these resemble those held at motorcycle rallies, I can't expect it. I'd never read Sir Walter Scott before, and his Waverly Novels are wry, insightful, and even funny. Ivanhoe isn't merely a medieval adventure but a forceful women's lib and pro-Semitic story. It should have been entitled, *Rebecca*.

You, too, can be warm if you irresponsibly abandon your family to live in poverty without hot and cold running water, electricity, and refrigeration. It also can be chilly, even though I know 70 degrees doesn't sound cold to you right now. But it is if you are naked and wet and have a 20-knot breeze for wind chill. We walked about three miles today, uphill and downhill, to bring home the bacon. My arms, shoulders, and back are aching, and I long for a hot bath with bubbles, but I'm going to have to fling myself into the chilly sea to get clean and then climb out into that 20-knot breeze to dry off. I must do it soon because the crab races at the beach pub are just about ready to start, and we want to be there for the first heat.

Pam's next letter to friends, a very long one recounting our extensive trip into the backcountry of Colombia, and finished in Puerto La Cruz, Venezuela, on May 1, 1996, begins:

It took two attempts to get out of St. Croix, but eventually, the wind velocity dropped, and we made a comfortable, albeit slow, passage to Blanquilla, a lovely, almost deserted island.

I caught our very first fish on this trip. People who have been living on the ocean for nearly two years should have caught a fish before, but we are not mighty hunters or anglers. Kent hates to touch slimy, smelly things and detests the idea of killing any living thing except mosquitos. I, on the other hand, don't mind this kind of stuff. I'm not particularly bloodthirsty, but if I like fish to eat, I shouldn't be too fastidious about killing them.

Kent isn't as crazy about eating fish as I am, so he always dragged his feet when I said we needed fishing gear. He made excuses about not knowing what kinds of line, hooks, or lures to get. He said he didn't know about the right knots or whether we needed sinkers, and he wouldn't ask other boaters who were successful fishermen, either. So, one day in St. Thomas' K-Mart, I bought a ready-made line on a hand spool, complete with a hook and leader. I also bought two pink rubber squids because some Austrian friends told me to get pink squid.

I trailed this line from St. Thomas to Culebra to San Juan to Vieques to St. Croix. I took it in only when we got near a port and were ready to turn on the engine, or if I was too seasick to clean a fish, or if it was dark. So far, I'd had no luck providing fresh food for the larder. The pink squid's tentacles looked chewed when I pulled in the line one day, but that was all. Kent smirked and told me I'd wasted my five dollars.

But the worm turned as we came into Blanquilla. I was hauling in the line when a little tuna took my lure. It was a foot-long black-fin tuna. Just as I lifted it over the stern rail, the hook slipped from its mouth, and it almost got free, but I managed to trap the wriggling body in the gunnels until Kent came to the rescue and threw it in the cockpit. I'd never cleanly killed a fish before, but someone had told us that the only reasonable use for French rum is to pour it down the gills of fish. We didn't have any French rum, but we did have rubbing alcohol, which put a quick and mess-less end to my trophy's struggles.

I didn't know that little tunas had so much blood. I beheaded the poor creature and filleted it, trying to remember a lesson in fish cleaning and filleting I'd been given in the St. Lawrence River. We only got about half of the meat we should have, but it made a lovely meal, and Kent agreed that this tuna was better than the canned stuff we'd been eating. I'm the one who's gloating now!

After two days of swimming and resting from our four-and-a-half-day trip, we left Blanquilla for Puerto La Cruz and chores. We efficiently checked in, had the laundry done, saw the doctor, had some blood tests, and went to another island just five miles away to swim. After that, we put the boat in a marina, packed our bags, and left for Mérida in the highlands of Venezuela.

Chapter 18

Colombian Sojourn

March 25–April 18, 1996

No man ever steps in the same river twice,
for it's not the same river and he's not the same man.
—HERACLITUS

We intended to spend some time in the highlands where Pam, who was miserable in the hot lower altitudes, could rest and re-cover. Traveling in Colombia, where we both wanted to go, was dangerous, but I hoped to show her the country I loved and the village where I had served in the Peace Corps thirty years before. Pam continues the story in her letter to friends:

> Airfares in Venezuela had just taken a huge jump, so we opted to make our trip by bus. We also thought we'd see more of the country. The first leg was to Mérida, Venezuela, a favorite tourist spot in the mountains about sixteen hours from Puerto La Cruz. I looked forward to being cool again. I was even willing to be a bit cold. We didn't know that we would be frozen by the air-conditioning on the bus that took twenty hours, not sixteen.
>
> Innocent gringos that we are, we didn't prepare for this trip the way the Venezuelans did, with blankets, earmuffs,

woolen socks, pillows, and gloves. I'm not kidding—that is
how the locals got on that bus. When I saw them carrying
all those jackets, blankets, and scarves, I thought it would be
cold in Mérida, and they didn't have room in their luggage.
The bus driver ran the air conditioning full blast for the
whole trip. We'd taken long pants, sweatshirts, and socks,
and we were returning our woolen thirty-year-old *ruanas* to
their country of origin, but these items were packed in our
luggage in the hold of the bus. We barely survived the trip.
The windows wouldn't open, so we couldn't let any warm air
in that way. Each time the bus stopped, I'd totter out, only to
have my glasses fog over in the warm air. We both got nasty
colds, which we tried to quell by two days in bed in Mérida,
forgoing the surrounding gorgeous mountain scenery and
charming old villages. Fortunately, our posada had cable
television with English-language movies. It was the first
television we'd watched in nearly two years.

When we thought we had a grip on the grippe, we
left Mérida for what our guidebook warned would be the
nastiest part of our trip into Colombia—Cúcuta, the border
town. This was no exaggeration, and we witnessed every
con the book warned us about. We got off the (thankfully!)
unairconditioned bus (an eight-hour ride from Mérida) at
the busy Venezuelan border town of San Antonio del Táchira.
We taxied into town, went to the immigration office for a
salida (exit permit), and headed toward the bridge to get a
Colombian *entrada*. We were warned to watch for the first
trick on the bridge. A thief would jostle a luggage-laden
tourist, and when the victim apologized and tried to maintain
balance, the thief would throw the bags over the bridge to a
confederate waiting below.

We took a taxi across the bridge as we were advised and
made it into Colombia with our bags. Our first success!

Then we found a little *busetta* to take us into Cúcuta proper
because we were warned that taxi drivers might rob us or
charge exorbitant rates and dump us by the side of the road.
We didn't want to stay in Cúcuta overnight. Like many border
towns the world over, it's dirty and dangerous, but we'd not
chosen the best time to travel. It was *Semana Santa*, when
Latin America was on the move and schools were closed
for Holy Week. The northeastern part of Colombia, with
its many religious centers, was the site of many traditional
processions. Pamplona, where we hoped to spend the night,
was booked up. So, we were stuck in Cúcuta, where we made
ourselves at home in the land of no toilet seats or hot water.

Our guidebook warned that Colombia was the most
dangerous country in the western hemisphere and that the
Cúcuta bus terminal was one of the most dangerous places in
the country. So, we took a cab from the hotel to the terminal,
where we were surrounded by men offering fake bus tickets
and insurance against guerilla attacks and bus banditry. They
spared no effort to separate us from our luggage. However,
having been warned, we were the epitome of knowledgeable,
competent travelers. Kent led us directly to the right bus
company, bought us authentic bus tickets, and led me
through the hordes of screaming thieves. It was a scary place,
and during the rest of our time in Colombia, I worried about
getting back through Cúcuta and its bus terminal.

As I silently bulled my way through the throng, Pam said over
and over, *"No me moleste!"* (don't bother me!). When we bought
our tickets, we were warned not to exchange them for anything
else. Once we got through the boarding gate with our bags, we
were let alone. To recover from the noise, commotion, and tension of running a gauntlet, we sat on a wall in the sun while we
waited for the bus. The same people who had been trying to rob

us five minutes earlier walked past, looked at Pam with friendly smiles, waved, and teased, "*No me moleste!*" We smiled and waved back.

Our first stop after Cúcuta was Bucaramanga, the capital of the state of Santander and the principal city near Kent's village when he was in the Peace Corps—a place he used to know quite well. For years Kent had told me that no matter how the rest of the world changed, Colombia wouldn't. However, we arrived in Bucaramanga at a new, bright, clean, well-organized bus terminal, and Kent was lost. Bucaramanga has grown a bit since 1964 and is now approaching a million people. As we got nearer downtown, Kent recognized a few streets. He was disappointed that our guidebook didn't recommend the hotel where he used to stay. Our guide is for budget travelers, and we're lucky to get our own bath, hot water in the mornings, and sheets changed since the last resident. Kent hoped that his old hotel, El Tay, would be plusher. However, the one person who admitted knowing anything about it warned us that it was extremely dangerous.

Kent wanted to treat me to the restaurant he always visited when he came in from the country, but it had moved, so we ate at an expensive but much inferior steak place. Thirty years of hearing how great the churrasco was at Di Marco's was not to be confirmed by the experience of eating a Di Marco steak.

I was disappointed in Colombian food. I'm sure there are some great places to eat, but good restaurants are as expensive as those at home. In ordinary cafes, the *comida corriente,* a set meal that includes meat, fish, or chicken, plus a soup (usually potato); yuca, plantain, potatoes, and rice with a bit of lettuce and a slice of tomato we could eat for $1.50 a plate. Guess where we ate? The two of us could eat for ten dollars a day, but the meals were heavy on starch, and we were careful about eating any fruit or vegetable we hadn't peeled ourselves.

Our breakfasts were usually taken in tiny street stalls and consisted of scrambled eggs and heavy-corn-based arepas. We longed for leafy greens. The beef we ate had been plowing a steep slope the day before, and the plantain, yuca, rice, and potatoes were all boiled plain, and I mean plain. There was no salt, pepper, or salsa. On occasion, if we asked, we would be given a well-used cup of *aji* (a chili/onion/green pepper salsa). The soups were best, if only because we didn't have to chew them unless we were unfortunate enough to get a piece of meat in one. I have discovered that I can live comfortably without yuca (a fibrous root vegetable).

Hotels are much like those in the U. S., and if we wanted comfortable beds, clean sheets, our own bath, hot and cold water all day long, toilet paper and toilet seats, towels, and television, we would pay American prices. We didn't. Our hotels varied in quality and price, usually between six and twelve dollars per night. We had clean sheets and our own bathroom, although the sheets rarely fit the bed, which was always remarkably bumpy with pillows stuffed with rocks. We were given ragged but clean towels about the size of an American face cloth. There was rarely a toilet seat, the shower floors were rarely mopped, the drains were the highest part of the floor, and the shower water often spilled into the bedroom.

We sometimes had hot water in the mornings in the mountains, but there was usually no hot water at any time of the day in the warmer cities. Our hotel in Tunja (10,000 feet) assured us that we would have 24-hour hot water, and the showerhead had a contraption that looked as though it might heat water if it didn't electrocute us first. We were thrilled because our colds had descended to our chests, and we were having trouble panting and coughing our way through the churches and museums at the high altitude. The hotel had neglected to tell us that after nine in the morning, there was no water at all. Tunja was going through a drought, and the cheap hotels were cut off. We managed to avoid the "love hotels," which rent rooms by the hour and never change their sheets. At least, we think we did.

We were stuck in Bucaramanga for a couple of days before Good Friday because even the bus station shuts down during this part of Holy Week [Easter was on April 7 in 1996]. We managed a trip to the remarkably well-preserved colonial pueblo of Giron, where we saw our first Holy Week procession. It was quite medieval, with the priest leading the group, altar boys swinging incense, and the men's religious orders dressed up in what looked like Ku Klux Klan outfits. They wore tall, pointed hats with masks, long robes, and wide hairy belts. The robes and hats varied in color from group to group. They carried their parish saints, newly dressed and polished for the occasion, on litters that took eight to ten men to hoist. The parishioners walked behind the saints.

Memories of Bucaramanga that I had cherished for years did not prepare us for our visit. The city had changed, and so had I. The central business district had deteriorated, and most of the life of the city had moved to the suburbs. Thirty years ago, I came to Bucaramanga for business and camaraderie with other Peace Corps volunteers. Now, Pam and I were alone, and I was no longer a 20-year-old enjoying my first overseas adventures. Neither my youth nor the old Bucaramanga remained. It did not help that many businesses and attractions were closed during Holy Week.

One evening as we enjoyed a cup of coffee at a sidewalk café, an odd little man started talking to us in gibberish. When he realized we were not comprehending him, he began to speak with gestures accompanied by guttural sounds. He sat down at our table, babbling and making puzzling gestures. The woman at the counter made the universal crazy sign with her hand; Pam rolled her eyes in reply and got up to go to the bathroom. I needed to go, too, so I hurried after her, worried that if I waited until she returned, she would be stuck alone with the crazy guy.

We had been warned about thievery and held tight to everything. When Pam and I returned to the table, the crazy man shook his finger, scolding us. I had left our bag (which contained all our money, passports, and cameras) on the table in plain sight of every passerby. This strange man kindly guarded it for us.

We survived other stupid mistakes. Our guidebook described several common tricks perpetrated on the unwary, and we witnessed some of these but, forewarned, congratulated ourselves on falling for none. In Cúcuta, pickpockets dropped money on the street in front of tourists and picked their pockets when they bent over to retrieve the coins. When we walked, money tumbled in front of us like confetti, and we laughed.

We ran out of Colombian pesos in Bucaramanga and needed to exchange some dollars, but banks were closed because of the Easter holidays. Our little hotel refused to exchange money, as did a nearby posh hotel, since we were not guests. However, we were directed to a men's clothing store not far away, which seemed odd. Not a single business was open along the deserted street. We were convinced we had been sent on a wild goose chase and almost turned back. But, lo and behold, we came to a business with its steel shutters rolled up and were able to open the door!

A pleasant female clerk greeted us as casually as if we had stopped in to buy a pair of slacks. I asked if we could exchange some money, and she said, "*Cómo no.*" A gentleman stuck his head out of a back room. "*Un momentito, por favor!*" The clerk offered us a cup of tea while we waited. She asked where we were staying, and we told her the name of the hotel, the room we were in, where we had come from and where we were going. We showed her how we carried big wads of cash in little purses we wore under our clothing and even bigger wads in our shoes. We were so relieved and grateful to have money that we forgot about caution.

When we left the store, we realized what we had done. We had been warned not to accept coffee or tea because it might be laced with a drug (*borrachero* or *cacao sabanero*) that could turn a person into a witless zombie who would follow anyone's instructions. Had anybody been interested in robbing us, we had provided all the necessary information. The whole setup had been odd, and we should have been on our guard. Pam, wondering if we had been drugged, ordered me, "Take off your pants!" right there on the street. When I said, "No!" she knew we had not been reduced to complete witlessness. Nothing came of our indiscretion, so the business must have been legitimate.

> There were uniformed men everywhere, hung about with automatic rifles, pistols, and billy clubs. At least four or five soldiers, local police, or *vigilencia privada* patrolled every street. Every bank, every good hotel, and every corner had armed guards. (As an interesting aside, in Trinidad, fabric stores had armed guards, and in Venezuela, paint stores usually had somebody with a gun sitting out front.) The buses we traveled on were stopped by the army at least once during each journey, supposedly to look for guns going to the guerillas.

Pam, with her rather boyish figure in her travel clothes—jeans and a sweatshirt—was dressed more like a man than a Colombian woman. Once, when we were forced off a bus, a young soldier with his automatic rifle ordered the men to line up beside the bus and the women to sit to the side. Pam started toward the women, but the young man prodded her with his rifle barrel and motioned her to line up spread-eagled beside me. I did not say anything, nor did Pam—I think she was intimidated by the rifle barrel. The young soldier patted me down and reached for her.

I said, "She's my wife."

He froze and turned beet red. There was laughter all around. He was within inches of having his hands on her. Pam and I started laughing. He waved her over to the women and self-consciously continued down the line.

As odd as it may sound, we didn't feel threatened by these searches. The army fellows were polite and even a bit apologetic. We were warned to check the political situation before venturing into new areas because the guerillas are still active in many parts of Colombia, and because they move around, it's impossible to say where they might be. We dutifully checked at every bus station and hotel and were always told that we would have *no problemas*. We did not travel at night because that is when buses are most often attacked, and we heard that Americans were especially disliked.

I thought the reports in U.S. papers about the dangers in Colombia were exaggerated. So, while we were briefly stopped, I asked the young woman next to me if there were *banditos* in the area. She looked at me as though I had lost my mind and said, "*Cómo no! Este es Colombia.*" (Of course, this is Colombia!)

I then asked if there were guerillas, too.

"*Sí!*"

But are they right here in Santander and Boyacá states?

"*Sí!*"

As soon as I could rejoin Kent, I told him we were mad for being where we were, and as soon as I got home, I was going to find a safe library to work in and only go out to weed my garden.

The people at the bus terminal were wrong about how long our trip would take. We would not get into the town of Málaga (our jumping-off point for Carcasí) until late at night. Málaga was not in our guidebook, but Kent assured me there would be a hotel. He was right. We found the nicest hotel of the whole trip with no trouble.

The Colombian mountains, where most people live, have kept the clearest Castellano in South America. They don't even call it Spanish. Even when listening to the radio, I could tell that if I had a better Spanish vocabulary, I would be able to understand. Kent began to chat with people, and his understanding took a quantum leap. Of course, we had to speak Spanish or die, as no one spoke English. The Colombians seemed reserved, and we wondered how dangerous it was for them to be seen talking to us, but if we needed help, they always graciously provided it.

The country is the most spectacular that I have ever ridden through. We spent most of our bus time on curving, steep, fascinating roads. Cúcuta was low, around 1000 feet. Seventy-five kilometers and three hours later, we were at Pamplona, 8000 feet. We saw every climate, mode of dress, agricultural technique, and architecture imaginable during the journey. Coconuts and sugar cane grew in the lowlands, the air was thick and hot, and people dressed like yachties. During a four-hour bus ride, we ascended through rain forests with lots of citrus and bananas to high plains where potatoes and wheat grew, and the *camposinos* wore woolen *ruanas*, long pants, and felt fedoras.

Each segment of our trip involved moving from one low-lying valley to another over two or three great spines of the Andes. What would have taken half an hour on an airplane took six to eight hours by bus. At one point, I looked down and saw seven levels of road zigzagging directly beneath my window. The drop-offs were so steep and the roads so narrow that I could rarely see the edge of the road when I looked out the window. The views were breathtaking, as valleys and ridges repeated unendingly into the blue distance.

Unlike the high Rockies in the U.S., these mountains are populated and farmed. I do not lie when I tell you that they plow and plant 60-degree slopes. Cows can fall out of their pastures and not stop until they reach the river in the valley 2000 or 3000 feet below. It's impressive to see cabbages growing on a hillside that looks too steep to walk up. When it gets too steep to grow row crops, they often stick in some yuca or bananas, which will produce at elevations close to 8000 feet.

The most romantic part of the mountains is the *páramo*.

Above 8000 feet, the land began to flatten, and gently swirling clouds surrounded us. Cows grazed, and the dominant plants looked like a cross between desert yuccas and jungle bromeliads. Nearly human height, they sported halos of white flowers. When the clouds parted at the high passes, we could see the rocky tops of the Andes. These mountains are older than the Rockies, and the peaks aren't

PÁRAMO

The Páramo is a high Andean neotropical, mostly uninhabited ecosystem above the tree line but below the snowline, with over 3,000 species of flora, including giant rosette plants, shrubs, and grasses. It is an important habitat for wildlife, including birds, such as the Andean Condor, and amphibians, insects, and mammals, including the spectacled bear and the Andean wolf. *Wikipedia, "Páramo." Last Modified 22 October 2022* as serrated. Few people live on the páramo, and its emptiness reminded us of Wyoming. We wished we had the time, the gear, and the energy to do some real trekking.

Colombia was a center for Spanish colonization in a way that Venezuela never was, so we saw some fine colonial architecture for the first time since San Juan, Puerto Rico. We toured churches and houses in every city and town. We saw one of the oldest and most richly decorated cathedrals in the country in Tunja and visited the village of Villa de Leyva, a national treasure preserved as an example of sixteenth-century architecture. Its central plaza is the largest in South America, and unlike most plazas, it has not a tree, bench, or bit of grass. Only a small well stood lonely in the center of a vast cobbled area. This plaza is also one of the few that isn't named Plaza Bolivar. It has retained its original name of Plaza Mayor.

We loved our trip, but the best part is the one I still haven't told you about. Kent did make it back to Carcasí, his home, when he was in the Peace Corps from 1963 to 1965. Returning to Carcasí has been on Kent's mind since we first came to the southern Caribbean. I, of course, wanted to visit there too, because I've heard about this place for thirty years. I think it's usually a mistake to go back, but Kent kept saying it wouldn't have changed. I was afraid he would be disappointed.

On the bus from Tunja to Málaga, our jumping-off point for Carcasí, I asked a woman returning from Bogotá if she knew the village. She responded that she did and that it was now ugly, almost abandoned, and the road to it was terrible. I must not tell Kent because if he was making a sentimental journey, this was something he needed to find out himself. But I did tell Kent. I was afraid that we wouldn't find a place to stay or eat if no one was left. Of course, Kent was not

COLOMBIA AND THE PEACE CORPS

In 1961 Colombia was the first South American country to participate in President Kennedy's newly established Peace Corps. From 1963–1965, I volunteered in the small, isolated Colombian village of Carcasí with fellow volunteer Ron Aulgur and our Colombian counterpart, Roque Garrido, in a program called Acción Comunal. Our mission was to empower communities by organizing self-help projects, such as building schools, sewers, bridges, and roads

Our living conditions were primitive. There was no electricity. We cooked on a Coleman camping stove, walked, or rode horseback to remote areas, and read by the light of gas lanterns. We bought groceries at the weekly open-air market and escaped to the larger town of Malagá via a wooden-bodied chiva every other month.

After a long hiatus, The Peace Corps returned to Colombia during the Obama administration after the Colombian peace settlements.

deterred, and the first thing the next morning, he checked on the bus to Carcasí. There was just one. It left at eleven in the morning and returned at the same time the following day.

Early in the morning, I walked to the corner to see if there was still a bus to Carcasí. A wooden-bodied *chiva* was parked in the usual spot.

"*Va a Carcasí?*"

"*Si!*"

In Spanish, I asked about the departure time and reserved two front seats (so I could fit my long legs in).

Pam was hesitant, but I was excited at the thought of seeing my old stomping ground again. Málaga had not changed much, although everything seemed smaller than I remembered. I looked forward to the bus ride through the country that was etched in my memories. I wondered who would be in Carcasí and whether we would find a place to eat and sleep. If Pam felt well enough, we could get a couple of horses and ride the old trails into the mountains.

We left some of our luggage at our hotel pending our return (which I fervently hoped would happen) and departed on what would be my first ride in a wooden-bodied bus that Kent said was just like the one he had ridden thirty-odd years ago. We got there early, so Kent could grab the front seat—the only one that would accommodate his legs— and discovered that the 11 o'clock departure time was only when the bus left its parking spot.

First, it circled the town square, picking up passengers, seven sacks of cement, and a parcel of lumber. It collected a few more people and bags of produce at the market and continued to pick up anyone who hailed it along the way.

This is true of any bus in Colombia, even the big cross-country buses. Any schoolchild or *camposino* can flag a bus down anywhere, although the big, carpeted ones probably don't take chickens or goats. Public transport is cheap and readily available in both Colombia and Venezuela. I wish that the U.S. would take a leaf from their books. But I suppose we won't follow this excellent example while cars are cheap. We saw few cars on the highways. But an hour's cab ride costs a dollar, the city buses about ten cents, and the cross-country buses are reasonable, so why would anyone want to drive? People are also kidnapped from private vehicles.

Carcasí was not even on our map. When Kent lived there, it was at the end of the road, with only pony trails and the páramo beyond, and after that, the high peaks of the Andes before the whole country descends into the Amazon basin. We traveled for two hours through spectacular countryside. I could see why Kent wanted to return.

As we bucked and grumbled up the awful road (Kent said it was better thirty years ago), I kept looking at a young woman who was well-dressed and well-spoken. She regarded us with suspicion. We were far off any tourist track. Most people in the cities had never even heard of Carcasí. I told Kent, over the clanging of the bus, that if he got a chance, he should tell her why we were on the bus. She probably wondered why two foreigners were going to the end of the road. Maybe we were police spies, guerilla supporters, drug runners, or people coming to steal children to sell?

So, Kent started talking with her, the bus driver, and the bus driver's helper. He explained why we were on the bus and asked about people he had known thirty years before.

From the three of them, he learned who was dead, who had moved to Bucaramanga, who was still there, and what they were doing. As we approached the town, the woman pointed out an old man walking on the road. It was Juan de Jesus, Kent's basketball-playing friend. The driver stopped so Kent could get out to visit.

Then the driver dropped us at the house and store of Don Dimetrio Duran, who was still running the little tienda where Kent had shopped all those years before. Don Dimetrio greeted us, took our luggage, and refused to let us go elsewhere. He said we could eat and sleep with him *con confidencia*, which made me think that the other place, if it even existed, might be dirty, dangerous, or unhealthy.

Thirty-five years ago, the bus (they call these local buses *chivas*) would have been packed with people returning from the market in Málaga; it would have been filled with livestock and produce as well as men, women, and children. There were only three passengers besides the driver, his assistant, and us. Most of the seats had been removed to provide space for cargo instead of passengers.

Carcasí had changed. Most of the houses were not lived in anymore, but they were still well-painted and looked cared for. The plaza was prettier than when Kent was there, and the people were better dressed and healthier-looking than the bent, tattered *camposinos* he remembered. Don Dimetrio said that many had moved away and that the *fincas*, little farmsteads that dot the mountainsides, were not producing as they used to. The young people were moving to the cities. We reveled in the lack of litter that characterizes most settlements in Colombia and enjoyed the lack of traffic. There are no cars in Carcasí, and everyone still gets around on foot or horseback. But Carcasí had changed. It now had electrical service and a little pavement on the streets. Kent walked and remembered old trails and reminisced with Don Dimetrio.

Carcasí in the distance.

Dimetrio was one of the people I enjoyed seeing most, even though I was closer to Juan de Jesus and others when I lived there. He was still the same, wearing his ruana, the traditional poncho-like garment rather than the blue jeans and T-shirts that were now ubiquitous. His small tienda near the plaza still sold the same products we used to buy from him. I felt I'd returned to the past.

We talked about people who left and where they were now, who was alive and who was not. I recalled the time when Dimetrio's brother was stabbed in a fight. Some men rushed to the taxi I had arrived in and wanted to take him to a doctor in Málaga. I retrieved my first-aid kit and pushed his protruding intestines back into his belly. I was trying to tape the wound closed when he died. He had a severe puncture wound in his chest that I did not even see.

I asked Dimetrio, "Is the animosity between the liberals and conservatives still as violent as it was?"

"*Si!*" It was still violent. Dimetrio told me rebels had come into town and blown up the mayor's office. "But they are opposed to the government, not the people."

His sympathies seemed to be with the rebels (the ELN, National Liberation Army). The federal police no longer had a presence in the village.

"What happened?" I asked

"They killed them."

We talked about more mundane matters.

"The town is not as pretty as I remember it. When I first saw it from the road, it looked gray." The red tile roofs had been replaced by Eternit (a gray, corrugated product made of compressed asbestos and cement).

"*No, no está tan bonito.* But it is so much better now. Vermin lived in those old roofs. It is much cleaner without the dirt sifting down from the mud that held the tiles in place."

We met the visiting dentist and received a tour of the community medical and dental facilities. It was a far cry from Kent's time when the butcher pulled sore teeth on market day. We worried that it might be dangerous for Don Dimetrio to associate with *Norteamericanos*, but the visiting nurse assured us that he wouldn't have problems for hosting us.

We were told the guerillas didn't bother the townspeople; they only blew up government buildings. I was at the low point of my cold and wasn't too agile at bounding around the town, which is built on the side of a mountain, so Don Dimetrio's wife Arminta brought chairs out into the street, where I was introduced to all the villagers. I think their store did an unusual amount of business that day. Almost everyone in Carcasí came to shake my hand.

It was an unusual trip, and I regretted not being more fluent in Spanish. I wanted to ask questions, but I had no way of asking or understanding the answers I might be given. Doña Arminta was a lively, educated, modern woman (she was Don Dimetrio's second wife and had been only a schoolgirl during Kent's time). Still, she didn't eat with her husband or son at supper or breakfast, nor did her female helpers. I suppose I ate with the men as a foreign guest, but I was dying to ask her why she didn't eat with us—tradition?— or did she prefer it that way.

We knew the guerillas had influence in this area, and we thought Don Dimetrio might be in sympathy with them. We wanted to ask political questions, and we thought he would be able and willing to answer them intelligently, but we didn't have enough time for serious talks. If I'd felt better, we could have found some horses and ridden into the *páramo* that Kent loved so much. We also worried that we wouldn't be safe from the guerillas.

Every time Kent and I walked from our host's house and

wandered off by ourselves, we were questioned, "You went alone?" with concern in their voices. When we returned to Mérida, we read in the newspaper that there had just been a shoot-out between the army and the guerillas a few miles from Caracsí. It may have been good we stayed just one night.

The visit to Carcasí was the high point of the Colombian trip, although Kent may have made a mistake in taking me to the mountains. Despite my miserable cold, which had even turned toward pleurisy, I was much happier up there. I felt so much better in the clear, crisp air that returning to the boat was harder than usual. We didn't make it to Bogotá, and we've seen nothing of the coast or the southern part of the country. We hope to visit Cartagena by boat in the future.

As much as I enjoyed visiting old friends in the village that had been such a significant part of my youth, I experienced a tremendous sense of loss. The young people I knew had become old men and women. Even the improvements: the dusty plaza converted into a park, the bits of paving on the streets, the new and improved buildings of the vocational school, and the electricity that made cold beers possible were oddly disturbing. I realized my youth had passed long ago and that nothing stays the same forever, not even Carcasí.

We returned to Málaga on the bumpy bus. This time it was packed. People rode on top and managed to stow a goat in the rear. The school kids were allowed, at no cost, to hang from the rear ladder and hitch a ride from the school to their homes. When one fragile old lady, dressed in her best, tried to pay the driver, he refused to take her money. She got off at a steep, twisting trail that led up the mountain. We spent another night in Málaga and one in Pamplona (a lovely colonial town) before returning to Cúcuta. This time we

In 2019 I again visited Carcasí and Dimetrio, who still owned the tienda.

quickly passed through the *entradas y salidas* at the border and caught the bus back to Mérida.

We thought we were done with armed inspections when we left Colombia, but we were surprised to be stopped just after San Antonio del Táchira. The army, or at least a group of people wearing camouflage fatigues and carrying machine guns, ordered all passengers off the bus and into a small steamy room where we emptied our luggage so inspectors could sift through every bit, searching for drugs smuggled from Colombia. Two young, gringo, hippie types got a thorough going over, including body searches. I was glad we looked old and stolid.

By the time we reached Mérida, we had been through four blockades.

We're back at the marina in Puerto La Cruz, and we're trying, rather unsuccessfully, to get ourselves ready to leave for western Venezuela and the western Caribbean. After much searching here, where batteries don't come in U.S. sizes, we have a new house battery for the boat. We've cleaned our fuel tanks and a few bits on the outside, done some varnishing and general grubbing, and purchased new swimsuits since the old ones have disintegrated. *(Conclusion of Pam's letter to friends, written from Puerto La Cruz, Venezuela, May 1, 1996)*

Chapter 19

Flying Serpent in Paradise

April–November 1996

It's O.K. They don't itch. —George Kent Kedl

What follows is another very long letter, this one written to sailing friends Ian and Maggie Staples more than six months after the the events described. It begins with the sail to Bonaire on May 15, 1996, and continues through our stay in Isla Mujeres in February 1997:

> From Puerto la Cruz, we sailed to Bonaire [May 15], where we stayed for only four days. The season was advancing toward hurricane time, and I wanted to get closer to the Rio Dulce in Guatemala. We were due for a reasonable sail instead of short hops, and we'd been looking forward to a real downwind run. We'd been on the wind for most of 6000 miles, and we wanted to see how *Coot* behaved on the 1100 miles from Bonaire to Guanaja, Bay Islands, Honduras.
>
> *Coot* handled just fine, as did the steering vane, but the trip convinced me that I didn't want any more long, downwind jaunts on her. We had to keep her shut tight, and it was a squalid, swampy stew below. I don't think I could take that for more than ten days.

Like many longtime married couples, we may each have assumed we knew what the other thought or felt. I selectively remembered old conversations, the Pacific charts we had collected,
and our investment in what we called the "Panama line" that we'd
need to transit the Canal. These memories reassured me that Pam
was willing to sail the Pacific. Her letter to Ian and Maggie about
not wanting to make passages longer than ten days should have
warned me that she didn't want to sail the Pacific or make any
other long voyages in *Coot.* But I continued to believe that sailing
the Pacific remained our common goal and interpreted what she
wrote to friends as idle chatter. I also rejected as hyperbole her
remarks about preferring the mountains to the sea and her dread
of returning to the boat.

> Kent thought he'd found his perfect tropical island when we
> reached Guanaja [May 25]. It's a charming place with friendly
> people. It's not got the heavy humidity of the mainland
> since the trade winds cool it nicely. There are lovely reefs
> for snorkeling and diving. There are good anchorages, not
> too many tourists, and a community of foreign settlers. It's
> reasonably affordable, although perhaps not as cheap as we'd
> like. Then we discovered the serpent in paradise. It didn't
> crawl upon its belly—it flew.
>   Guanaja was rife with no-see-ums and sand fleas of
> enough variety to be about at all hours, not just at sundown.
> They were the reason people built their houses over water.
> We had washed a lot of paint off the boat during the passage
> from Bonaire, so we snugged ourselves into the mangroves
> to do some repainting down to the waterline, and there we
> got the full effect of the insects. Kent refused to use repellent,
> although he was soon covered with thousands of red spots.
> "It's O.K. They don't itch," he said. So, I left off my repellent,
> too, as I hate the sticky stuff. Then, by the third day, the itch

began, the red spots turned a pus yellow, and we suffered as
we never had before. We decided we wouldn't buy property
in Guanaja.

We were so miserable that we were driven to thoughts of suicide. We finished painting by the end of the fourth day and moved
back to the breeze, away from the insects. But the bites drove us
crazy for days afterward. We didn't dare scratch for fear of infection and scarring, so we doctored ourselves with calamine lotion,
Honduran beer, and Venezuelan rum.

We anchored in Guatemala's Rio Dulce from June to
November to wait out the hurricane season. From Livingston,
the Rio Dulce runs inland for seven miles to a small lake
called Golfete. The route was a dream of a jungle tour. Steep,
vine-hung cliffs were stitched with snowy egrets. Indian
families paddled under the vines in cayucas (log dugouts)
with freeboards of an inch, maybe two. Howler monkeys
screamed from the trees. Golfete was fed by jungle rivers, and
quiet, comfortable anchorages stretched over ten miles. *Coot*
could navigate the rivers, and it was a kick to see how far we
could push her upstream. Wealthy Guatemalans built elegant
holiday homes along the western end of Golfete and the Rio
Dulce. We saw jet skis, big, fast motorboats, and cayucas
from which the occupants cast large, weighted nets with the
grace of ballerinas. There were hundreds of foreign cruising
boats, several marinas, and the kinds of restaurants and hotels
found in holiday places. However, the town of Fronteras
was a grubby crossroads between the more developed part
of Guatemala and the free-for-all life of the Petén jungle.
It was a real frontier town where cowboys kept pistols in
their pockets, and scabby dogs lay in the dusty street until a
"chicken bus" disturbed them.

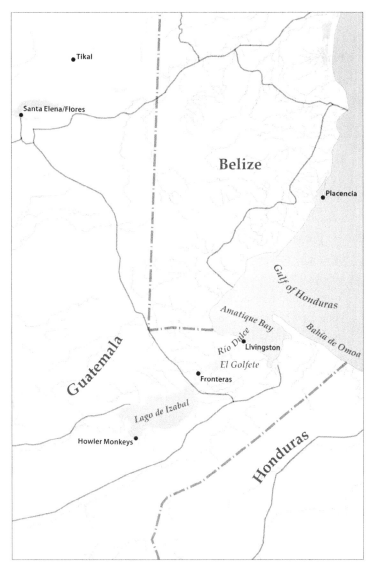

The Rio Dulce, where Guatemala, Belize, and Honduras meet

The chicken buses were a delightful (I use this word a bit tongue-in-cheek) part of Guatemalan life. They are old Bluebird buses made in Storm Lake, Iowa, around 1950 and designed to carry about 40-50 American school children. In Guatemala, they carried upwards of 100 adults, their chickens, trade goods, and tourists packed so solidly it was possible to stand up and sleep. The tops were loaded with produce and extra people. They were cheap, efficient, ran everywhere, and we used them all the time. West of Fronteras was Lago Izabal, another navigable lake that went 25 miles further inland and was fed by jungle rivers.

It was up one of these rivers while I was traveling alone by dinghy that I had the singular honor of being shit upon by howler monkeys. I deserved it, as we had gone to this place to get a good look at them. We'd heard them in Trinidad and Venezuela but never gotten close enough to see. Kent was stuck babysitting the big boat when I had my adventure, so he forced us up every other river in Izabal, hoping that he could have the same experience.

We were told that an excellent place to see the monkeys was up a little stream at the western end of Lago Izabal.

"I want to get so close that they throw their feces at me," I told Pam.

When a person gets too close to the monkeys for their comfort, that is what they do. We made the trip on our own, against the advice of just about everybody. Others warned us that the locals lusted after the small outboard motors on dinghies. These motors were the right size to power the dugout canoes, and they advised us to keep the motor and the dinghy locked

A single-hander friend who made the same trip was awakened early one morning by an odd thumping sound on his hull. He found his dinghy bumping into the bow and wondered, "How did it get there?" Then he noticed the motor was missing. The thieves had cut the painter and taken the dingy ashore to cut the steel cable that secured the motor. Knowing that their victim had no way to get to shore without a dinghy, they had considerately taken it back to the boat, anchored it with a rock, and left.

We planned our excursion so we would not have to leave the boat unattended. I took the dinghy first while Pam stayed to watch the boat. I promised to return in an hour so she could have her turn, but I missed the entrance to the creek. I retraced my track, looking more closely for the stream. I found it but had little time left to explore. I saw no howlers.

With my directions, Pam found the stream right away. She caught glimpses of the howlers along the banks. Then she turned off the motor to let the dinghy drift with the current. A howler ran along the bank ahead of her. She spied some monkeys lined up on a branch that arched overhead. Because she was wearing her wide-brimmed Chinese tea-picker hat, she had to tilt her head far back to look up at the monkeys. She saw what they were about to do, just in time to close her mouth and hunker down under her hat. Plop, plop, plop came a shower of shit. The monkeys did not need to chuck their feces; they just let them drop.

When she returned to the boat, she had a big, I'd like to say, "shit-eating" grin. She didn't have to tell me she'd seen the monkeys.

"I see you got close enough to have a good look at them,"

Two fecal chunks were stuck to her hat, and the dinghy boasted several piles of souvenirs. I was terribly jealous. I never did get that close to the howlers.

One of our most precious times in Guatemala was our trip by chicken bus to Tikal, the impressive Mayan ruin in the Petén. We wanted to be on the top of Temple IV at dawn, so we arose at three to take a *buseta* the seventy kilometers from Santa Elena to the park. Our headlights caught a jaguar crossing the road—the first memorable event of a memorable day. We didn't reach the top of the 160-foot temple by dawn, but we were there when the mists began to rise and reveal other temples in the complex. Tikal isn't just fabulous piles of old rocks; its setting is also impressive. We felt like explorers as we moved through the jungle. There were few people around. We seemed to share the place only with spirits. A fox crossed our path, oscillated turkeys were plentiful, spider monkeys showed off their babies, howlers screamed but stayed out of sight, and coatimundis rustled in the undergrowth. If you ever get a chance, go!

We visited Tikal before the road from Fronteras to Santa Elena was improved, so, it took the better part of a day. The notoriety of the road kept down the number of visitors. From the top of Temple IV, the tallest of all Mayan ruins, we looked down on the macaws, parrots, and toucans flying beneath us. The roar of howler monkeys filled the jungle that extended as far as we could see. Spider monkeys jumped among the tree branches far below.

We glimpsed more temples jutting above the forest canopy before they sank beneath the mist again. As the fog gradually burned away, the shadows created by the low angle of the sun brought the jungle and the ruins to life.

We wandered freely and, with the help of vines, pulled ourselves up to the tops of unrestored temples. Short trails through the thick jungle led us to temples we could have walked past without seeing.

When I returned to Tikal with Andy a few years later, much had changed. The new road made the drive to Santa Elena quick and easy. The number of visitors had increased dramatically, and there were restrictions on where we could go and what we could do. Climbing to the highest level of Temple IV and exploring on our own was no longer allowed. Still, Andy and I enjoyed our visit, despite the wet blanket I thoughtlessly threw over his experience by describing how it used to be.

When we returned to Fronteras from Tikal, we had engine trouble, so we stashed *Coot* in a marina, ordered parts, and took off for the cool Guatemalan mountains. The Rio is hot and humid in the summer, even though it is the best hurricane hole in the western hemisphere. We enjoyed the Mayan villages, the crafts, the old churches, and especially the cool of the higher elevations. As we neared the Mexican border, we thought that instead of returning to the hot and humid river, we could keep going all the way to the U.S. Bus travel in Mexico was comfortable and cheap. We could go home and visit the kids! So, we made a whee of a two-month trip through Mexico and back from July 15 to September 14, 1996. We enjoyed it so much that we are thinking about retiring in Mexico.

Pam happy in the cool highlands of Guatemala

We traveled by the seat of our pants, with no plans and no schedule. We had packed just a few clothes for a short trip to the cool highlands, but we didn't go back for more. At the Guatemalan border, we realized that there was nothing between Arizona and us but Mexico. Jake had returned from the Peace Corps and was working as a prep cook in a Tucson restaurant. We had not seen him for more than two years.

We took buses north, stopping along the way. In San Cristobal de las Casas we tried to find a room for the night, but the town was fully booked for a leftist convention. Madame Mitterrand, Comandante Marcos, and other prominent figures were in town. So, we returned to the bus depot, took the first bus north, and found a room in the next town, Tuxtla Gutierrez. We enjoyed Oaxaca, Mexico City, Guanajuato, and San Miguel de Allende. We crossed the border at Nogales, Arizona, took another bus to Tucson, and rousted Jake out of bed.

It was a strange reunion since our circumstances and his had changed since he left for the Peace Corps. We no longer had a family home for him to return to, and we learned he was struggling to bring his girlfriend, Cathy, and their new daughter, Melanie, from Papua New Guinea to the States. He hesitated to search for a permanent teaching job until he had them with him.

We bought a cheap used car in Tucson, drove to Wyoming and Minnesota to visit family and friends, returned to Tucson, left Jake the vehicle, and took buses back to the boat to complete the work on the engine. Our short jaunt to the highlands to cool down had turned into a two-month-long adventure.

Chapter 20

Salt Water Again

November–December 1996

. . . now and then a giggling trail of mermaids
appeared in our wake. We fed them oatmeal.
—TOVE JANSSON, *Moominpapa's Memoirs*

We were ready to return to the saltwater and sea breezes by
mid-November. One advantage of the Rio Dulce's freshwater
is that all the marine growth falls off the boat's bottom when
we enter saltwater. We sailed to Belize and, on the outer reefs,
found the best snorkeling we've ever enjoyed.

⁓

People often asked us if we were afraid in the situations we found
ourselves in foreign countries, but our biggest fear was getting
ourselves into trouble with the boat. We had rather complicated
and ambiguous instructions for getting into the north end of
Lighthouse Reef in Belize. Boater acquaintances George and
Nancy sailed to the reef with us, but rather than waiting for good
light, they headed in, got into trouble, and had to back out. They
then tried another way in and ran aground. Someone from the
lighthouse had to pull the boat off the reef.

We waited until the light was good. I identified the marks as best I could and headed in. We were to turn right toward the end of a small cay at the second stake, then make two more turns to get into the anchorage. As we approached the second stake, Pam, standing on the bow pulpit, directed me to move not to the right but to the left, where she saw what appeared to be the channel. Trusting her judgment, I did what she said.

After that turn, I had no idea where the purported channel was. From the cockpit, I could not see down into the water. I called to Pam, "It's all up to you now!" and settled back to follow her directions. I got mixed up in one tight spot and put the tiller to the right, which turned the boat to the left when Pam said, "Right." Pam caught the mistake and sorted me out with only inches to spare.

The channel that Pam had chosen got narrower and narrower. She had me slow down until we were hardly moving. I was steering inches to the left and inches to the right. I saw no channel. There was nothing but coral beneath the surface on either side of us. We crept on, and, lo and behold, Pam's path took us through the reef! Our keel must have been inches from touching bottom or getting wedged between banks of coral. When we snorkeled back that way later, I couldn't see how we'd done it. We were embarrassed by our awkward navigation through a channel not described in our guidebook, but the other boaters were impressed. We were the only ones to get in unassisted! I had finally learned to listen to Pam.

> We came to Lighthouse Reef in Belize partly to see Honey, a wild dolphin that frequented the anchored boats and played with swimmers. Sure enough, on our first morning, when I went into the cockpit for my first cigarette of the day to wait for the coffee water to boil, who should be lurking by the dinghy but Honey! I roused Kent, who climbed into the dinghy to stroke her, but she kept rolling over on her back and

slipping just out of reach under the dinghy. Kent took this as an invitation to play, so even though it was only six a.m., he put on his mask and jumped in, rolling about, trying to look playful and dolphin-like. She ignored him but didn't seem frightened or inclined to leave the vicinity of the boat. Then he saw what she was interested in—she was masturbating against the skeg on the outboard motor! We watched her for a while, giggled, and thought about the self-centeredness of humans. She soon abandoned us to check out other dinghies and their outboards as they were dropped into the water. As weird as she was, it was still a treat to touch and swim with a wild dolphin.

In our minds, we changed her name from "Honey" to "Horny" and thought the incident was amusing enough to tell our English friends, Mike and Jane,[1] whom we had been bumping into since meeting in the ICW years before. From their faces, we knew what they were thinking: How disgusting! These Americans can't resist making bad jokes about nature's marvelous creatures.

After they lowered their dinghy (with a much larger motor than ours), Honey visited them and did the same thing. They were genuinely surprised that we had not exaggerated, took a video of her affair with their motor, and brought it to show us. We later learned from a marine biologist that Honey's behavior was not unusual.

"Dolphins are very sensual creatures," she told us.

However, we saw no reason to disabuse other boaters of their belief that Honey had genuine affection for them.

---

1. We first met Mike and Jane on *Colleen* along the Intracoastal Waterway about the same time we met the other Brits. We kept in touch with Jane over the years, and in 2013 Linnea and I also visited Jane at her home in Cargreen. Jane had three husbands, all named Mike. We knew the second Mike.

People cruise for all sorts of reasons, and maybe sometimes for no reason. George, whose impatience had led him to run aground on the reef, was hard-driving, friendly, and occasionally funny but sometimes too close to the edge. As we gunk-holed the cays and the reefs, we often encountered George and Nancy. They came to our boat to share tepid rum and water, and we went to theirs for cold beers. As a result of a childhood accident, Nancy had a prosthetic leg, but that didn't slow her down. The first time they came aboard *Coot*, which was not the easiest boat to board without a gate in the lifelines, George boarded first and then directed Nancy, pointing, "Good foot here, wood foot here."

When we talked about the volcano that had recently destroyed much of Montserrat, George said, "I'm glad. I wish the whole island would sink into the sea!"

I thought he must be joking, but he was still angry about the inefficient clearing-in process he and all of us experienced there.

"When I get back to the States," he said, "I'm going to kiss the ground."

We left Lighthouse Reef for Belize City at the same time as George and Nancy. It was a beautiful clear day with no waves in the lee of the reef, and we had a nice 15-to-20-knot breeze on our nose. Pam and I tacked back and forth, enjoying an exhilarating sail, fortunate, happy, and free with no worries. We were looking forward to whatever came next in our unpredictable lives.

While we sailed, George motored, and even though we traveled a greater distance and had a smaller boat, we stayed well ahead of him. I thought if he didn't sail in such perfect conditions, he must not like to sail.

When we arrived In Belize City, we thought we'd save on cab fare by clearing in together. Nancy and Pam stayed with the boats. But when George and I showed the immigration officers our passports, they told us that Pam and Nancy had to come in person, too. George exploded. He turned bright red, almost purple, the veins stood out on his neck and temples, and he demanded to see the young clerk's superior. He made such a commotion that all business in the office stopped. I was embarrassed. There was no other way: we had to get Pam and Nancy.

George berated the driver as we taxied back to the boat. His poor one-legged wife had to appear at immigration in person! The driver, perhaps to shut him up, sympathized. In the heart of town, the driver pointed out the Belize secretary of state walking down the street. George insisted on stopping, jumped out, cornered the secretary, and carried on about how immigration was mistreating him and his wife.

"Belize will lose millions of tourist dollars if you don't fire all those dimwits in the immigration office!"

The beleaguered secretary tried to soothe George, admitting that, given his wife's disability, the immigration people could make allowances. He would talk to them about it. But George was still irate when we got back to the boat.

As soon as Nancy saw us coming, she said to Pam, "Oh, oh. Things did not go well—I can tell from the color of George's face."

She sighed and waited for George's tirade. After that incident, we avoided George and Nancy.

Chapter 21

Camalot and *Lo Entropy*

January–April 1997

Don't let it be forgot, that for one brief,
shining moment there was Camelot.
—JACQUELINE KENNEDY

We first saw *Camalot* (I don't know why it was spelled that way) from a long way off because her masts stood taller by half than those of any other boat in the anchorage at Placencia, Belize. Although we did not meet Marsha and Val then, we formed an opinion about them. We would typically want to meet the owners of such an unusual boat, but the shouting we heard across the water made us think they were bickering, unpleasant people.

A month later, we were in the immigration office in Isla Mujeres, Mexico, attempting to clear in without revealing (another story) that we had just come from Belize when Marsha and Val arrived. Although we did not recognize them, when they told us their boat was *Camalot,* we worried they might mention seeing *Coot* in Belize. Fortunately, they did not, and our clearance proceeded smoothly. When we chatted briefly, they shattered our initial impression of them. They were congenial and invited us to come to their boat for cocktails and penny-ante poker.

That evening we learned that Val, a swashbuckling fellow who never spoke softer than a shout (nor did Marsha, who had to keep up with him), had been a Navy test pilot.[1] Upon retirement, he bought *Camalot* and began cruising. He and Marsha ran charters on *Camalot*, sailed around the world, and had many marvelous adventures.

Marsha, who left the United States in disgust when Nixon was elected to a second term, was a real character in our country-bumpkin eyes.

One morning, before the VHF radio net began, Marsha, who rarely used the radio, called and asked Pam to come over. She did not sound well. Pam hurried to their boat and found Marsha, sweating from every pore, bright yellow, and in terrible pain. Pam insisted we take her to the clinic. Val was away in Florida attending his mother's 100th birthday party.

Marsha told the doctor she knew she was having a gallbladder attack. The doctor wanted to talk to Val, but Marsha would not let anything interfere with his trip. After three days of waiting in the clinic without eating or drinking, the attack subsided. Marsha walked out and thumbed a ride back to the boat.

When we saw her the next morning, she said she felt better and that it was all for the best, anyway. "I don't believe in Western medicine, and I've heard of a psychic surgeon in a little village about six hours away. So, when Val returns, I'll go to him and have my gallstones removed." I asked if she really believed in such things, and she said, "Of course." As in, doesn't everybody?

She had once watched a psychic surgeon in the Philippines take worms out of a woman's intestines. "He reached right through

---

1. Val and Marsha Schaeffer: There is an obituary for Val in the *Washington Post*, 19 August 2006. I have more stories about Marsha, illustrating her pluck and ingenuity, but when I recently let her read them, she said most of them were wrong, so allowing truth to get in the way of good stories, I've reluctantly left them out.

the skin with his bare hands and took out the worms, and then he simply pushed and patted the skin back together again."

When Val returned from Florida, Marsha and a friend went to the village where she had her gallstones removed by the psychic surgeon. When she arrived she found a line of people waiting. She was told to buy an egg from an old crone. When her turn came, she presented the egg to the psychic. He broke it, studied it for a few moments, and declared that she had gallstones.

He told her he could remove the stones, leaving her gall bladder intact. He had her lie on her back and pull up her shirt to expose her belly. I asked if she watched the procedure, but she said she had not wanted to. She felt a slight scratching on her stomach, and then the surgeon told her he had removed the stones, and she was cured. Was there any wound? No, not really, just a few scratch marks that would soon disappear. She lifted her shirt to reveal a couple of scratches. While she told her story, Val laughed and shouted, "She's cured, she's cured," and then laughed even harder. Marsha was utterly unflappable. She knew she had been cured.

A day or two later, we called over to say goodbye as we left the anchorage. Marsha claimed to be okay but seemed a bit subdued. Pam and I speculated that she may have had a minor attack and lost her faith. We sent a letter or two to them at a Florida address but never heard back. Then, a couple of years later, we returned to Isla Mujeres and found *Camalot* still anchored in the same place.

Val and Marsha came right over. Had Marsha cured her gall-bladder? Val immediately answered yes. She had not had an attack since her visit to the psychic surgeon.

But *Camalot* was in such poor shape that they had not been able to get her to Florida and had been forced to return to Isla Mujeres each time they tried.

Marsha was a fount of information and helped us provision for our visit to Cuba. She had all the angles worked out. Marsha knew which buses to take and which to avoid when we took the ferry to Cancun for serious shopping. She bought certain items at one store and some at another.

Pam, who bought only half as much, could not keep up with her. When they finished their shopping with dozens of bags to carry, Pam expected to take a taxi back to the ferry landing. But no. Marsha stood at just the right spot at the bus stop to enter the rear door. She got the other passengers to help load her bags. The crew happily helped her with all her stuff at the ferry dock. Val met her with the dinghy. It was then an easy matter to load up directly from the ferry. I wish I had thought of that a few days earlier and had Pam meet me with the dinghy when I lugged two number twenty-seven deep cycle batteries several blocks to the dinghy.

After leaving Isla Mujeres that second time, we didn't see them again and doubted we would ever hear from them. However, we kept them on our mailing list and sent an occasional note telling where we were and what we were doing.

Some years later, we unexpectedly got a phone call from Marsha. She and Val had finally gotten the boat to Florida, sold it, and now lived in a lovely house. Val was not well—he had some neurological problems that made him weak and unable to speak. The Western doctors, of course, said there was nothing they could do for him. Nevertheless, Marsha knew what to do: get him to her psychic surgeon in Mexico. Even though Val was too weak to travel, she could circumvent that problem because she had a friend who did astral travel and would take Val to Mexico via astral projection. I don't know how a psychic surgeon could work on an astral body, but then, I don't understand how he works on a physical body, either.

Shortly after moving to Las Cruces, New Mexico, we had another call from Marsha. Val had deteriorated again, so she took him to Mexico to see her psychic surgeon who had moved on to wherever psychics go when they die. Fortunately his former assistant worked on Val for several days until he improved enough to swim again in the beautiful Mexican waters.

When Pam told Marsha that she, herself, was having some health problems, Marsha said she had just purchased a new machine that would be able to help her. She needed Pam's date and place of birth to tune the device so it could send waves of help. Pam dutifully gave Marsha the information but she didn't improve. We heard from Marsha one last time and learned that Val had "given up" on her and passed on. She promised to send more help to Pam.

———

We met another unusual boat at Isla Mujeres. *Lo Entropy*, a steel vessel flying a British flag, was large and slab-sided with two enormous triangular masts of steel rods that formed a radio-tower-like structure. Rust streaked the white-painted topsides, even though the boat was quite new. Our English friend Mike had seen it under construction in Bristol a couple of years before.

Shortly before we arrived, *Lo Entropy* had dragged her anchor, damaging another boat named *Rapture*. The port captain would not permit *Lo Entropy* to leave the harbor until her crew, Alan and Ian, paid for the damage. This required them to sell some of their gear.

They listed the items they had to sell on the early morning radio net. When I went to look at the self-steering windvane they advertised, Alan gave me a hand up, and I stepped into an ankle-deep pool of rusty water. The gunnels had no scuppers to let the water out, but Alan did not seem to notice. He enthusiastically told me about the boat as we splashed our way to the pilothouse. I didn't want the windvane, but Alan wanted to show me around.

The huge hold was full of bags of old sails and some large foot-wide rolls of Velcro tape that must have been made for some commercial purpose. The boat was made entirely out of used and salvaged parts. Its engine and the crane on the deck came from the truck used in the boat's construction. The only new metal was the plating on the hull. As they were finishing the boat, their money ran out, so they put on a quick coat of paint and called it good. Alan and Ian had put their life savings into the venture. I don't believe that either of them had sailed before setting out on *Lo Entropy.*

We never saw the captain of the boat, who was reported to be in Cuba. Alan said they planned to set up business as an island-trading schooner and complete work on the boat as the money came in. They had sailed downwind from England to Mexico, with stops in St. Maarten and Cuba, blowing out numerous sails. When one gave out, they threw it away and put up another. They collected old sails of any shape and size and used them up as they went.

The engine was connected to the propeller shaft by two fan belts. The dinghy was a little Sunfish they sailed back and forth. They had once had a proper dinghy, but during the night they dragged, they dropped a large anchor on it, sending it and their outboard motor to the bottom.

Later the sunfish was stolen, and they drove *Lo Entropy* up on the beach and climbed down a ladder to get to shore. When the time came to leave, they managed to get her off the beach. They paid for *Rapture's* rigging and planned to leave for Jamaica, where they were to pick up a couple of new cars and haul them to St. Maarten. Alan estimated it would take two weeks to get to Jamaica, sailing directly into the trade winds. Pam did not think he had ever sailed into the wind before.

They needed deckhands and posted a notice for crew. I could not imagine who would want to go with them, but we saw young backpackers reading the notice. *Lo Entropy* practiced sailing into the wind in the channel between the island and the mainland, tacking back and forth for hours, seemingly staying in the same spot. We left and did not see them go.

A year or two later, we spied *Lo Entropy's* unusual steel masts in the boatyard in Trinidad. Anxious to learn how their venture had gone, we found Alan in the sandblast area. Ian was no longer with him and he seemed to be taking care of everything alone. We learned that when Lo Entropy arrived in Jamaica after an exceptionally long passage, the crew was arrested for lacking the proper papers. They convinced the authorities that they were innocent of any criminal intention and set out again for St. Maarten. The deal to haul the cars fell through, but they got a contract to transport goods from St. Maarten to Venezuela, where they were to pick up a consignment to carry back.

As they approached Venezuela after another long, slow passage, they heard news on the radio about a drug bust on the docks. Details in the story convinced them those drugs were the consignment that they were supposed to pick up. So, instead of continuing to Venezuela, they turned east and beat their way to Grenada against the trade winds. They were short of food and unprepared for another long passage. They were skeletal by the time they reached Grenada. They had motored against the currents in the *Bocas* with great difficulty to reach Trinidad, and Alan was now trying to come up with enough money to save the boat from rusting away.

When Pam ran into a very discouraged Alan at a phone booth, he told her his family would no longer accept his calls. He had used his last penny to keep *Lo Entropy* afloat. Now he was at the end of his rope and weighed maybe half of what he had when we first met him in Isla Mujeres. Pam gave him $20 for groceries. He thanked her and said he would pay her back, but Pam said not to bother. Later, we saw him carrying groceries back to his boat. When we left Trinidad a month later, *Lo Entropy* was anchored in the harbor. We called as we passed, but nobody answered. I would like to think that Alan made a go of his venture in the end, but it certainly looked like *Lo Entropy* had run out of energy.

LO ENTROPY

Curious about what had happened to *Lo Entropy*. We found there was more to her remarkable story. A movie, *The Cuba Connection* (see citation in the resources), shows the building of the boat and tells a little about the background of the original crew that built her, including the instigator of the whole project, Geoff Boerne, who owns the ship and has continued to keep her afloat. He tells me that some of the details of my account are incorrect. *Lo Entropy* sails into the wind easily, and Ian was an experienced and competent sailor. Nevertheless, he says I should leave my story the way it is because it was my impression formed by my long-ago acquaintance with Alan. So, with Geoff's permission, I haven't let the truth get in the way of my story this time.

Chapter 22

Chance Encounters and Ill Winds

February–April 1997

Tis an ill wind that blows nobody any good.
—Traditional

[February 1997] We're now back in Mexico with *Coot*, and each day our plans change. We'd hoped that we could get the kids to come down here. The fares to Cancun from Minneapolis, the icy capital of the frozen north, are reasonable. However, the boys couldn't make up their minds to come, so we got out our pilot charts and decided if we're ever going back to Venezuela for the big haul-out *Coot* desperately needs, we'd better do it while the winds are favorable. That meant we should have left here last month— when we were collecting charts and guides for the south coast of Cuba.

As you can see, we don't know what we're up to, but we would like to get to South America again. We bypassed Cartagena, and we're still regretting it. We'd like to go there, put *Coot* up somewhere safe, and do a little overland travel to Ecuador, Peru, Bolivia, and now with you in Chile, travel even farther south. We've always wanted to see Chile. Kent even applied for a job there back in 1966. However, we're quite sure now that we won't do it in *Coot*. I've discovered that I enjoy traveling by bus more than by boat.

We, especially Kent, are envious of your travels. However, I've talked him into putting the Pacific out of mind. We sold all the Pacific charts we'd collected in Trinidad and Venezuela. I somehow can't imagine our working with a Marquesan woodcarver as you did, and it's that kind of thing that makes your voyages special. You'll have to keep us posted on real adventures outside the Caribbean Lake.

I'll send this to Valdivia [Chile] and hope it arrives before you leave for your English summer. We'll want a complete account of your travels by tandem. Best of luck with weddings and operations. Forgive me for taking so long over this rambling epistle, but I'm having so much fun with the computer working again that I couldn't stop. *(Conclusion of Pam's letter to Ian and Maggie, written from Isla Mujeres, February 2, 1997)*

Pam mentioned that she had talked me out of sailing the Pacific. I'm sure she thought that was true. I did acquiesce in selling our Pacific charts when another boater made a generous offer to buy them. Sailing the Pacific required committing to continue our life on the boat. We were both getting bored with sailing around the "Caribbean Lake." Sailing back toward Europe or down the Atlantic coast of South America would be difficult because of the direction of prevailing winds and currents, but I was still hoping that Pam would eventually agree to the Pacific.

We were not forthright with each other. I always tried to avoid confrontation and did not tell Pam how much sailing the Pacific meant to me, and she did not tell me how adamantly opposed to it she was. She made weak excuses, saying our water tank was too small, or the French islands would be too expensive, although neither of those drawbacks would stop us. We could carry plenty of additional water in jerry cans, and we knew how to get by cheaply when we had to. I hoped that if I could get her to Cartagena, Colombia, a jumping-off place for the Panama Canal, I could convince her to go to the Pacific.

Pam saw the boat as one of my projects, and although she enjoyed seeing new places and meeting new people, she resented the time and resources we spent on the boat's long haul-outs and our endless "traipsing to hardware stores." I didn't realize how much seasickness, discomfort, pinching pennies, and anxiety tempered her enjoyment of our life on the boat. She must have been frustrated with me for not understanding how hard it was for her.

We spent three months in Isla Mujeres from January through March 1997, waiting for Jake and Andy to visit (they didn't) and trying to decide what to do next. Pam's long letter to our Brookings friends Ruth and Terry Branson was written on February 21.

It's great to know that the Mexican mails still work occasionally. And, as you can see, my computer is fixed. Mexico is the most civilized place we have been for some time, and we've been taking advantage of this by hemorrhaging money. We do best financially when we're in a place so remote that we can't even buy beans. Then we manage to get by with what we've got, but the moment we enter even the smallest village, our pockets empty.

We love to hear stories of miserable winters. They make us feel we made the right decision to leave that unholy part of the world, i.e., anything above 20 degrees north. Phyllis writes that they warn the snowmobilers about decapitating themselves on overhead power lines because the snow is so high in Minnesota. Serves them right, I say. We're trying to figure out a way to decapitate jet skiers. Maybe we could string sky-blue cables between the cruising boats.

You feel the same about people building expensive houses on slide-prone slopes as we do about people who keep expensive boats in hurricane-prone areas during the summer. If these fools want to throw money away, they could throw it in our direction. You suggested that if they were intelligent enough to have a half-million-dollar house, they should be smart enough not to build where they do. I suggest this demonstrates that acquiring a half-million-dollar house or boat doesn't require intelligence.

It's not been a Caribbean dream of a winter here. Those nasty storms in the Great Plains keep some force through the Gulf of Mexico and even down here. We've had a week or more of 25-knot winds with gusts near 40, rain, and squalls. We're anchored about as far from shore as one can get at Isla Mujeres, and our low, slow dinghy makes for a very wet ride for groceries or happy hour.

Not much has happened since we wrote about the monkey shit and the masturbating dolphin. We had a great sail from Ambergris Cay, Belize, to Isla Mujeres. So great that we arrived 12 hours earlier than we'd anticipated and had to lay off Cancun for six hours, waiting for it to get light.

We've spent most of our time fixing broken or malfunctioning stuff, and it's been too chilly to snorkel the reef, which is just a few hundred yards off our stern. Although we see hordes of pale, northern tourists in the water, we've become wimpy enough to demand calm weather, 82-degree water, and sunshine before we immerse ourselves.

Just as soon as we got here, gremlins attacked all sorts of systems that, until now, had worked quite well. At one point, all the lights seemed to go on the fritz. Not just the regular reading lights, but all the navigational lights on the mast and the flashlights went kaput. Even the kerosene lamp sprang a leak. All the batteries decided to commit mass suicide. Six flashlights, the multimeter, the shortwave radio, and the new expensive house battery we'd just bought in Belize all joined hands and drank the pink lemonade[1] in unison. Kent spent a lot of time tracing wiring and checking continuity while standing on his head in tight places. We ferried to Cancun and lugged heavy things back.

Then we decided we'd go to Cuba. We borrowed and copied charts and guides and began to provision. We heard that boaters can't buy anything in Cuba, not even bread or an onion. It's not that the Cubans don't have these, but it's all rationed and impossible for foreigners to obtain. It's okay for people who stay in expensive hotels on a package tour, but difficult or impossible for travelers like us. We now have the boat so loaded with canned goods and fuel that the galley sink won't drain because it's below the waterline. We invited a couple over for supper last night and worried that having two extra bodies on board might send us into a final plunge.

We planned to go to Cuba because the south coast has pleasant, unspoiled cruising. We collected charts and purchased a cruising guide from author Nigel Calder, who was passing through. A friend sewed us a Cuban flag. We stocked up on as many supplies as we could carry so we could be as self-sufficient as possible for the next few months. I had the engine's injectors serviced, bought new batteries, and had the boat so loaded that the water was practically lapping over the gunnels.

Because of delays over several weeks, the seasonal southeasterly winds had set in by the time we left, making it a beat

---

1. Pink Lemonade? Pam's reference here is to the red "kool-aid" that the followers of Jim Jones's religious cult at Jonestown, deep in the jungle near Georgetown, Guyana, drank to commit mass suicide in 1978. For an extensive discussion of what happened, see Wikipedia, "Jonestown." Last modified 22 October 2022.

to windward to get to Cuba. The winds were strong enough to build up substantial waves, and the current worked against us, too, making for rough sailing. We tacked back and forth but made little headway. The overloaded boat struggled, and Pam swore she could hear it groan with the slap of every wave. After three days of pounding, Pam suggested that we return to Isla Mujeres. The distance we had traveled in three days would take just one to return. We could see Cuba, but it would take a day to reach Maria La Gorda, where we intended to clear in.

Pam had her arguments prepared. I thought it would be a shame to give up all the hard-won ground we had covered, but Pam reminded me that we would still not be out of the southeasterly wind. Did I want to beat into it for two or three months as we cruised the whole length of Cuba? We were both tired, and I saw Pam was suffering. I didn't have the heart to insist we continue. So, despite my misgivings, we turned around. The boat took off like a horse going home to feed, and we were back to Isla Mujeres in a day. We never did get to Cuba.

Isla Mujeres isn't the most exciting of ports. Its proximity to Cancun's glitzy tourist industry doesn't lend itself to the kind of primitive exploring that Kent and I enjoy. The other boaters are mainly Americans who haven't done much traveling. It's only two or three days from Key West, so people can get down here and back quickly if there are fair winds and seas, which we haven't had lately. Most of our European friends have moved toward Cuba or the States in the last month, so we're forced to become acquainted with retirees who travel in packs, mostly motoring from marina to marina, where they will stay for two or three or four months and then turn around and motor home. They organize potlucks (Kent and I always attend because the food is often delicious as the ladies try to outdo one another), bridge tournaments,

and bazaars to aid the local Red Cross. They spend the rest
of their time traveling by taxi the two or three blocks to
the grocery store and complain that the clerk doesn't speak
English, and the store doesn't have familiar brands.

We have had a sobering event here. A few mornings ago,
we were having our coffee and waiting for the local VHF net
to come on when we heard that a boat coming from Belize
had lost someone overboard during the night. As the drama
developed, we realized that *Sea Level* had suffered a tragedy
that all of us fear. When the husband came up to relieve his
wife at the end of her night watch, she wasn't on the boat. The
Mexican navy searched, some boats went out from here, and
a plane was hired to search, but she was never found.

Kent went around in a daze and, on occasion, reached
over to pat me. We've tightened up our night-watch
procedures. Yesterday afternoon, while the people from *Sea
Level* (it's now only the father-in-law and the husband) were
doing paperwork in Cancun, their boat went adrift. I suppose
they didn't anchor as carefully as they should have when they
came in after the search. Kent grabbed Chris off *Rapture,* and
they went off in the dinghy to re-anchor it. We've heard of
two nighttime over-boards, and several boats lost sailing into
reefs at night. *Cruising World* doesn't say much about this
stuff.

We're still up in the air about plans. The truth is we are
on something like plan 23. We were charted and provisioned
to go to Cuba. Then we decided to go to Venezuela to a
yard where it is dry enough to sandblast. We got out the
Venezuelan charts and then began to hear horror stories
about the yard in Venezuela, sandblasting in general, and the
escalating crime rate. Venezuela is 1400 miles to wind. Scratch
Venezuela.

We regretted that we didn't get to Cartagena, so we got

out the Colombian charts. Kent was ready to clear out of Mexico yesterday if the weather had cooperated. But it didn't, and I got increasingly nervous about sailing 1000 miles into the wind in the bumpiest seas the Caribbean has to offer.

Boatyards would be scarce in Colombia, and it would be difficult and expensive for the kids to visit. We are woefully lonely for them. We should find lucrative employment if we are going to help Jake get back to Papua New Guinea to retrieve Cathy and Melanie.

Plan 23. We stay here into April when the northers should have quit blowing, and the south easterlies are prevalent. This would give us a pleasant ride to Florida and on to the Chesapeake. We'd look for work, earn some money, and maybe do some maintenance on the boat. *(Pam's letter to Ruth and Terry Branson, written from Isla Mujeres, Quintana Roo, Mexico, February 21, 1997, concludes)*

Those months in Isla Mujeres were difficult. As Pam wrote, sailing plans did not work out. Even though we'd run away to sea, we hadn't escaped from family obligations. Jake was having trouble bringing his family together and getting settled after the Peace Corps. Because we sent him money to bring Cathy and Melanie home from Papua New Guinea, we couldn't afford to fulfill Pam's long-held dream of flying to Peru to visit Machu Picchu.

Andy was dissatisfied with his college theater program and decided to drop out and go to work. We learned that Jake and Andy were confiding in my brother Doug and his wife Phyllis about problems we knew nothing about. I wondered if my cruising dream was mere self-indulgence. We needed to take a break from the boat and reconnect with our family.

It seemed that all aspects of our lives needed maintenance. We lacked a clear understanding of what we wanted to achieve in our sailing life and how we were going to do it. Maintaining the boat was more expensive and time-consuming than we'd anticipated, although we were living more simply and inexpensively than we had in Brookings. I still thought we could make life on the boat work, but Pam was increasingly doubtful. Her next letter, written to family and friends in December 1997, summarizes our time on Isla Mujeres and other escapades, notably omitting our aborted Cuban misadventure.

Chapter 23

Family Affairs
and Complications

May–December 1997

Home is the place where, when you have to go there,
*they have to take you in. —*ROBERT FROST,
"The Death of the Hired Man"

Pam's Christmas letter to friends and family was written from
Shark River, Florida, Everglades National Park, December 1997:

> We are presently sitting at anchor about four miles from the
> sea, up the Shark River in the Florida Everglades. It's a breezy,
> sunny day. Last night was so calm and clear that the stars were
> reflected in the unruffled water, and it was so quiet I could
> hear the dolphins breathing as they went about their night
> fishing. It's too bad that the no-see-ums and the mosquitos
> can zero in on human targets when the wind is light.
>
> Kent and I haven't had an exciting sailing year. We've
> often not followed through with what we planned and been
> disappointed with what we did. On New Year's Eve (1996),
> we were on Cay Caulker in Belize. We enjoyed Belize, but we
> spent much of our time ducking northers in the mangrove

cays, which aren't fun places to be when reefs and snorkeling in clear waters beckon only a few miles away.

After Belize, we sailed to Isla Mujeres, Mexico, on one of the nicest, quickest sails we've ever had. We enjoyed Isla Mujeres — for far too long. It was good to meet again with the cruisers we'd lost track of farther south and meet new people who were heading south, but we got stuck, hoping that our children could find time to visit us while we were there. Neither of our boys made it down. It's a bit off-putting to realize that one's children have their own lives and can't drop everything to visit their aging parents whenever the parents find it convenient. We spent nearly three months at Isla Mujeres on the off-chance that one of them would be able to take advantage of the phenomenal fares the charter cut-rates offer from Minneapolis to Cancun as an escape from the northern winter.

In April, we left Isla Mujeres for a windward jaunt to the Dry Tortugas, where we stayed for over a week, waiting for the wind to change. It's a pleasant place to get stuck, and we were able to add to our bird list, that is, if we kept one. It was the sooty tern nesting season, and the island was aswarm with Bermuda-shorted folks with more money in lenses hung round their necks than I've seen in a Mercedes showroom. The ranger in the park office took one look at us and said, "You must be off a boat. You're certainly not birders."

Finally, we arrived at Ft. Meyers, where we bought a 1988 Samurai Suzuki from a kind former professor of Kent's and prepared to haul out at Glades Boat Yard in the Okeechobee Waterway. We needed the car because Glades is about as far from civilization as it is possible to be in a boatyard. It is also the most exotic place we've ever been. Even the language was foreign, and the only word I clearly understood was "Ma'am." We chose Glades because we thought the center of south

Florida was unlikely to be hit by a hurricane. It was also cheap and had a storage yard where we could leave *Coot* after we stopped some deck leaks.

We didn't realize the Gulf and the Atlantic weather systems fight it out directly over Glades Boat Yard, creating BIG winds, lots of rain, lightning, and, on occasion, tornados. One morning I awoke to the news that there had been an earthquake in the vicinity (actually, it was in Alabama or Georgia). We, of course, had opened up the boat, taken up the decking, hauled the hatches out, and ended up waiting three weeks for a welder to show up to weld all the holes shut. Duct tape and plastic sheeting are not the definitive answer to deck leaks.

We didn't expect to find a place like this so close to the fleshpots of Miami, but the wildlife was extraordinary. Our catalog of bugs exceeded those of the jungles of Guatemala. When we first arrived, the love bug season had just begun. I'll bet you thought that was just the name of a movie featuring a Volkswagen. You were wrong. These innumerable insects appeared to be two-headed; then, I realized that the larger bug was lugging the smaller one through the air by the tail. They mate in mid-air, with the larger female dragging the male around until she is exhausted, whereupon they both fall to the ground and become food for their unlaid but presumably fertilized offspring — a typical family, I think.

The love bugs lasted about three weeks and, during that time were responsible for innumerable deaths on highways and murders perpetrated by folks maddened by having them fly into their ears, eyes, and mouths. They like hydrocarbons and hang out over roads and in the locks along the Okeechobee Waterway, where engine exhausts provide a rich environment. A forty-foot powerboat was hauled into the yard a day or two after we arrived, badly damaged from running up on the side of the canal after exiting a lock filled with love bugs. The owner said the love bugs did it. We said he shouldn't have let them drive. This little episode cost him more than it costs us to live for a year, but then his engines suck up 80 gallons of fuel an hour, so he must have a different kind of bank account than we do.

Once the love bug season was over, we became more aware, painfully aware in some cases, of the variety of less abundant species. Of course, there were mosquitos, but not as many as in South Dakota and Wyoming. There were no-see-ums, so small and light that one doesn't know they've taken up residence. Then one becomes aware of an itch as bad as participating in a procession of flagellants.

We also encountered something Kent and I call the slow bug. It's about the size, shape, and color of a flea, but it's easy to catch and squash. It came at night when we were reading and crawled under our backs or thighs and nipped. This one doesn't leave a welt and is preferable to mosquitos and no-see-ums.

We had a grasshopper the size of a Shetland pony, painted the danger colors of yellow with a red saddle, and unintimidated by humans. I kicked at one, and it kicked back. There were palmetto bugs (huge, flying cockroaches), German cockroaches, and a bug that imitates the German cockroach and flies; yellow jackets, which sting, and mud daubers that don't but build little mud nests inside and outside of the boat. Into these, they insert a paralyzed spider and deposit eggs. There was a little bug about the size and shape of a ladybug with a red head and an iridescent blue-black body. A thumbnail-sized bug liked to crawl up my leg toward my crotch at night and then start to whirr like a helicopter—we called this the crotch bug, and it usually got our attention quickly. It didn't bite. There were also houseflies and the Famous Florida Fire Ant.

Larger species abounded as well. Bunny rabbits leaped about the yard at night. One or two resident alligators made fishing from the dock unprofitable, as they tended to make off with the catch before it left the water. We were told not to wade on the shore of the canal as there were water moccasins. The yard was in the middle of a cow pasture, fifteen miles from the nearest village. The most common breed, an odd animal with bizarre horns, seemed to be a combination of Brahma, Hereford, and Longhorn.

The birds almost made up for all the weird stuff. There were Snowy and Cattle Egrets; and Louisiana, Great White, Green, Great Blue, and Yellow-crowned Night Herons. We saw Anhingas, Cormorants, Gallinules, Sandhill Cranes, and Caracaras, which look like eagles or hawks but walk on the ground, tipping over cowpats. Then there were all the twittery little birds that I couldn't identify and, my favorite, the Mockingbird. These last have such cheerful, musical, and varied songs that I was grateful they hung about the boats in great numbers.

We eventually got the boat not seaworthy but storage worthy. We filled her with formaldehyde gas to discourage mud daubers and mildew and departed in the Suzuki for points north. We were looking forward to a cool, relaxing summer in the Black Hills of South Dakota in my family's cabin.

We'd told ourselves that we wanted to make Minneapolis in one hop. What, after all, is another night watch or two? We'd forgotten how aged and stiff we'd become, and the Suzuki was not designed for lengthy freeway travel. In the middle of Illinois, we took a turn that put us a hundred miles off course. I begged for a motel, and Kent agreed. We stopped briefly in Minneapolis and caught a glimpse of Andy before continuing west to Brookings, South Dakota, to meet our granddaughter and daughter-in-law for the first time. I won't comment on the granddaughter except that she is the most beautiful, intelligent, and charming family member. Our daughter-in-law is lovely, and Jake is delighted with his family.

We eventually made it to the Hills with bottoms as stiff as a Brit's upper lip, loaded with all the Mexican canned goods, black beans, and rice with which we'd provisioned the boat for Cuba and never used. The Black Hills had the coldest, rainiest summer in years, and rather than painting and repairing, we got sick and huddled in front of the fireplace, trying to keep warm. Over the next three months, Kent put three coats of varnish on the cabin, painted the trim, rebuilt the porch, whacked weeds, and nailed up sagging ceilings. I managed to kvetch my way through hacking undergrowth, bronchitis, three sets of visitors, and a family feud that had been brewing for years and finally ripened this summer.

I visited both my brothers. When I arrived at Pete's, he said, "When Bob dies, I'm not going to his funeral." When I went to Bob's, he told me, "I have given my wife instructions that when I die, Peter is not to be informed of or invited to my funeral, and I'm not even including him in my obituary." Their relationship deteriorated from there. Since I was nearly as crazy as my brothers, it was up to Kent to shuttle back and forth to patch things up, only to fail in our efforts to keep the cabin as a family concern. My beloved cabin is now on the market.

It was a relief, finally, to clear the cabin of our personal stuff, load a truck, go to Brookings, load Jake's property, and haul the whole shebang to Bigfork, Minnesota, where he had finally gotten a job that paid enough to feed his wife, his child, and himself. We passed through Minneapolis again, got another brief glimpse of Andy, and climbed back in the Suzuki (still hauling most of the Mexican food) to return to *Coot*. The Suzuki performed flawlessly, and we had a whee of a time with her in the Black Hills. In the past, while driving the back roads, we have destroyed clutches and transmissions and punched holes in every automobile system that conducts fluids to its innards. It was a treat to have a proper vehicle at last.

We returned to Glades the second week of October and were supposed to be in the water a week later, but Kent discovered quite a deep tear in the rubber hose that connects the packing gland to the stern tube. He said we had to replace it. Ah, simple words. After nearly a week-and-a-half with his tummy on the head's seat and his head and shoulders through a hole to the engine compartment, Kent managed to free the flange from the prop shaft with specially made pullers and a lot of heat from a torch.

Ultimately, we had to pull the engine to replace a miserable four inches of rubber hose. Of course, once the engine was out, we needed to paint underneath it, and because we had the paint out, we painted the quarters. So, out came all the cockpit lockers, their contents, and masses of hoses, cables, and wiring.

At every haul-out, I sincerely, loudly, and bitterly question why we do this thing called boating. Kent looks at me with grease, paint, and sweat, defining the anxious lines of his face, and says nothing.

What could I say? Haul-outs are difficult, especially if you are not into projects the way I am. Listening to me grunt and swear was not pleasant for Pam, who had no way to escape. She enjoyed visiting new places, meeting people, and even sailing in good conditions. She was proud of her ability to crank the winch, trim the sails and do her part in handling the boat. Despite sea-sickness, anxiety, and discomfort, she took pride in our passages and enjoyed recounting these experiences. But the haul-outs, boat chores, and their expenses, plus the separation from our families and worries about finances, diminished the pleasure of our cruising life. I sensed she was ready to quit, and I did what I could to keep her happy without giving up the boat.

> We got the whole muddle back together with a new propane installation, salt-water pump, fan, galley light, chain, overhead, and wind generator. We plugged leaking holes, painted the topsides and bottom, re-caulked, varnished, and painted parts of the deck and, and . . . It was almost Thanksgiving when we flung the boat in the water and motored out of the Okeechobee Waterway. As we passed under the bridges in Ft. Meyers, the dolphins came to meet us. They cavorted around the boat for half an hour, so vigorously they splashed the deck and us.
>
> We are now a week and a half out of the yard. We've yet to see a manatee, but we saw our first wood stork and our first white ibis. The bald eagles and osprey share our anchorage along with dolphins. We want to get south, make another circumnavigation of the Caribbean, and try to get it right this time. Do write and tell us how you are all doing and where all of you are.

From the Shark River, we sailed to Marathon, Florida. While kedging off a mud bank that I had twice run into on *Jacana* (you'd think I'd learn), we got a call on the radio from Lew and Anne Tucker[1]—the people who were so helpful to us in Castleton-on-Hudson when we were starting out in 1994. Once we were free of the mud bank, they came for an evening visit. They left the next day on an around-the-world voyage that lasted seventeen years.

---

1. Lew and Ann Tucker were starting their circumnavigation when we met for the third time at Christmastime in Marathon. In 2014, Linnea and I joined them in Scotland for a two-week sail to London. They have since retired to Roatan in Honduras.

Chapter 24

Back to Sea Again

December 1997–August 1998

*I must go down to the seas again, to the lonely sea
and the sky / And all I ask is a tall ship and a star to
steer her by. —JOHN MASEFIELD, "Sea-Fever"*

Marathon was filled with boats, but nobody we knew. There were plans for a Christmas party in the marina, but neither of us looked forward to it. We looked at the weather forecast and decided we would rather be at sea alone than pretend to have a good time with a large group of strangers. We left Marathon on Christmas Eve for what we hoped to be a non-stop passage to the Virgin Islands. The passage took our minds off Christmas without family or friends, but we both felt we were sailing to nowhere, leaving everything and everybody that we cared for behind. How different it was from a few years earlier when we set out for the Caribbean and our grand experiment with such optimism and anticipation.

We wanted to get to the Caribbean fast and thought we could sail straight from Florida to St. Thomas without stopping in the Bahamas. We departed on Christmas Eve with a promising weather forecast, sailed through the Bahamas without a problem, and were well out in the Atlantic in a few days.

Then the winds picked up and shifted to the east and south of east. We sailed close-hauled as the apparent winds built to twenty-five knots. As the waves grew bigger, the boat was as much under the water as on top of it. Leaks developed around the main hatch combings, and the water we inadvertently let into the boat every time we stuck our heads out to have a look soaked the interior. The noise from the wind and the crashing waves was so deafening that we could hardly make out "Metal Mickey" (the nickname for the mechanical voice of NOAA weather). The boat stood up to the beating quite well, but I was concerned about a nut that came off the bolt holding the mast to the tabernacle. I did not have a spare, and should that bolt work its way out, we would lose the mast. I kept an eye on it.

After several days of rough sailing, we decided that instead of trying to reach St. Thomas, we would bail out at the small island of Culebra that lies between St. Thomas and Puerto Rico. As we approached the longitude of the eastern end of Puerto Rico, we saw we might not make it to Culebra before nightfall, but we were so tired and desperate to get into a harbor that we decided to try. I went on watch, and Pam went below. The weather turned even worse, and she knew she would never be able to hear if I called for help. So, instead of going to our regular berth, Pam lay down on the cabin sole at the foot of the companionway ladder. The floor was so wet that she sloshed back and forth with the motion of the boat. When a wave broke over the coach house and sent a spurt of water onto her head, she'd had enough. When I looked down the hatch and saw her sliding back and forth on the sole, I knew it was time to heave to even before she suggested it.

Instantly the motion of the boat turned gentle, the wind ceased to howl, and the waves (except for an occasional break-ing one) stopped washing over us. We cooked our first hot meal in days, and I wrapped wire around the problem bolt in a way I hoped would keep it in place. I dried the combings around the hatch well enough to seal the leaking seams with duct tape. We remained hove-to for a day and a half, and although we lost hard-won ground, we finally got some much-needed sleep.

By the time we turned back into the wind and started sailing again, we had been blown back about half the length of Puerto Rico. The winds did not let up, and we spent two days getting back to where we had been before. By then, we were as exhausted as we had been the first time we arrived at that spot, and the timing was now even worse for reaching Culebra in daylight. So, we shortened the voyage once more and headed to Isleta Marina near Fajardo, Puerto Rico.

We arrived in sorry shape on January 6, two weeks after our departure from Marathon. We had blown out our genoa, paint was washed off the hull, the large metric nut needed to be acquired and installed, deck seams needed to be replaced, and, most of all, we needed a rest.

Looking back at that passage, I can see several things we did wrong. We allowed ourselves to get too tired to think clearly. Heaving to and losing so much ground when we didn't know if the weather would improve cost us too much. I don't know why we didn't sail into San Juan and anchor. We had been there before and could have found our way into the harbor, even after dark. Or, we could have taken a shorter respite for a hot meal and made the timing better for arrival in Culebra.

After reorganizing the boat and replacing the missing nut, we made the short hop from Isleta Marina to Culebra, where a fellow in a bar asked us, "Which boat is yours?" The island was filled with tourists, and we had put on our best clothes to come ashore. How did he know we were from a boat? Was it our tans? Was it our healthy good looks? The strings on our glasses?

"How do you know we're from a boat?" we asked.

He hesitated for a moment before he said, "It's the mildew odor."

A few weeks after our exhausting passage, Andy came, and we

arranged to meet him on Culebra, which he would reach via a connecting flight from San Juan. The day he was to arrive, we left the boat and walked a short way to the small airfield. It started to rain, and the terminal was locked, so we stood outside under a porch and waited. The plane did not come, and the rain poured down. After an hour or more, we walked around the building, finding several workmen in a baggage area. They told us the plane would not be coming because the FAA had grounded the feeder airline for safety violations—the weather had nothing to do with it.

We had no way of contacting Andy, and we didn't know if he could find his way from San Juan to Fajardo to catch a ferry to Culebra. He was loaded down with a huge sail we had ordered to replace the blown-out genoa. I walked to the airport every time a plane flew in, and to the dock to meet each ferry. To our relief, Andy arrived on the afternoon ferry one day after the plane was to have come. He handed me the huge wrapped-up sail and said, "Here! It's your turn now." The package was as big as a surfboard and weighed at least thirty pounds.

I don't know why we had worried about Andy. He got along fine, even carrying the awkward sail. He crossed San Juan to another airfield to catch his feeder flight, discovered it was canceled, and met another stranded passenger. That person had friends who gave them both a lift to Fajardo, put them up for the night, and drove them to the ferry the next day.

It was just as well that Andy had not arrived as scheduled because when we went to pick him up at the airport, we had forgotten to close the forehatch, allowing the rain to pour on our berth and into our bilges for well over an hour. We came back that afternoon to a sopping mess. It took a day to dry everything out so Andy would have a place to sleep.

We sailed with Andy from island to island over the next two weeks. We visited some of our favorite anchorages in the Virgins, stopped for a few days in St. Maarten, climbed to the top of Saba, and into the crater on Statia. We watched an eclipse of the sun at St. Croix—had we been just a degree further south, we would have seen a total eclipse. At the end of his vacation, we left Andy in St. Thomas to catch his flight to Minneapolis. We made sure he was wearing his shoes.

The paint problems that had started on our long sail to Guanaja the year before continued to plague us. The undercoating and the filler used when the boat was first built were beginning to give out, so we were constantly patching our topside paint. When we got to the Virgin Islands after the long sail from Florida, we found we had a bigger problem than ever, despite all our work at Glades. We now had raw steel exposed to the saltwater beneath the waterline.

We could not afford to have the hull sandblasted and repainted anywhere in the Virgin Islands. We called all around the Caribbean, and the best place to have the work done was in Trinidad. But we needed to paint the exposed steel before we could sail there. There was not enough tidal range in the Virgins to careen the boat to expose the steel below the waterline. We had to figure out how to do it while we were still afloat.

Hurricane Hole is an extremely well-protected bay on St. John with several narrow fingers of water. We took *Coot* to the end of one of those fingers where we could take lines to shore on either side. We pulled the masthead to port and the keel to starboard, tipping the boat enough to expose all the raw steel on the starboard side. Hurricane Hole is now a nature preserve, and it would be impossible to do there now what we did in 1998.

When the winds were right, we sailed directly to Trinidad, where we had the hull sandblasted and recoated with multiple layers of paint.

Chapter 25

The Macareo River

September 1998

The water, the canoes, the people, and the bark of the
mangroves along the river's edge were all the same earthy
tone, so the naked people were invisible against the jungle.
—GEORGE KENT KEDL

From Trinidad and Tobago, we headed south to Venezuela and the Macareo River in the delta of the great Orinoco. Several boaters had found their way up the river before us, and their reports inspired us to make what turned out to be a memorable excursion. During the high-water season, the Warao Indians, a hunting-gathering people, come down the river to fish. People from the yacht club told us that most of them spoke only their native language and were so desperately poor they didn't have clothes and paddled dugout canoes, their only means of transportation. If we were going up the river, we should take some things to them. We did not have much, but we sorted through our clothing and put together a bag of old T-shirts and pants. We had some medicines and band-aids we thought would be useful, things we could spare or replace. We got advice from several people and sketches of the uncharted river's mouth. Another boat anchored at a yacht club decided to join us. These folks had boxes of things to give away.

The Warao live in open, thatch-roofed bamboo houses perched on stilts along the banks of the river. A cluster of three or four dwellings and three or four families constitutes a village. Even though the river is in Venezuela, most people did not speak Spanish, so our ability to communicate was limited. We traveled in the high-water season when no land was above water, and the only way people could move was via their dugout canoes.

The water, the canoes, the people, and the bark of the mangroves along the river's edge were all the same earthy tone. The naked people were almost invisible against the jungle. They matched their environment so perfectly that the sound of the paddles tapping against the side of their dugouts as they slipped through the water was frequently the only notice that we were not alone on the river. They moved through their watery world with hardly a wake. We, by contrast, were intruders. With its small diesel engine that chugged and spewed its way up the river, our unnatural vessel seemed like a scream in a church. Their lives made our attempt to achieve a simple, unobtrusive life seem lame.

We anchored just inside the river's mouth the first night, close to one of the Warao dwellings. Soon after we arrived, a young woman and her little brother (who did the paddling) visited us. She spoke some Spanish so we could talk to her, and although she was rather shy, she welcomed us and asked where we were from and where we had been. We asked about her family and what they did. She invited us to visit. I wanted to see the dwelling and meet her family. So, we put our dinghy in the water and motored over.

The home was a bamboo platform on stilts just high enough to escape flooding from the river at its highest. It had a thatched roof but no walls. All activities were conducted in the open. There was no dry land within miles, and the water was 10 to 12 feet deep. The mangrove jungle growing up through the water defined the edges of the river. There were some elderly people, a young couple, and two or three children, including an infant crawling about. The young woman was the only one we could speak with. Although it may have been nothing more than the language barrier, I felt our visit made the others uncomfortable.

I was struck by how close the family lived to the water; their dugouts were what a bicycle was to me as a kid — the contrivance I climbed aboard as I stepped out the door. The young woman mentioned that she did not know how to swim, and when I expressed amazement at her remark, she pointed out that the fish in the water made swimming unwise. I knew there were piranhas in the area, so I asked, guessing that the Spanish word for "piranha" would be similar to English if those were the fish she was concerned about, but she did not recognize the name.

The bamboo floor seemed strong enough, but there were wide gaps that I thought the infant might slip through. There was nothing to keep the child from crawling off the edge, but no one seemed concerned. Surely, they knew what they were doing. Pam and I said goodbye and dinghied downstream to our boat. The current had become so strong, and we were moving so fast that I worried that our little motor would be too weak to carry us back upstream if we missed the boat. I relaxed only after we had a line tied on.

The next day, when the current slowed, we moved up the river and anchored in front of a cluster of bamboo structures. We were immediately surrounded by dugouts banging into the side of our boat, filled with young kids and older people, all with their hands out. Pam and I brought out our paltry items and gave them to those who seemed to be in greatest need, although they all looked similar, dressed in T-shirts received from previous boaters. As soon as we were out of stuff to give away, they left us for the boat of our companion, who brought out his boxes and had a grand time distributing his treasures.

We thought how silly it was. There was no need for our cast-off T-shirts. The begging had become a kind of business. One woman insisted that we write down a list of things to bring the next time we came, including, to our amusement, French perfume.

We thought better of the Indians farther up the river than those lower down who had become beggars. I don't know how dependent the Warao were upon the charity of boaters. I was told they took most of the stuff they received upriver to Tucupita, where they sold it in the market. The reliance on cast-offs from boaters had changed their lives, whether for better or worse, we didn't know.

In the more remote areas upriver, the Warao were comfortable without clothing. They did not beg, nor did they approach us, except on one occasion when a man asked if we had any medicine for his sick wife. She looked ill, huddled in the back of the dugout. I wished I had some medical knowledge and could have been of genuine assistance. He was the only Warao we saw who looked in need of help. We gave him some cough medicine, hoping that might make her feel better.

The river ran against us at five knots during low tide but slowed to one or two when the tide was high. We could make progress motoring upriver only at high tide and had to anchor to keep from going backwards when the tide was low. Great floating 'islands' of water hyacinths and debris drifted past, collecting logs, animals, and virtually anything in their paths. They were larger than our boat and would have gathered us up, too, had we not stayed out of their way. Moving the boat at night was out of the question. We had to find a place to anchor where the current would carry the masses of flotsam away from us. One night we unwisely anchored below a stream that, when the current reversed, ejected a steady train of debris and batches of floating water hyacinths that snagged on our anchor chain and accumulated alarmingly.

We used a boathook to remove the plants as they built up, but we fell behind and quickly exhausted ourselves. We feared that the drag of the plants might cause the anchor to break loose or the bow to be pulled underwater. We realized that with a long anchor rode, we could steer the boat with the tiller and swing from side to side, thus avoiding most of the flotsam descending upon us. We spent the night, one of us with a flashlight on the bow, watching the debris emerge from the rain and gloom, and the other at the tiller steering to avoid the patches of flotsam, rather like a racing-car videogame in slow motion. It was a long sleepless night, but when morning came, we still had our boat.

Further up the river, we explored several *caños* with the dinghy. These narrow streams allowed us to get deeper into the jungle. We followed one in the dinghy for a mile, estimating whether *Coot's* mast could clear the branches that arched overhead and taking soundings to make sure her keel would clear the bottom. About a mile in, we found a spot where the *caño* divided into two and would give us enough room to turn and tie off the boat. We decided to take *Coot* in. Her mast wove through the branches, breaking occasional twigs that fell to the deck. The growth along the sides tried to snag our lifelines, but we kept going. At last, tucked into this place where the wildlife was undisturbed, we were as alone with the natural world as it was possible to be and still have our own little home with us.

Each morning a toucan perched on a branch beside our cockpit, clacking his bill in what we presumed was an attempt to attract a mate, although he may have been begging for Fruit Loops. To ensure he was seen to his greatest advantage, he flew into the sunshine on the other side of the *caño* and repeated his whooping, clacking, dancing routine. Flocks of macaws flew through the jungle, and pairs of flying parrots woke us in the morning with their raucous squawks. In late afternoon when the sun was low, flocks of scarlet ibis on their return to the rookeries downriver created a Fourth-of-July-like display of fluttering red bursts as the sun glinted off their wings.

> When we needed to rest our necks from watching the toucan,
> there were hummingbirds, dragonflies, and crazy hoatzins
> thrashing their way through the thick foliage along the
> caño. (Christmas letter to friends, written from Cartagena,
> Colombia, December 15, 1998)

The howler monkeys gave the jungle a lion-like voice. The alligators and piranhas kept us from enjoying the fresh tannin-colored water, but we did not begrudge them their space. We were the intruders. Surrounded by the jungle alive with birds and critters, we quietly read and watched, binoculars in hand, and whispered to each other for fear of breaking the spell.

After eleven days, we left the Macareo River and set out for Cartagena, Colombia, making many familiar stops along the way. We anchored once again in small, uninhabited San Francisco Bay on the north coast of Venezuela to rest and fill up with fresh water from a lovely stream that flowed into the bay. We were by ourselves until a Venezuelan fishing boat arrived and anchored much closer than was safe. Fishermen and cruisers did not have the best relations. Fishermen had used this spot for generations to fill up with fresh water, and now, as often as not, the place was invaded by cruising boats. We had been warned to be careful of the fishermen.

The boat had many onions slung in netting, and we needed some, so we rowed over. Four or five men puttered about in the cockpit, but as we approached, all but one slipped behind the cabin. The cook, who was cooking, could not get away. They may have assumed we were coming to complain about where they had anchored. Pam pointed at the onions, held out a pack of cig-arettes, and asked how many they would want for some onions? The scowling cook's face morphed into a smile, and the others came back smiling, too.

They wanted to chat. They asked where we had been and where we were going. It turned out they were leaving shortly, heading home to Margarita. They were from Pampatar and urged us to anchor there. We told them that we always anchored at Por-lamar, the next bay over, because we had been told Pampatar was not safe. They reluctantly agreed that thievery was a problem (no doubt perpetrated by fishermen on the lookout for boat gear), but they assured us that we would be safe there. We parted on friendly terms and with more onions than we could eat in a week. It was much better than the tension and mistrust that would have prevailed had we not asked for a favor. As a typical American male, I found it difficult to ask for help, but doing so often broke the ice and established friendly relationships. It would have been nice to have had a reciprocal interaction like that with the Warao.

Chapter 26

Cartagena and Beyond

September 1998–March 1999

It is not true that people stop pursuing dreams
because they grow old; they grow old because they stop
*pursuing dreams. —*GABRIEL GARCÍA MÁRQUEZ

Christmas letter to friends, written from Cartagena, Colombia,
December 15, 1998:

Our passage through the Venezuelan offshore islands
has been pleasant this time. We hung out—working and
swimming a little and reading a lot—mostly just keeping
expenses down so we'd have money to travel when we got to
Colombia. Curaçao was agreeable, although we spent little
time there, only stopping to pick up provisions and get mail.
Then came our sail to Cartagena, which cost us our windvane
steering, a broken boom, and two days of hard hand-steering,
hour on, hour off.

According to the pilot charts, the rhumb line from Curaçao to
Cartagena passes through the area of the Caribbean with the largest waves. Weather is an important factor, but the forecasts cannot accurately predict it for the entire passage. We left Curaçao

with a nice breeze on our stern. But after scooting past Aruba, waves began to build, and we raced down their faces. Even though the boat was yawing back and forth in the quartering seas, the self-steering wind vane held the course reasonably well.

After a day or two, we were sailing wing-and-wing with the working jib and one or two reefs in the mainsail. During the lighter winds, I had done a lazy-man's job of preventing the boom from swinging out of control. Instead of running a line from the end of the boom to the bow, I had taken the lower end of the kicking strap and attached it to the deck at the shrouds. This secured the boom in light conditions and was much easier than putting on a proper preventer. However, my shortcut would have dire consequences.

I was below, logging our position before waking Pam for a watch, when I heard an explosion followed by a terrible clatter. The boom had broken at the kicking strap (most likely because the boom had dipped into the water during a roll). The sail was flogging back and forth, dragging the broken boom across the deck and coach house, making a terrible racket (I did not need to wake Pam). I dropped the mainsail and tied up all the loose pieces while Pam took the helm because, for some reason, the self-steering was no longer working. After taking care of the main, I saw that the wind vane was still holding steady, flopping back and forth just as it should, but the quadrant did not move. When I looked over the stern, I discovered the paddle had broken off and vanished. I had neglected to run a line from the hole in the paddle to the boat. We would have to find or build a new paddle.

With days to go, we had to stay at the helm, watch on, watch off. I realized how much work the steering vane had been doing to keep the boat on course. We continued slowly, under jib alone. Without the mainsail, the boat was unbalanced, making the steering so heavy that we had to trade places each hour. We got little rest. We arrived in Cartagena more exhausted than we had ever been after a passage.

> It seems like more than a year since we left Marathon, Florida, to head back south on Christmas Eve. It's been high adventure mixed with periods of sheer boredom or unpleasant work, with some remarkably fine experiences in between. We have adopted the Hobbit's view of adventures and seek no more of them. Our adventures invariably involve broken gear, and the cost of repair and replacement cuts deeply into the funds we try to save for pleasant experiences. For now, the boom is repaired, and the windvane is about to be. We enjoy Cartagena and are doing our personal hull maintenance, visiting doctors, dentists, and optometrists between excursions to the *conventos*, fortifications, and museums.

Pam wrote about Club Nautico to Gary Green, a New Zealander we'd met in Trinidad, who wanted to know if Cartagena was worth visiting:

> The conveniences of Club Nautico make life easy here. We are provided with water, garbage disposal, a safe dinghy dock, affordable laundry, cold beers, and a reasonable grocery store. Bank machines are a block away. The only drawback is that the harbor water is even richer than Chaguaramas, and Norm, the marina's owner, charges the boats at anchor a couple of U.S. dollars a day for all his amenities. It's quite reasonable, as he pays *mucho* to haul off our garbage, and we can take all the showers and water we want. Since we've been here, we haven't heard of theft problems in the anchorage or on the street in town, although it's not unknown. The area around the marina

seems so safe that we walk comfortably at night. *(Excerpt from Pam's letter to Gary Green, written from Cartagena, January 25, 1999)*

Pam needed to replace a crown she'd lost in Trinidad, and I needed a more permanent repair for one I'd super-glued back on. One of the marina members was a dentist, and Norm introduced

GARY GREEN

We met New Zealander Gary Green on his boat *Heartbeat* in Trinidad, where he told us this story: In 1970, he and two friends set out from Taiwan, where they'd had a boat built. They met a barmaid in Guam who decided to tag along. After weathering several small storms, they ran into the Big One in the middle of the Pacific. The boat rolled over, lost its keel, and sank. They freed the life raft and partially inflated it. All were battered, and one dislocated a shoulder. The raft overturned, and they lost their safety gear, water, and food. Rescue was unlikely because they were not in shipping lanes. They collected water from the canopy, but the orange coating flaked off and made it undrinkable. They caught a turtle, but a shark leaped up and grabbed the meat they'd set on the canopy to dry. Only Gary was strong enough to continue pumping air into the ever-deflating raft. When he thought they couldn't last another day, they were rescued by a Russian fishing boat. Gary was nervous about the Russian fishermen, but they were treated very well. Years later, we learned that *Heartbeat* sunk in a cyclone in Fiji in 2017. We don't know where Gary is now. His story did not inspire Pam to sail the Pacific. Gary is also mentioned in *Beer in the Bilges*, 2012, by Alan Boreham and others. When we contacted Alan in 2022, he knew nothing more of Gary.

us to her husband, who was sitting at the bar. The husband drove us to several appointments. Each time, he picked us up at the marina, drove one of us to the dentist's office, and took the other around to do errands. We got two crowns, a filling, and cleanings for $250. The dentist apologized for the expense but said that her materials came from the U.S. and were expensive.

Some weeks earlier, when we were in the Chaguaramas anchorage, I had lost a filling. I found a young Brazilian dentist cruising with her husband and ten-year-old daughter by inquiring on the morning radio net.

When I arrived at their boat, everything was laid out on the table by the settee, where I lay back on pillows that supported my head. The water for the drill came through a plastic tube threaded through the hatch from a dish on deck. The little girl's job was to start and stop the water with a clothespin.

It took more than two hours to drill out the remnants of the old filling and put in a new one. The little girl became bored and forgot to pay attention to the clothespin, so sometimes water ran into my mouth without stopping. It was challenging to work in the busy Chaguaramas anchorage, where passing boats made waves that came up under the long flat scoop on the stern, hit with a sharp slap, and made the boat bounce. The dentist jumped with every slap. Despite the difficult working conditions, she replaced the broken filling with one still in my mouth over twenty years later.

Norm, an Australian, and his Colombian wife Candelaria owned the Club Nautico Marina. Candelaria and her friends were often high on marijuana, but Norm seemed strait-laced and business-like. When their son went away to school, they let loose his pet boa constrictors. The boas took up residence in the restaurant's thatched roof, where they continued to grow and keep the place free of rats and mice. In one corner of the restaurant was a large cage with three toucans named Heckle, Jeckle, and O.J.

CLUB NAUTICO

In 2019, Linnea and I walked through Getsemani to Manga to see if Norm's Club Nautico was still there. No longer a place to be avoided, Getsemani is now a barrio of lively backpacker hostels and late-night action. Its evil reputation changed when Pope Francis visited the church, and the authorities cleaned up the area. Club Nautico was still operating, but a modern building replaced Norm's palapa-roofed structure. One wall in the new building sported photos of Norm and his family and told the history of the enterprise. We were told that Norm and Candelaria occasionally stopped by. We had a drink on the terrace for old times' sake. The club now has a state-of-the-art web page.

When we asked, "Why O, J.?" Norm explained that there had been four toucans, but the bird called O.J. had killed his mate. One morning we noticed only two toucans in the cage. "What happened to Heckle?" we asked. Earlier that morning, Norm had found one of the boas with a large, toucan-sized lump in its middle, resting in the cage with the remaining two frenzied toucans.

Norman and Candelaria prepared an extravagant Christmas buffet and invited all the boaters on the docks and at anchor for an evening of celebration. Pam and a flutist from another boat performed a pleasant duet. Then we all went to the center of town to watch the festivities, leaving Norm and Candelaria behind. I have always regretted deserting them like that. Norm and Candelaria were very generous, and we failed to show our appreciation.

Cartagena is an exceptionally well-preserved city with reconstruction and renovation in full swing. So many buildings are under repair that we worry that we'll be hit by falling masonry when we walk in El Centro. They must have some super experts on colonial renovation. We're amazed when we visit a museum in a building brought back from near total decay to see every detail of beams and window frames recreated. We marvel that they replace the old flooring with the same massive floor joists and then lay brick or stone paving over it. The roofs look as heavy as the floors, and the three-foot thick walls carry that weight.

Except in the areas near a couple of the old *conventos* converted to luxury hotels, the sidewalks are a crazy patchwork of holes that you could drop a horse down. I like to peer into windows and doorways and look up at the balconies. I can't do that here, or Kent would be looking for a new mate. For now, we dodge wiring hanging from the buildings. I expect they will someday close the streets, take the paving up, and lay in all the services correctly. *(Excerpts from a letter to Jeff and Sue Grant, written from Cartagena, Colombia, March 6, 1999)*

Seeing a good opportunity, Norm bought some wrecked boats for very little after hurricane Luis hit St. Maarten. He put a couple of them back together well enough to sail them to his marina and refurbish them to sell. One morning he was delighted to have sold one. We did not know who bought it. It was anchored nearby for several days, although we saw no one on board. One morning it was gone, and a few days later, it was back again, although we still saw nobody on the boat. A Colombian coast guard officer came by shortly after, asking if we had seen anybody. We grew suspicious.

Andy came to visit at the end of January. Early on his first morning with us, we were awakened by the noise of a dozen or more policemen boarding the nearby boat and breaking down the companionway hatch. What was going on? We were away most of the day, getting bus tickets for our trip to the interior and showing Andy the city.

The next morning, as we passed through the restaurant on our way to the bus, someone handed us a newspaper. A picture of police officers in front of a pile of plastic bags was splashed across the front page. They had confiscated over a ton of cocaine from the boat and arrested Norm because the vessel was still in his name.

We tied *Coot* to the dock and left for the mountains of Santander and Boyocá the day after the raid. Andy had already had one Colombian adventure—a drug bust—and we were off in search of another—a guerrilla attack. We tried to inform ourselves about the hot spots in Colombia and planned to stay out of the hottest of them, but the guerrillas move around, and it's almost impossible to know which areas they will be infesting. Some people said not to go by bus under any circumstances, while others thought bus travel was okay during the day, but we should stay west of the Magdalena River. We ended up traveling by bus at night east of the Magdalena, from Cartagena to Pamplona in sixteen hours.

Pamplona is a small city famous for its historic buildings and Holy Week celebrations. We enjoyed wandering from church to museum and from an empanada stand to an ancient market. There is a modern art museum housed in a beautifully restored colonial villa. We stayed one night and then went to Bucaramanga over one of the most beautiful mountain roads I have ever traveled. We zigzagged down the hillside from 9,000 feet to about 2,000 feet and saw every type of tropical and temperate crop and plant in five hours. Thirty-five years ago, Bucaramanga was Kent's center when he traveled back and forth from his *pueblito.* He still remembered his favorite restaurant—DiMarco's. Three years ago, we had been unsuccessful in locating it. This time he was determined to find it and treat his wife and son to their famous steak. We found it, we ate, and I don't think we'll be back.

Our next stop was Tunja, a high (10,000 feet) state capital and one of our favorite Colombian cities. The tourists haven't found this place yet, and it has an authentic feeling. Many splendid colonial houses and churches remain, although modernity is creeping in. Tunja sits on a high plateau that has the feel of our western mountains. The air is crisp and dry. We apologized to Andy about taking him someplace cold, but he said 50 to 60 degrees didn't bother him at all. The hotel, even though unheated, provided plenty of blankets, and Andy was happy to stay in one place for three nights. We traveled to Villa de Leyva one day, a restored village that made us think we had fallen into the 17th century.

In our hotel room, Kent found a current Bogotá phone directory and, for a lark, looked up a couple of names of people he had known thirty-five years ago. A Roque Garrido was listed. Kent called, and it was his old Colombian colleague from *Accion Communal* with whom he worked in the Peace Corps. Roque said, come, I can't put you up as my apartment is too small, but I can feed you and get you from the bus station. We hadn't planned on going to Bogotá, but this was too good to pass up. We stayed four days, visiting the fabulous gold museum, the salt cathedral, churches, other museums, Roque, his Dutch wife Ines, and his son Francis. Kent and Roque reminisced until Ines and I put a stop to it.

Andy, fortunately, lost out on another Colombian experience—Bogotá muggers. We walked through an iffy neighborhood, trying to find the bus to Zipaquirá and the salt cathedral. A traffic policeman told us it was dangerous for us to be walking in the neighborhood. He put us on a bus and told the driver where to drop us. We made it to Zipaquirá without further incident. We returned to Cartagena on an eighteen-hour bus ride directly from Bogotá. Roque and Ines warned us that the guerrillas were now stopping buses and taking ordinary tourists as hostages. However, we thought traveling through the Cauca valley, far west of the Magdalena would be okay. As it turned out, the route took us along the eastern side of the Magdalena quite close to a troublesome spot that even

ROQUE GARRIDO CELIS

When I said goodbye to Roque upon leaving the Peace Corps almost fifty years ago, I gave him my work boots to replace the street shoes he wore in the campo and did not foresee much of a future for him. In 2019, Roque and I met for a third time. He and Ines still live in Bogotá, no longer in a small apartment in the heart of the city but in a large, modern house in an outer suburb. Linnea and I visited him and Ines at the beginning and end of our five-week ramble through Colombia. They sent us warnings about the dangers awaiting us in various areas as we traveled. We appreciated their concern but kept to our plans, much as Pam and I did when we took buses through places Roque would not even fly to. Whether we were wise in either case, I do not know, but we survived.

Their son Francis, a family man with an impressive inter-national career, joined us at their lovely home for a delicious traditional Colombian soup that Roque had prepared. Shortly after our return to Albuquerque, we were shocked to learn that thieves had broken into their home, held them at knifepoint, trashed everything, and stolen their cash and valuables. Roque and Ines were so traumatized by the experience that they thought they might have to give up their lovely house and move back into their small apartment.

we knew should be given a wide berth. But Andy's luck (or unluck) held, and we returned to *Coot* tired but unharmed.

Andy left early this morning, and I can hardly keep from sobbing. I think about how long it will be until we see family again. However, now that we are done with the tourist stuff, we will have time to write. We think Andy had a good trip; at least we enjoyed having him. (*Excerpts from Pam's letter to friends and family, written from Cartagena, Colombia, February 23, 1999*)

Seeing Roque again after more than thirty years was the kind of contact I sought but rarely found in our travels. Roque met us at the bus terminal and drove us to our *pension*. Then he took us to his apartment for dinner, where we met his wife Ines and son, Francis, who was Andy's age. Roque had met Ines not long after I left Colombia in 1965. Francis was about to be married, so it was a busy, inconvenient time to drop in on them. Roque had recently retired from *Acción Comunal*, the Colombian agency for rural community development. We had worked together in Carcasí when he was just starting as an extension agent. He eventually ended up in the headquarters in Bogotá.

I wish we had been able to spend more time together. I was curious about his thoughts about the United States and its association with Colombia (and, by extension, with other Latin American countries). Roque was not happy with American interference in Colombia, and he was distressed about Colombia's current situation. In an effort toward reconciliation and peace, the Colombian president had given FARC (Revolutionary Armed Forces of Colombia or *Fuerzas Armadas Revolucionarias de Colombia*), the long-standing Marxist rebel group, governance of a portion of the country they already controlled.

In the sixties, the name "*Tirofijo*" ("Sure Shot"—Pedro Antonio Marin, also known as Manuel Marulanda) frequently showed up in the papers. Trained as a highway engineer, he had become

Roque, Ines, and Kent in Bogota in 2019

disgruntled with the Colombian government, and now as the head of FARC, he officially governed part of the country.

This unpopular attempt at reconciliation was not destined to last long—the next elected president would reverse the policy and fight harder than ever to defeat FARC.

Roque blamed the United States for many of Colombia's problems. He explained: "Americans are addicted to drugs. Because they refuse to acknowledge drug addiction as an internal problem, they treat it like a foreign invasion and declare war on it. They use military intimidation and other forms of coercion to stop the drug trade overseas.

Once the pretty plants, due to American demand, became a cash crop worth ten or twenty times more than any other crop that could be grown, what was a poor, struggling Colombian farmer to do?"

So much money was involved that if a farmer refused to grow coca, the drug cartels eliminated that farmer and found someone else who would. FARC grew in power and stature when it taxed the drug cartels to use the highways they controlled, thus providing money for their revolution.

As Roque saw it, Americans (not Colombians) had a drug problem. Rather than dealing with the addiction problem at home, they sent the Marines into Panama to bomb poor neighborhoods and supply arms to Colombia, which helped turn the actions of outlaws into civil war. The United States often backed corrupt and dictatorial regimes regardless of the consequences to the country's citizens.

This resentment toward the United States contrasted with Roque's attitude in the early sixties when he saw the United States as a good-hearted benefactor whose foreign policy was exemplified by the Peace Corps, the Alliance for Progress, the Rockefeller Foundation, CARE, and other groups.

The largest celebratory demonstrations in the world after 9/11 occurred in South American cities. After my conversations with Roque, I could see why that might be. He may have thought the United States was, at last, getting a little back (as awful as it was) for its bullying and self-serving interference around the world. I had expected Roque and I would simply rehash old times, but I was given much to think about.

COLOMBIA AND U.S. DRUG POLICY

A guest opinion essay in the New York Times on 7 September 2022 by Johns Hopkins University professor Christy Thornton chronicles the international effects of four decades of failed United States drug policies. In her essay, "The U.S. Has Led the War on Drugs Abroad for Decades, and It's Been a Staggering Failure," The author argues that the policies have not only failed to reduce the supply of illicit substances they have made them more dangerous.

We returned to Cartagena and news of Norman after our two weeks away. It wasn't good. He was still in jail. Rumors and gossip were flying. We heard that Norman had sold the boat for a good deal more than the bill of sale indicated, that he had bought Candelaria new jewelry, a penthouse apartment in Manga, and a trawler. It was said that he couldn't account for where he got the money, that he didn't have a name on the bill of sale and wouldn't give the authorities one because they (whoever "they" might be) had threatened his wife and family if he revealed it. We heard that the brother-in-law, who allegedly set up the deal, had tried to commit suicide by slitting his wrists. We don't know what, if anything, is true, but Norman is still in jail a month-and-a-half later, and everyone says he's in deep shit.

Now we're waiting for better weather so that we can get out of here. We're not sure where we're heading. We will set our waypoint for Guanaja in the Honduras Bay Islands, but who knows where we'll stop if the going gets rough. We have some charts for the San Blas Islands, but I am not keen on stopping there, even though Kent would like to. We should make directly for Florida, put the boat on the market, and get jobs. However, the thought of this is so oppressive that we procrastinate. Maybe another hurricane season in the Rio Dulce of Guatemala wouldn't be so bad. *(Pam's letter to Joe and Signe Stuart, written from Cartagena, March 12, 1999)*

After we left Cartagena, we occasionally talked to other boaters who had been there recently. We were told that Norm got out of prison after a year or two and had gone back to Australia. Candelaria and her brother were still running the marina.

Cartagena was the jumping-off point for the Panama Canal and the Pacific. I desperately wanted to pursue this path, but clearly, Pam did not, even after meeting and talking with boaters heading that way, which I hoped would inspire her to want to do the same. She may have resisted visiting the San Blas Islands because they were perilously close to the Panama Canal and would tempt me even further. She knew that I wanted to keep cruising indefinitely and see more of the world by boat.

When we set out for Guanaja instead of sailing to Panama, I gave up my dream of the Pacific for the third time. The first time was on *Jacana* when we headed from Jamaica to Belize, the second on *Coot* when we sailed from Bonaire to Guanaja, and now, a third time, we headed toward Guanaja. This was not a decision we sat down and discussed. I knew that Pam did not want to sail the Pacific, but I was unwilling to give her up and go off on my own or force her (as if I could!) to go with me. Indeed, these choices never crossed my mind. According to Pam's law of threes, my dream of the Pacific should have been dead, but deep down, it was not.

Nevertheless, I was starting to accept that our cruising life was ending, and I was not going to get to the Pacific. Nothing Pam did or said in recent months indicated she'd be willing to go through the Canal, and neither of us wanted to continue going around and around in the "Caribbean Lake." Pam's mind had already turned to reestablishing ourselves on land, and she dreaded the uncertainties: where would we go? What would we do? Could we find a way to make a living at our age? Breaking away from the States twice was difficult but going back was no less so.

Even if we gave up the idea of spending the rest of our lives seeing the world by boat, I could not get rid of *Coot*. I had fallen in love with boating, and my affection for the *Coot* was as strong as ever.

Chapter 27

Aftermath of Hurricane Mitch

March–June 1999

How inappropriate to call this planet Earth when it is
quite clearly Ocean. —ARTHUR C. CLARKE

On Thursday, March 18, we left Cartagena, arriving in Guanaja on Wednesday, the 24th after a reasonably uneventful trip. Kent is working hard, chipping and grinding on our rusty gunnels, and I'm trying to keep out of the way. The most comfortable thing to do is play with the computer, and I wanted to talk to you anyway. We have no idea when or how we will send this as an email. However, they say that Roatan will have email cafes and all the mod-cons, so I'll assume my play will have more use than just avoiding some nasty work.

I'll say upfront that we didn't break anything or injure ourselves, so we count it a successful voyage. The knotmeter/log quit functioning, but that seems part of the aging process that *Coot* and her masters are going through—much akin to the non-functioning language-learning centers of my brain. I assume they are there, but they're just not working anymore.

We left Cartagena with no wind and a lumpy sea and motored for three hours. At the end of that time, we were able to put up everything we had, including the big genny and full main, to catch the beam wind. We were down to a double-reefed main and working jib within the hour, dipping the boom in the water on every third roll. We did 140 miles that first day. Kent cursed every extra pound he had acquired in Cartagena, and we both wished we hadn't given our muscles such a complete rest. By Saturday (we'd left on Thursday), the winds were back down to the 15-20 knot range on the beam, and we had a pleasant sail. Early Sunday morning, we made our first waypoint at the northeast corner of Providencia (Colombia). We headed for the next, northeast of Cayos Cajones, leaving the Quita Sueno bank to starboard and Arrecife, Alagardo, and Media Luna to port. Of course, the wind turned more northerly. We had to beat, but as the wind was no more than fifteen knots, it was reasonably comfortable.

In one eight-hour period, we made only eight miles to the good. We considered coming around the southern side of Alagardo and Media Luna, nearer Cabo Gracias a Dios and south of the Vivorillos, but we were afraid we'd lose our wind entirely if we got closer to the coast. There are also some reefy bits we felt shy of. Maybe I'm getting to be a nervous old lady, but I was a bit worried about traveling through waters full of Nicaraguan fishermen, who haven't the most hospitable reputation. As it was, we saw only about six fishing boats during the night.

Early Tuesday morning, we turned west to head directly for Guanaja, just as the wind turned gently east. We put up the spinnaker and waddled on. We were afraid we wouldn't make Guanaja before dark on Wednesday and would have to lie offshore all night. We'd done that three years ago and would rather not repeat the exercise. The wind slowly increased. We dropped the spinnaker and got the hook down in El Bight by late afternoon.

Three years ago, we were told by local sailors that between the mainland and the islands, it always blows five to fifteen knots higher than elsewhere. We wanted to get through the reef in good light. The water is usually opaque, and a difference in color means it is likely too shallow to sail over.

Now for Guanaja. We slept and took it easy on Thursday and didn't even try to clear in. The immigration officer wasn't there on Friday, so the port captain told us to not worry about checking in until we got to Roatan. On Friday, we went into the settlement on Sheen Cay. We feared it may have been destroyed by hurricane Mitch six months before. We couldn't imagine a place three or four feet above sea level surviving those winds and seas. There is some damage, especially to the less substantial structures that ring the cay, but everything looks remarkably good. Most buildings didn't get water on their floors and kept their roofs.

All services are as available as they were three years ago. Diesel and gasoline are available. We will jug it, but I think it is possible to bring the boat into a dock and fill up. The grocery stores are packed with goods. I think there's more than there was three years ago. Canned stuff is high in price, maybe 10% more than Cartagena, and fresh stuff comes from the mainland only about once a week in tired condition. There is electricity, so it is possible to buy frozen and refrigerated foods. The phones work, or at least one did, although there is still interruption of service. The walkways that serve as streets are all tidy, even though there are piles of debris where something collapsed. People look well-fed and

HURRICANE MITCH

Mitch was the second most deadly Atlantic hurricane on record at the time. It caused over 11,000 deaths in Central America in October 1998. Much of the damage was caused by flooding. Honduras was especially hard-hit, with over 7,000 deaths. We were farther west, sailing to Venezuela and Colombia from Trinidad, when the hurricane hit, but we did experience some rough weather. *Wikipedia, "Hurricane Mitch." Last modified 13 October 2022.*

relaxed. We get our sweet water from a hosepipe that comes down to a dock near some friends' house here in El Bight. We're told that it's there for the taking and doesn't need any treatment except filtering.

The damage outside of the settlement on the cay is varied. Trees on the upper half of the hill look like a giant hand stripped them of foliage, and the palms on the beach are tattered or down. Most places on the southeast-facing hillside look good. The bar, perched on the reef on the eastern side of El Bight, where we used to go for sundowners, is gone, although its blue washhouse looks intact. The hotel on the beach, run by a German fellow, is missing its roof and some walls and has no electricity, but Hansito had his fortieth birthday party there on Sunday and invited all of us to partake of beer, chicken, and great salads. We attended and saw people we'd met three years ago.

The German farmer on the low ground lost all his fruit trees, but his house is fine, and his lettuces are coming up. A couple who had built three houses in Mangrove Bay

on the north side of the island were totally wiped out and
spent three days huddled on the ground under a plastic bag.
Mangrove Bay was the worst hit, with 200 houses destroyed
by winds and high seas. Savannah Bight and Brick Point, both
a little northeast of us, were also severely hit. Few boats are
stopping, and people here want to get the word out that it's
fine to come.

We're still not sure of our itinerary. We'll go on to Roatan,
but from there, we're undecided. We should just head up to
the States and start to reorganize ourselves. We're halfway
between Florida and Cartagena here, and it seems like an
omen that we should go all the way.

Do drop us an email if you get the chance. We may not
be able to receive it for a while, but we'd like to hear how
things are going with you. Also, if you return to Cartagena,
we'd be interested in knowing Norman's status. *(Pam's letter to
boating friends Bob and Julaine Cleland, written from Guanaco,
Honduras, April 1, 1999)*

[April 12, 1999] The chipping and painting took a little longer
than expected, and it was pleasant to see friends again. We
spent a couple of days at Port Royal, Roatan. We'd heard on
the net that Velella, a boat we'd known in Mexico was there,
and we wanted to say hello. Jack and Sheryl are managing an
elegant private estate while its owners are back in the States,
divorcing one another. It was a kick to see how the other
half lives, with washer/dryers, freezers, gardeners, cleaners,
boathouses, caretakers' houses, and original carving on all the
doors. They have their share of problems, as you can imagine,
trying to keep up all this elegance on a relatively primitive
Honduran island. The thought of designing, constructing,
and maintaining cisterns to receive and hold nearly 100,000

gallons of water is overwhelming. There are generators, dive compressors, and solar collector arrays to service. It must be worse than having a boat.

We would have stayed there and done some more work on *Coot*, but that end of the island has no roads, and we still haven't checked into Honduras. The winds have been whooping since we arrived, and the anchorage at Port Royal got bumpy. We had to keep the forehatch closed because the waves would splatter us in bed.

Today we are in French Harbor, anchored near the yacht club. Three years ago, it was thriving, with several boats at the dock and several anchored. It's quite handy to the road and the grocery. The club had closed, and we were the only boat there. The anchorage is nicely protected, and we can keep the hatches open, but it's a spooky neighborhood, and we feel lonely and vulnerable. Tomorrow we'll go to Brick Bay, where we'll have easy access to the road and the bus to town. We'll finally clear into Honduras. (*Pam's letter to Bob and Julaine Cleland concludes, written from French Harbor, Honduras, April 12, 1999*)

The Honduran islands Roatan and Utila were a bit like a tropical 1960s Haight-Ashbury. Brick Bay, a cove with anchorage for two or three boats, mostly belonged to a hotel, but a few docks belonged to a small marina. As we headed into the wind to anchor, Brian, the marina owner, was taking some scuba divers out on a rough, hard-chine steel boat. He invited us to tie up at his marina, but we declined.

He had bought the marina sight unseen and was trying to get it and a dive operation going. When he arrived, he found the steel ketch sunk at the dock and the marina abandoned and run-down. He raised the boat and got it running, although his efforts to mask the odors of mildew and rust with marijuana smoke were not entirely successful.

He repaired the docks so he could rent them and intended to turn part of the building into a restaurant. He gave us access to his hand power tools, internet, fresh water, and garbage pickup and encouraged us to use his dock as a work area.

He smoked marijuana, had a dozen projects going at once, and worked as hard as anybody I have ever known. Unfortunately, he also rode a motorcycle.

One day we noticed one of his eyes was severely crossed. He'd been run off the road on his motorcycle, but there was no serious damage, he said, just a scratch in the paint. What about the eye? Had he seen a doctor? He looked at me like I was crazy. He would not trust any doctor on the island, and it was nothing to worry about. He could still see to work. He was sawing with a skill saw as we talked, and he said, "I just have to remember which fingers I see I should saw on the right side of."

He had headaches but thought aspirin and eye exercises would soon take care of them. Then he told us that if he did not get better, he would give his brain surgeon in the States a call. Asked why he had a brain surgeon, he told us about another accident that he had also ignored. When his girlfriend couldn't wake him one morning, she took him to the hospital emergency room, saving his life by minutes.

Shortly after we left, we heard that Brian's headaches had worsened. He was flown to Tegucigalpa, where emergency surgery relieved pressure on his brain. He was unable to get permits to open the restaurant, ran out of credit, and had no money to pay his debts. Officials were about to serve papers and take away everything he owned. So, he threw his tools and his cycle on the boat and escaped in the night. Years later, our friend Bruce

Blossman,[1] who owned a cabin just above Brick Bay, ran across Brian in Florida. He was as busy as ever, wheeling and dealing on some new scheme.

---

1. Bruce Blossman (1935–2007) and his wife Eleonor Hellman were avid sailors on their boat *Horizons*. Their paths crossed with ours in varied and unexpected ways. I still have an autographed table-cloth Bruce and Eleonor created for Pam's birthday at Susana's Laguna. We all eventually retired to New Mexico. Bruce and I were in the Peace Corps simultaneously—while I was in Co-lombia, he was in Tunisia with our good friend Ross Burkhardt, through whom I met Linnea. An obituary for J. Bruce Blossman, published in the Santa Fe New Mexican on 16 August 2009, is also available on Legacy.com.

Chapter 28

Decisions

July 1999–November 2006

And all I ask is a merry yarn from a laughing
fellow-rover / And quiet sleep and a sweet
dream when the long trick's over.
—JOHN MASEFIELD, "Sea-Fever"

When we left the Bay Islands, we had to decide whether to return to the States and go to work or go back to the Rio Dulce in Guatemala to wait out another hurricane season. We decided to head to the Rio Dulce, stopping first in Belize to enjoy snorkeling at some of our favorite anchorages, shortening what we knew would be a lengthy stay in Guatemala.

On our first visit, Tom Owens Caye was a wonderful place to snorkel. The fish were the biggest anywhere. We met a grouper as large as Pam and saw eagle rays with wingspans of six feet. Schools of fish and lobsters' antennae poked out of every third hole. We enjoyed some of our best snorkeling days in the company of some avid spearfishermen. Pam worked her magic to get several meals of fresh fish.

Now, only two years later, we anchored in the same spot, but there were no other boats. We entered the water, expecting to see the wonders we had seen before, but the coral was dead, and we saw no fish or any other living things. The little cay had been scoured of life. We did not know whether this depredation had been caused by boaters, local fishermen, damage from Hurricane Mitch, or coral bleaching, but the reef was dead.

We moved to Glover's Reef, an atoll outside Belize's barrier reef, where we worked our way through the coral to visit a World Wildlife Fund research station. We picked up a mooring buoy and went ashore to look around. The station supervisor told us we were free to snorkel so long as we did not take anything away. The WWF had policed the area for years, and the contrast between the reserve and the rest of the reef was stark. I was reminded of a National Geographic aerial photograph of the border between the Dominican Republic and Haiti. A straight line marked the border, with a rich tropical forest on one side and an eroding desert on the other.

There were huge lobsters under every coral ledge and so many fish that it was hard to see through their schools. There were many varieties of corals, and things growing on top of each other wherever we looked. The whole reef must have once looked like this. Even in economic terms, the degradation of the reef was a significant loss. Once, it may have provided a good living to fishermen and good sport for some, but I doubt there are enough fish outside the reserve to provide a decent living now.

Some boaters complained that sailing was better in the "old days."

They said, "I used to anchor here and gather up a dozen large lobsters in half an hour. Now you have to spend an hour to get two or three small ones."

I wonder if they considered the effect of taking a dozen lobsters. If they collected two or three an hour this year, what did they think they would find next year? They were fishing for fun, not because they were eking out a living for their families.

The night sail from Glover's Reef to the mouth of the Rio

Dulce took us through a spectacular electrical storm that lit up the sky like daylight. Several lightning strikes hit so close to the boat we could see the water glow. Why were we not struck? Our well-grounded aluminum mast was the tallest thing for miles around. We would have enjoyed the spectacle more if we had not been so concerned about how much replacing burned-out electronics would cost. But God protected us fools again, and we survived to write about it.

We left the boat on the Rio Dulce for a month, took chicken buses into Honduras to visit the Mayan ruins at Copan, hiked into the cloud forest from Gracias a Dios, and checked in with the Peace Corps office in Tegucigalpa about participating in the Crisis Corps to help clean up after the Hurricane Mitch.

We looked at places with an eye to living there someday. We made a game of it. Pam was looking for a place with a good library, art, and music, a climate where the pine trees grew next to the palms, and the bougainvillea bloomed year-round. If it was a university town, we went to the campus to see what was happening. We visited the art galleries to see what cultural activities were available. We made the trip into the mountains of Honduras to find a small, unspoiled village where we sat on the town plaza surrounded by simple, old stone buildings, sipped beer, breathed in the cool mountain air, and watched people carry on their daily activities. We enjoyed the local markets and coffee each morning at a *tienda* where we stayed long enough to chat with the proprietor and become "regulars." My Spanish was rusty after over thirty years of non-use, and Pam's, although more recently studied, was more limited. Nevertheless, we traveled easily and were grateful we spoke as much as we did.

Public transportation was less expensive and more efficient than in the United States because most people did not own cars. Some places had special tourist buses, but they cost hundreds of dollars for what we did for tens. We chatted with the other travelers on the local buses. We had unexpected delights, such as a stop at a crossroads high in the Guatemalan mountains before daybreak, where we waited for a pick-up truck to take us to the next town. We sat on a rock beside the dusty road, breathing in the warm, dry mountain air while the sun penetrated the darkness and burned off the mist to reveal the majestic Fuego, Agua, Pacaya, and Santa Maria volcanoes. Our fellow Mayan travelers also ceased murmuring as the panorama emerged, ghostlike, from the shadows.

While we waited in Tegucigalpa to hear back from the Peace Corps, Pam went to a medical clinic for a checkup. She had not been feeling well, and the doctor strongly recommended a hysterectomy.

We looked at the hospitals in Tegucigalpa and thought about the rough trip back to the boat. Bouncing around in the back of a pick-up would not be good after surgery, so we looked for a hospital in Guatemala City. We cut our Honduran travels short, sought recommendations, and settled on a doctor who was the faculty head at a small, rather elegant, private university medical school. He had been trained in Israel and spoke good English. He confirmed the diagnosis and the need for surgery, and we decided to proceed.

We called my brother to find out what such a procedure would cost in the States. The estimate was $25,000 plus the cost of the anesthesiologist and hospital days beyond one. The estimate in Guatemala was $2,500 for everything.

On the morning we went to the doctor to make the final arrangements for the surgery, I was pick-pocketed on the bus. I had stupidly put the pouch I usually wore under my clothes into my front pants pocket. The pouch contained my passport, credit cards, driver's license, and cash. Pam discovered the thief had first rummaged around in her purse, but she had kept her valuables under her clothing and lost nothing.

We continued to the doctor's appointment and afterwards canceled the credit cards, replaced my passport at the U.S. Consulate, and reported the theft to the police. We had no way to pay for the hospital and the surgery after we canceled the credit card, so we asked the doctor if the hospital would accept a personal check. The answer was no. The surgery was scheduled for the first thing the next morning. But the doctor said, "It's no problem. I will pay the hospital bill for you, and you can pay me by personal check."

He knew that we were transients off a boat and that it took some time for a check from the States to clear. We did not have a phone number or even an address to give to him. What chance would we have of a doctor in the United States doing that for us?

We took a semi-private room in the hospital following Pam's surgery. I stayed with her and helped with Spanish. The hospital gave me meals, towels, and slippers as if I were a patient. We were waited on hand and foot for four days. Then we moved to a ground-floor hotel room nearby, where we stayed for a week, so Pam didn't have to climb stairs. She managed the bus ride back to the boat without a problem. The boat was docked so she could step in and out without needing to climb in and out of the dinghy. As surgeries go, Pam had a good experience.

When we returned to the river, we fought colds and flu, worked on the engine, played volleyball, visited friends, and waited for the mail. We received word that Andy was coming on December 30th and would stay for two weeks, so we canceled plans to sail to Belize for the holidays. Instead, we would show Andy Tikal, Copan, and the highland villages of Guatemala.

When Andy arrived, he and I traveled to Tikal and Pacaya, a volcano not far from Antigua and Guatemala City. It was on Pacaya that I felt old for the first time. I could hardly make it to the top of the mountain. Andy, tired of waiting for me, clambered ahead with other people. When I finally reached the top,

I discovered I had inadvertently climbed to one of the higher points of the irregular rim surrounding the crater. This was the leeward side, and the sulfur fumes were so intense I began to choke. With my lungs burning, I quickly descended and worked my way around to windward, where I found Andy and the other climbers.

I was not only exhausted but frightened. The volcano's gurgling sounds turned into a roar and threw buckets of molten lava high over our heads every thirty seconds. The only thing that kept the lava from landing on top of us was a light breeze. I wondered if the wind ever changed direction. When my feet began to burn, I realized that the pebbles of lava rock we were standing on were still red-hot inside and had been spit out of the volcano hours before. When I looked at my brand-new shoes later, I found holes melted through the synthetic rubber soles.

Andy was not only tireless; he was fearless. He followed the most daring and foolhardy to the brink of the crater, where he could see the lava thrusting up from the volcano's innards. I was relieved when we finally started down the mountain. I tried to convince myself that I was old and overly cautious and that it was silly to be fearful when the others did not seem to be.

A week to the day after our climb, Pacaya erupted on January 16, 2000, forcing the evacuation of all the villages in the area and closing the airport in Guatemala City for a week. Had we been on the mountain then, we would have been vaporized. My temerity may have been warranted. Perhaps I was not older so much as wiser.

After Andy flew home from Guatemala City, we left the boat at Fronteras and again traveled to Guatemala's cool highlands. From there, we continued to Mexico, where we met old friends. We played bridge in Guanajuato and San Miguel de Allende with Ron Reed (a friend since grade school) and his wife, Helen. We also met Ruth and Terry Branson (who first introduced me to sailing in Brookings) in Morelia (where Pam had once studied Spanish).

During our stay on the Rio Dulce, I got the sad news that David Nelson, my friend and colleague in the Department of Philosophy and Religion at South Dakota State University, had suffered a stroke. He would have to retire. Nothing was settled, but a temporary return to my old job in Brookings was possible. Accepting this position would solve several of our immediate concerns. We would have a place to go and some income. We'd also be close to the boys. The temporary aspect of the job was appealing because I was no longer looking for a career.

Between March 13 and April 7, 2000, we sailed north from the Rio Dulce to Isla Mujeres, Mexico. On the way, we anchored on the Chinchorro Banks off the Mexican coast to make some repairs to sails and canvas. Blustery weather was forecast, so we sailed to Bahia Espiritu Santo on the mainland, where we could tuck in behind a reef and out of the waves. A couple of other boats did the same thing. However, when we tried to anchor, we discovered the bottom was hard-packed sand, and the anchor would not dig in. We did not want to be near another boat in case we dragged, so we anchored half a mile beyond the others. I dived down and dug the anchor into the sand by hand as best I could, dumped out a lot of chain, and figured if the wind came up, we could drag for a mile before getting into trouble. We were in a beautiful spot behind the reef and virtually alone.

We took our afternoon salt-water bath from the dinghy, and while I rinsed off with fresh water on the boat, Pam took a swim to the reef about 50 yards away. There she attracted the attention of a large, attentive barracuda. Pam believed that a barracuda would not attack a person who watched it, so as she sculled backward to the boat, she kept her eyes on the closely trailing fish. She reached the dinghy and was about to leap out of the water to safety when she heard someone call, "Hi there!"

The other boaters had dinghied over to invite us for a sundowner. Pam shouted, "There's a huge barracuda down here sniffing at my feet, and I don't have any clothes on. I'm jumping into the dinghy in two seconds — please go away!"

As they turned away, Pam flew into the dinghy so fast she looked like a large brown and white-striped flying fish.

After three weeks in Isla Mujeres, we sailed to Ft. Meyers Beach, Florida, then took the Okeechobee waterway to the Atlantic, with no problems other than almost losing our mast to a railway lift bridge. From Florida, we sailed to North Carolina, retracing the route we had joyfully taken six years before through Beaufort, Elizabeth City, the Great Dismal Swamp, and the Chesapeake. It should have felt like the energy-filled reprise before a musical's intermission, but our mood was somber. Although I did not know it, we were not heading toward an intermission but starting the final act of our life on the boat.

We hauled *Coot* out of the water at the Coan River Marina, just off the Potomac in Virginia, worked on her, prepared her for winter storage, and reluctantly returned to Brookings, where I filled in for David Nelson for what turned out to be two years. We lived frugally in an apartment, and I was able to buy back retirement years. I'd soon be eligible for Social Security, and we would have a more secure retirement income. Those two years gave us time to ponder what we wanted to do next. Neither of us wanted to stay in Brookings. Most of our friends were gone, and Pam was ready to leave after one year. But the extra money I would earn by staying a second year would be good. I was thinking of practicalities for once, but I had not yet given up the idea of returning to live on *Coot*.

Brookings was within visiting distance of Andy and my brother Doug and his wife Phyllis in the Minneapolis area. Jake and Cathy, who were soon a family of seven, with three daughters of their own and two of Cathy's children from Papua New Guinea,

were a little over an hour away. *Coot* needed major repairs, so I
returned to Virginia that first summer to work on her while Pam
stayed behind in Brookings. During the second summer, as we
contemplated leaving Brookings for the third time, we went to
Virginia together to check on *Coot*. On impulse, we bought a
1940s Cape Cod house in Kilmarnock. We left Brookings, and I
worked on both the house and the boat. We adopted two cats,
Max and Minnie, which I should have taken as a sign that we
were destined to be landlubbers since we'd vowed never to have
another cat on a boat.

We could have stayed in Kilmarnock, but Pam injured her
back while gardening. Once again, health issues and their cost
controlled our decisions. Because we had better health insurance coverage within the State of South Dakota, we moved to
Sundance, Wyoming, near the Black Hills and the South Dakota
border. After only a year-and-a-half, we sold the Kilmarnock
house, fortunately doubling our money. We moved to Sundance
and bought another place, which I also fixed up. Pam had surgery
on her back in Rapid City, South Dakota, and wrote that the dry,
dusty air of Wyoming felt more like home than green, humid Virginia. By now, she relied on inhalers to breathe and finally broke
her terrible addiction to cigarettes.

Sundance would be our permanent home. We could sail *Coot*
in the winters and leave her in the Rio Dulce or Roatan during the
summers. Maybe we could even sail to Panama and the Canal. In
October 2006, after two years away from *Coot*, Pam and I drove
from Sundance to Virginia with the two cats. While I worked
on the boat, we again lived in it on jack stands at the Coan River
Boatyard. The cats were not happy and managed to escape. Minnie returned, but Max did not. We were heartbroken to lose the
big timid cat we had come to love.

I finished work on *Coot*. We dropped her into the water and
anchored her off the boatyard. The boat rocked gently. It was

wonderful to be back on the water. We sat in the cockpit and toasted the launch with glasses of wine. We had no plans, but I hoped we'd sail to Roatan or the Rio Dulce.

Then, Pam looked in the bilge to make sure that it was dry.

"Kent, I think there may be a leak."

I saw a tiny trickle.

"Maybe it came through the drain hose for the chain locker."

We searched all the lockers in the cabin sole and found dampness on the hull beneath one of the portlights (windows). During the years on land, rainwater leaked around a portlight and rusted a small hole in the hull. It was nothing major, but at that moment, all the anxiety and tension that Pam had lived through during our cruising years came screaming back.

I called the boat yard on the radio and asked to be hauled out again. The travel lift was still at the haul-out dock where it had dropped us in the water just an hour before. Once the boat was hauled and I was setting up the jack stands, Pam put up a ladder, boarded the boat and packed her bag. With hardly a word, she took the car and fled to her sister-in-law Corkie in Washington, D.C.

Pam never saw the boat again.

I patched the hull and, with a friend, sailed *Coot* to a brokerage in Deltaville. She sold quickly to a young couple who wanted a steel boat to sail in Arctic waters.

Our sailing life was over.

Epilogue

Pam was ready to settle down in dry western air with an immovable basement beneath her feet. Her family life had been put on hold long enough. I decided I would be content doing whatever she wanted, wherever she wanted to do it. It was her turn, and I was ready for a quiet life of puttering. While we lived in Sundance, Pam wrote about what home meant to her. It did not include a boat or the sea:

> Wyoming has always been home with a capital H. Being able to see that big, painfully blue sky was as necessary to me as coffee first thing in the morning. I liked the desiccated texture of my skin. Feeling sticky was practically immoral, certainly unhealthy. Dust, dry fine-grained dust, was better than the most expensive unguents. It buffered the extremes of cold and heat. I wanted to breathe it as the only accompaniment to the thin air. The smells of Wyoming still seem to me the cleanest—pine, sagebrush, and, of course, dust. The astringent air absorbed anything fetid or rank, even the sulfurous odors of the oil refinery. The sounds were comforting as well. Wind in the pines, a meadowlark singing from a fence post, the coal train whooshing and clicking by. My best summer days were spent on my gentle old horse, Buster, picking our way through the prickly pear and sagebrush toward a stand of pines in a distant fold of hills for a picnic amidst the shale and sandstone outcroppings. The winters were filled with the dry, squeaky snow from which it was impossible to make snowballs.

Pam took up photography and created beautiful photo collages of expanses of snow fences winding over snow-covered hills and golden prairies ambling beneath towering clouds. One of her photos won a third-place award in a Washington Post contest. But Pam was restless, even though she was related to half of the people in Crook County. Perhaps it is true that you can't go home again.

We spent three months in Mexico but decided we did not want to live there for good. In 2008, on the way home to Sundance, we passed through Las Cruces, New Mexico, and bought another house on impulse. Travel to Mexico would be convenient from there. We made a quick trip back to Wyoming, packed our stuff, sold the Sundance house, and moved to Las Cruces. During this move, it became apparent that Pam was seriously ill with what turned out to be an auto-immune disease. After an extremely frustrating and unsuccessful year and a half of trying to navigate the American medical system, Pam died on June 14, 2009.

After Pam's death, my life was empty. To fill time, I hiked in the nearby mountains and desert, haunted junk stores, bought and refurbished old typewriters, and built some furniture. Then I met Linnea, who rescued me from aimlessly puttering my life away.

We married in 2011. I moved to Albuquerque and found a new life of friends, travel, adventures, and a loving home that I thought I would never have again. We live in just the kind of home Pam always wanted and travel to places, and in ways Pam would have enjoyed. Happy as I am, I think about her often and regret that she is not here to enjoy the dust-scented air and the basement firmly beneath my feet.

I still dream of setting out to sea again, of basking in the Pacific, but at the age of eighty-two, I realize that is not realistic. I am no Ulysses, ready to cast off, saying, "'Tis not too late to seek a newer world." But who knows?

Kent, with Andy, Jake, and the three granddaughters in 2013.

Pam's Black Bean Recipe

Adaptation of a Recipe from Ruth Branson

Ingredients:

¼ pound bacon

¼ pound salt pork

2 pounds (5 cups)
  dried black beans

8 medium yellow onions

3 medium green peppers

2 cups olive oil

2 teaspoons baking soda

2 tablespoons white wine
  vinegar

1 pint hard cider or
  dry white wine

Salt

Pepper

MSG

Whole bay leaves (6-7)

6 cloves garlic (or more)

For Garnish:

1 sweet red onion, chopped,
grated aged cheddar, and a mild
white cheese such as Monterrey
Jack, plus sour cream. Serve
with the beans over rice.

Directions:

1. Boil 4 quarts of cold water in a 6-quart pot

2. Wash the beans, dribble them into the boiling water, and let them boil hard for 4 minutes.

3. Let beans soak for 1 hour and stir in 2 teaspoons of baking soda. Or, let soak overnight

4. Wash and drain the beans and put them in a 6-quart covered oven-proof pot. Add the wine (or cider) and enough cold water to cover the beans. Cook in a 300-degree oven.

5. It's also possible to cook the beans in a pressure cooker, crock pot, instant pot, or over low heat on the stove. We used the pressure cooker and the stove-top burner on the boat.

6. Mix onions (peeled and chunked) and peppers (cored and
    coarsely chunked), bacon and salt pork cut into ½ inch cubes.
    Add them to the 2 cups of olive oil and sauté until slightly
    brown. Then add this mix to the beans, stir in the bay leaves,
    vinegar, peeled and minced garlic, and salt, pepper, and MSG
    to taste. Keep covered and add boiling water when the water
    level drops below the beans. Cook 4–5 hours.

Pam's note: The above is the proper recipe, but if I want to serve
this on Saturday night, I might start soaking the beans on Thursday night. Sometime Friday morning, I prepare the beans for the
oven and let them simmer most of Friday afternoon and part of the
evening. I stir the whole mess often as this encourages the beans to
absorb the horrendous amounts of fat this recipe contains. Stirring
often also allows the cook to taste the dish and correct the season-
ings. Sometimes I take the cover off for a while and let some of the
water escape. When the water gets low, I often add wine instead
of water. It's pleasant to keep the wine bottle at hand for both the
cook's and the beans' convenience. On Saturday morning, latish,
as I may be a little hungover from my time with the wine, I put the
beans back in the oven (or on the stove). I let them sit out all night,
unrefrigerated, absorbing oil. Keep stirring, adding wine, and tasting on Saturday until the guests arrive. If the amount of wine you're
going through seems excessive, use water, but don't have it boiling.
I believe that the constant heating and cooling makes the beans
more flavorful. I hate to say it, but the MSG improves the flavor
dramatically. I've tried it with and without. By the time the company arrives, the cook will not want to eat much. But that's okay, as
someone at the table needs to be mobile to serve the dessert, which
better not be much richer than a single grape per plate. The baking
soda I added so dutifully in the soak cycle does absolutely nothing
to prevent the formation of gas. Eat this meal only with close and
tolerant friends.

Coot's Log

We always kept written logs on our boats, and as the years went on, they became more detailed. We had two, one for sailing and general notes and a second for the engine and mechanical issues. I don't know if sailors today keep handwritten logs, but I thought readers would like to see a sample page of *Coot's* from 1996.

The sailing log was kept in a spiral notebook that lay flat on the chart table. It has eight columns on one page for recording data and space for remarks on the facing page. The day and date are written across the page. The first column lists the time hourly during passages. The second notes when the engine is turned on and off. The third column indicates whether we are charging the house battery, the engine battery, or both. The fourth column contains the log (like the odometer reading in a car) is noted each hour during a passage. The fifth column has the hourly compass reading, and the sixth the average speed on the knot meter. The seventh column estimates the average wind speed and direction, and the eighth the barometric pressure reading. The remarks include the latitude and longitude of our position, and sometimes the sail configuration, the cross-track error from the GPS, the names of our departure and arrival points, and notable occurrences such as sighting or speaking to a ship. When we anchor, we note the time, place, and depth of the water.

When we were not on a passage, we recorded the engine running time, the quantity of fuel and water added to the tanks, battery charging, propane (for cooking) bottle changing, and such details as times we left the boat and returned to it.

In the separate engine log, we recorded the hours we ran the engine and kept a running total so we would know when to

TIME	ENG	BAT	LOG	HEAD	SPEED	WIND	BAR
	MONDAY		JUNE	17			
09:15	ON	BOTH	481.8				30.16
11:12	OFF		483.7				
2 hrs. running				10 hrs. since fill			
	Thursday, June 20, 1996						
08:35	ON	BOTH	485.7				20.8
14:16	OFF		508.5				30.09
5¾ hrs. running				15¾ hrs. since fill			
	Fri, June 21, 1996						
16:00	ON	HB	508.5				
17:00	OFF		508.6				32.09
1hr. running or more				17 hrs. since fill			
✳	SATURDAY JUNE 22, 1996						
08:47	ON	BOTH	508.6				30.16
10:31	OFF		513.7				
10:59			515.7	270T			
13:01		—	524.0	270°C	4-5	E 10-15	30.13

change the oil and filters in the engine and the transmission. We
also recorded the total hours the engine had run since the rebuild
in Clayton, New York, when the several filters in the fuel line were
changed, and a running total of the hours on each one. We used
the engine running time to gauge how much fuel we had in the
tank because we had no fuel gauge or dipstick on *Coot*, although
we had a dipstick on *Jacana*.

Remarks
Going to lower Monitor — filled = water

Bock in Cochino Grande.

going to , Utila
anchored Utila (4.6 - 5.6 on DS)

reachoring, after dragging
reanchored Ino (DS° of 2.8)

Going to Water Cays —
heading S. to 16°N & then to Tres Puntas,
15° 59.98   86° 56.5 turn 270° T to Tres Puntas
15°59.85'N. 87° 06.3'W (.2)

Coot's log from June 17 to June 22, 1996, among the Bay Islands in Honduras.

Glossary of Nautical Terms

Terms, as we used them, on *Jacana* and *Coot*.

Aft: toward the back of the boat; opposite of forward

Anchorage: the area in a harbor where small boats anchor

Apparent wind: the speed and direction of the wind as it appears from a moving boat

Backstay: rigging wire aft of the mast to prevent its tipping forward

Baja filter: a brand name for a fine mesh filter and funnel used to filter diesel fuel

Ballast: heavy material placed low in the boat to provide stability

Bar: 1. large mass of sand and earth formed by the action of water, often found at the entrances of large rivers; 2. a place boaters go to drink beer and tell lies

Batten: a sail batten; a stiff stick placed in a pocket of a sail to enhance its airfoil shape, necessary on sails with roaches

Beam: 1. the width of a boat at its widest point; 2. the horizontal direction perpendicular to the centerline of the boat

Beam reach: sailing with the wind coming from the beam

Beat: sail to windward on alternating tacks

Belay: attach a line to a cleat or other object to secure it

Bend: 1. a knot used to join two lines; 2. to attach sails to spars

Bilge: the lowest space inside a boat where loose water will tend to run or collect

Block: a pulley

Block and tackle: two (or more) pullies threaded together with a line to give mechanical advantage in hoisting or adding tension

Boathook: a hook mounted on a stout pole for pushing or pulling the boat or for snagging lines in the water

Boom: 1. a horizontal spar attached to the aft side of the mast to which the foot of the sail is attached, 2. a moveable spar used to stretch out the foot of a foresail (see **Pole**)

Boom vang: In our boats, a block and tackle with one end attached to the boom several feet aft of the mast and the other end at a point lower on the mast to put downward pressure on the boom to control the shape of the sail (also called a kicking strap)

Bottom paint: special paint containing anti-fouling ingredients to inhibit marine growth on the underwater portion of the hull

Bow: the front of the boat (the pointy end)

Bowline: the "king of knots," used to make loops at the end of lines, noted for its ability not to slip loose and yet to be (relatively) easy to untie even after being under strain

Bridge deck: the deck between the cockpit and the companionway hatch. It prevents water from going below should the cockpit fill with water when the boat is pooped.

Broad reach: sailing on a reach with the wind coming from behind the beam (when the wind is on the quarter)

Cabin sole: the floor in the cabin

Cable: 1. the chain attached to an anchor, 2. the distance of 200 yards (240 yards in the U.S.)

Cap shroud: a shroud that attaches to the masthead

Capsize: to turn the boat upside down in the water (not a good thing)

Careen: tilt a boat on its side, usually on a beach, to clean or repair the hull below the waterline

Cay: 1. a low, sandy, small island on a coral bank, also known as a key 2. In England, what we would call a "slip" in the States (a place to dock a boat, often between two piers) spelled quay as well

Chainplates: the metal fittings attached to the hull to which shrouds and stays are attached

Clearing in/out: dealing with Customs and Immigration officials (and, sometimes, other officials as well) when entering or leaving a foreign country

Cleat: 1. a fitting with arms upon which to belay a line 2. a variety of devices involving cams or teeth to grip a line

Clew: the corner of a triangular sail to which the sheet is attached; the corner furthest aft (see **tack** and **head** for the other corners)

Close-hauled: sailing as close to the eye of the wind as possible

Close reach: sailing on a reach with the wind coming forward of the beam

Club racer: a boat designed to race in clubs

Coaming: a protrusion on the deck meant to deflect water

Cockpit: an open compartment surrounded by coamings containing an opening in the deck with a footwell whose sole is above the waterline, where the wheel/tiller, compass, engine controls, sheet winches, and various instruments are often located

Companionway: a set of steps (called "ladder" on a boat) leading down into the cabin

Courtesy flags: a small version of the host nation's flag

Cruising chute: a lightweight foresail that is not attached to the forestay, in size somewhere between a genoa and a full spinnaker

Depth sounder: an instrument using sonar to measure the depth of the water

Deviation: Compass error caused by conditions on the boat, such as magnetism of the hull or stored metal objects; the amount of error often varies with the heading and must be compensated for using small magnets or a deviation card that lists errors for each heading

Dinghy: 1. a small boat, often an inflatable, carried or towed to serve as a tender for a bigger boat; 2. as a verb, to travel by dinghy (probably a use made up by sailors)

Dodger: a hood, lower than the boom, over a companionway hatch; can be canvas or rigid

Dorade: a cowl and box intended to allow the passage of air belowdecks while keeping water spray and wash out; a ventilator

Double-reefed: the sail reduced in size to the second row of reefing points

Downhaul: a line used to stretch the luff of a sail

DR: "dead reckoning," navigating using log, compass, and chart

Draft: the depth of water needed to float the boat; the distance between the waterline and the bottom of the keel

Drop boards: boards placed in the companionway hatch to keep water or other unwanted things out

Electrolysis: chemical decomposition of metal caused by passing an electrical current through a liquid or solution containing ions

Ensign: a flag indicating the nationality of the boat

Ephemeris: a table giving calculated positions of celestial bodies

Ether: a highly combustible gas

Eye of the wind: the direction from which the wind comes

Fender: an (often) inflatable bumper tied along the side of the boat to protect it from docks, other boats, or anything else that might mar or scrape it

Flog: the rippling and shaking (like a flag in the wind) of a sail when the clew is not sheeted tight

Foot: 1. The bottom of the mast; 2. The bottom edge of a triangular sail from the tack to the clew (see **luff** and **leech** for the other edges)

Forecastle: the cabin, or the hold, furthest forward in the boat

Foresail: a sail that is set forward of the mast, often attached to the forestay

Forestay: rigging wire that supports the mast leading forward of the mast

Forward: toward the front of the boat; opposite of aft

Freeboard: the height of the hull measured from the waterline to the lowest point along the gunnels

Gaff: the spar to which the head of a four-cornered, fore and aft sail is bent

Gaff-rigged: a boat rigged with four-cornered, fore and aft sail, controlled at its peak by a spar called a gaff

Galley: the kitchen on a boat

Gooseneck: the flexible fitting that attaches the boom to a mast

GPS: The Global Positioning System, developed as part of President Reagan's "Star Wars" military defense plans, based upon signals sent from earth-orbiting satellites deployed and maintained by the U.S. Airforce

Gringo: a contemptuous term to refer to North Americans (mostly) and Europeans in Spanish-speaking Latin American countries; Pam often used this term to refer to the same groups self-deprecatorily

Gunk-hole: poke around, explore

Gunnels: the top edge of the hull often protruding above the deck and thus requiring scuppers to drain water from the deck

Genoa: a large foresail attached to the forestay (by hanks, in our case) whose clew comes aft of the mast

Gybe: move the stern of the boat through the eye of the wind, also spelled **Jibe**

Gypsy: a wheel on a windlass for gripping chain

Halyard: the line used to raise a sail

Hank: a clip used to attach the luff of a sail to a forestay

Hard: "on the **hard**" means up on dry land

Harness: a piece of equipment made of straps and belts worn to attach oneself to the boat with a tether; a safety harness

Hatch: an opening in the deck providing access to spaces below

Haul the sails: modify the position of the sails

Head: 1. the top corner of a triangular sail to which a halyard is attached (see **Tack** and **Clew** for the other corners); 2. a marine toilet; 3. the top of the mast, **masthead**

Headstay: rigging wire attached to the masthead leading forward

Hitch: a knot used to attach a line to a rod or a post

Hold: The lower part of the interior of a ship's hull, especially when considered as storage space, as for cargo

Hove-to/heave-to: a technique to slow the boat and keep it pointing into the wind with sails still set

ICW, Intracoastal Waterway: a 3,000-mile inland waterway along the Atlantic and Gulf of Mexico coasts of the United States, running from Boston, Massachusetts, southward along the Atlantic Seaboard, around the southern tip of Florida, then following the Gulf Coast to Brownsville, Texas. https://en.wikipedia.org/wiki/Intracoastal_Waterway

Jackline: a line run from bow to stern to clip safety lines onto when working on deck

Jib: a foresail hanked to the forestay but not overlapping the mainmast

Jibe: change the direction of the boat when the wind is from the back, bringing the boom from one side of the boat to the other (often with a bang, so watch your head)

Kedge: 1. move the boat by pulling a line attached to an anchor; 2. a small anchor carried for kedging

Ketch: a two-masted sailboat with the mainmast forward of a shorter **mizzen mast** stepped forward of the rudder post

Keel: the lowest longitudinal part of the hull containing ballast

Key: a small, low, sandy island on a bank of coral, also called a cay

Kicking strap: on our boats, a block and tackle system attached between the boom and lower down on the mast to put downward pressure on the boom to control the shape of the sail (also called a boom vang)

Knots: 1. nautical miles per hour; 2. when tied in a line: stopper knot, hitches, bends, or loops plus other specialty knots

Knot meter/log: an instrument that would be the speedometer/odometer in an automobile

Ladder: often just a stairway on a boat

Latitude: the distance north or south of the equator measured from 0 to 90 degrees North or 0 to 90 degrees south of the equator, which is 0 degrees

Lay-a-hull: a method to weather a storm: take down all sails, batten all hatches, lash the helm to leeward to keep the bow pointing up, let the boat drift, go below, and pray

League: a distance of about 3 miles, although definitions vary

Leech: the aft edge of a triangular sail from clew to head (see **Foot** and **Luff** for the other edges)

Leeward: the side away from the direction of the wind; opposite of windward

Lifelines: 1. the fence that runs around the edge of the deck; 2. a line thrown to a person overboard

Life sling: brand name for a rig to retrieve a person from the water

Lines of latitude: circular lines around the earth parallel to the equator used to designate the distance north or south of the equator

Lines of longitude: great circle lines passing through both poles of the earth designating degrees of longitude east or west of Greenwich, England; also known as **Meridians**

Log: 1. a book used to record such things as wind speed and direction, boat speed and heading, barometric pressure, sail configuration and changes, times of departure and arrival, plus any significant happenings on the boat; we kept a separate engine log recording hours-run, oil and filter changes, breakdowns and repairs, 2. a reference to the distance run

Longitude: the distance east or west of the prime meridian which passes through Greenwich, England, measured from 0 to 180 degrees East or 0 to 180 degrees West of Greenwich

Lower shroud: a shroud attached to the mast at a spreader and attached to a chainplate often forward or aft of the mast's beam

Luff: 1. the forward edge of a triangular sail from tack to head (see **Leech** and **Foot** for the other edges); 2. to steer closer to the wind (luff up)

Main: mainsail; the sail connected to the aft side of the mainmast and extended on a boom

Marine head: a special toilet on a boat that requires valves and pumps

Mast: the tall, vertical spar to which standing rigging wires (shrouds and stays) and sails are attached

Mast step: the place where the foot of the mast is secured

Masthead: the top of the mast

Meridian: great circle lines on the earth that pass through the poles. Lines of longitude

Minute: one-sixtieth of a degree; in latitude, equal to one nautical mile

Mizzen mast: a mast usually shorter than the mainmast that is stepped aft of the mainmast

Nautical mile: the distance of one minute of latitude; 6,076 feet (longer than a statute mile that is 5,280 feet)

Off the wind: sailing with the wind coming from aft the beam

Oilies: raingear

On the wind: sailing with the wind coming from forward of the beam

Outhaul: line used to stretch the foot of a sail

Packing Gland: Prevents water from leaking around the drive shaft

Painter: the line attached to the bow of a dinghy to tie it to something

Peak: the upper aft corner of a four-cornered fore and aft sail

Pitchpole: to capsize a boat lengthwise, usually with the stern going over the bow (not a desirable maneuver)

Pole: a boom used to stretch out a foresail to increase the surface exposed to the wind

Pooped: when a wave breaks over the stern and fills the cockpit

Port: the left-hand side of a boat when facing forward

Portlight: window or porthole

Q flag: the flag flown when entering a foreign port requesting pratique— that is, clearance with customs and immigration. It is the plain yellow flag representing the letter "Q" in a set of signal flags

Quarter: either side of the boat aft of the beam. Quartering sea refers to waves hitting the back corners of the boat.

Quay: a concrete, stone, or metal platform lying alongside or projecting into the water for loading and unloading ships

Reach: sailing when the wind comes from the side of the boat (see **close reach, beam reach,** and **broad reach**)

Reef: 1. to reduce the amount of sail exposed to the wind (see **Single, Double,** and **Triple reef**); 2. a ridge of coral, rock, or sand just above or below the level of the sea

Reefing points: a row of eyelets or short lines in a sail used to tie up the unused portion of a sail when reefed

Rhumb line: a straight line on a Mercator projection; a course that maintains the same angle with the meridians (rarely the shortest distance between two points on the globe)

Rigging: The system of masts and lines on sailing vessels; **Standing rigging** consists of such things as masts, shrouds, and stays that are, more or less, permanent structures; **Running rigging** consists of halyards, sheets, topping lifts, and such that are used for manipulating the sails and the spars

Rigging screws: turnbuckles on the stays and shrouds to adjust their tension

Rigging tape: tape similar to electrical tape for wrapping sharp, pokey things that could cause injury or damage

Roach: the part of a sail that extends beyond a straight line between the head and the clew

Roadstead: a reasonably sheltered place, outside any harbor, where ships can lie at anchor

Rode: line that attaches the anchor to the boat; can be chain or rope or a combination of each

Roll up: An inflatable dinghy that can be deflated and rolled up to be stowed, unlike an inflatable dinghy with a rigid bottom

Rolling hitch: a knot used to attach a line to another line or a pole when the strain runs parallel to the line or pole

Rudder: A hinged flat door-like surface dragged vertically in the water toward the rear of the boat used for steering

Rudder post: the vertical or near-vertical post to which the rudder is attached

Running: sailing with the wind coming from the stern

Running rigging: lines and blocks used for modifying the sails: such as halyards, sheets, downhauls, outhauls, boom vangs, and others

Safety line: a tether connecting the harness to a secure place on the boat

SALT: Strategic Arms Limitation Talks, a treaty between the USA and Soviet Union to limit nuclear weapons (1972 and 1979)

Schooner: a two-masted sailboat with a (usually shorter) foremast stepped forward of the mainmast, carrying fore and aft sails

Scupper: an opening in the hull to allow water to drain overboard from the deck

Sheet: 1. the line attached to the clew of a sail to control the sail; 2. the act of taking the sail under control with the sheet

Shroud: the rigging wire that supports the mast laterally

Single hander: a person sailing alone, without a crew

Single-reefed: sail reduced in size to the first line of reefing points

Slip: 1. a place to dock a boat, often between two piers; 2. In England, a place to launch a boat from a ramp

Sloop: a single-masted sailboat carrying a jib and a mainsail

Skeg: a fin-like structure behind a fin keel to which the rudder post is attached

Snubber: a line made of stretchy material to either tie down or contain something or to take the shock off something under strain

Snuffing sock: a sock-like tube of cloth that, when lowered, will inclose and collapse a lightweight sail, or, when lifted, will allow the sail to deploy

Sole: a floor on a boat

Spar: a rigid, stout, wooden, or metal pole used to support sails such as the mast, boom, and gaff

Spreader: a horizontal, rigid bar attached to the mast to spread a shroud from the mast

Spinnaker: a large, lightweight, balloon-like foresail (often colorful)

SSB: abbreviation for single-sideband radio

Sta-lock: a brand name for a mechanical fitting used to connect rigging wire to other fittings

Stanchions: the upright posts that support the lifelines

Standing rigging: stationary rigging, often wire cable, used to support spars, such as stays and shrouds on a mast

Starboard: right-hand side of a boat when facing forward

Stay: The rigging wire that supports a mast fore and aft; forestay and backstay

Step: the place where the mast is attached to the boat

Stern: the rear end of the boat

Stopper knot: a knot tied in a line to prevent it from passing through a block or other opening

Sun Shower: a one- or two-gallon plastic water bag, clear on one side, black on the other that is placed in the sun to warm the water. It is then suspended so one can shower using an attached short length of tubing connected to a nozzle.

Swing a compass: a procedure to adjust the compass or produce a deviation card (deviation is compass error caused by conditions on the boat that deflect the needle or card and keep it from reading the correct magnetic reading, it often varies depending upon the boat's heading)

Tabernacle: the structure that holds the mast employing a pin so the mast can be raised or lowered by pivoting on the pin

Tack: 1. change the direction of the boat by moving the bow through the eye of the wind; 2. the lower corner of a triangular sail that is attached to the deck or the mast (see **Clew** and **Head** for the other corners); 3. The position of the boat relative to direction of the wind, as in port tack when the wind comes from the port side or starboard tack when the wind comes from the starboard side

Tether: a strap clipped on the harness and a secure part of the boat; also called a safety line

Tiller: a bar attached to the head of the rudder post used as a lever for steering

Topping lift: a line attached to the outer end of the boom passing through a block at the masthead that takes the strain off the luff of a sail when raising or lowering it

Topsides: the hull between the waterline and the gunnels

Transom: the more or less flat bulkhead forming the stern of the boat

Triple-reefed: sail reduced in size to the third line of reefing points

VHF: abbreviation for very high-frequency radio

Waterline: the line along the hull where the water meets the floating boat. To raise the waterline, one paints the bottom paint higher on the hull

Whee: an expression of joy or delight

Winch: a mechanical device in which a line winds around a drum or a chain is gripped by a gypsy to pull it taut or haul it in. It can be powered by either a crank or a motor. On a boat, used to raise a sail, haul a sheet or other line to make it taut as well as for retrieving the anchor

Windage: air resistance of a moving object or the force of the wind on a stationary one

Windlass: the winch for retrieving the anchor

Windward: toward the wind; opposite leeward

Wind vane: a mechanical device mounted on the stern that (in our case) runs lines to the tiller or wheel and is set to steer the boat at a specific angle to the wind; a paddle dragged in the water provides the force needed to steer

Wing and wing: sailing downwind with the mainsail and foresail on opposite sides

Working jib: a foresail about the size of the foretriangle, the space defined by the mast, forestay, and deck.

Yachties: people who sail yachts—not always a flattering term

Yawl: a two-masted sailboat with the main mast forward of a shorter mizzen mast stepped aft of the rudder post

Timeline and Itinerary

JACANA, 1984–1985

1984	
September	*Jacana 2* purchased, Isle of Jersey, England; Pam goes back to Brookings, South Dakota, with the boys
September 18–19	Kent, David, and Gary depart on *Jacana* from St. Helier, Isle of Jersey
September 20– October 5	*Jacana* makes passage to Gran Canaria with stops in Cameret-Sur-Mer, Baiona, Spain, and Porto, Portugal. Rough sail in the Bay of Biscay
October 5– November 14	Pam and Andy return to *Jacana* in Gran Canaria; David and Gary depart, and Jake remains in South Dakota, as family prepares for the Atlantic crossing
November 14– December 7	*Jacana* crosses the Atlantic from Gran Canaria to English Harbor, Antigua
December 14–16	*Jacana* sails to Nevis, Basseterre, St.Kitts and meets Hirta
December 21–28	Christmas in St. Barts
December 28–30	Île Fourche, St. Martin, Anegada Passage
December 31, 1984	*Jacana* arrives in Charlotte Amalie, U.S. Virgin Islands, and has a close call with cruise ship on Kent's 44th birthday

Jacana *Timeline and Itinerary, 1984–1985, continued*

1985	
January 5	Jake arrives at Lindbergh Bay, St. Thomas, U.S. Virgin Islands, with Hugh and Diana Randall
January 8–20	Family sails with the Randalls to Caneel Bay, Jost Van Dyke, St. Martin, Île Fourche, St. Barts, Virgin Gorda, The Baths, and Spanish Town, Tortola, with two crossings of the Anegada Passage.
January 20	Randalls depart from airport, and Jake and Kent watch the Super Bowl in Charlotte Amalie
January 23– February 7	*Jacana* sails in the Virgins: Road Town, Norman Island, Virgin Gorda, Marina Cay, Jost Van Dyke, Red Hook, back to Charlotte Amalie, and on to Culebra
February 9–14	Passage from Culebra to Villa Marina, with stops in Ensenada Honda and Isleta Marina
February 18	Villa Marina to Sun Bay, Vieques
February 22– March 1	Sun Bay, Vieques, to Fajardo, Puerto Rico and over land to San Juan
March 9–16	Ponce, Puerto Rico, to Boca Chica, with stops in Boqueron and Mona Island
March 20–30	Jacmel, Haiti
March 30–April 2	Jacmel, Haiti, to Montego Bay, Jamaica

April 7–13	Half-Moon Bay and Lighthouse Reef
April 13–25	Belize City to Isla Mujeres, Mexico, with stops in Goff Cay and Cozumel
April 25–May 11	Isla Mujeres, Mexico, with inland trip to Mayan ruins
May 11–14	Boca Grande Key to Key West, Florida
May 16–20	Newfound Harbor Channel to Ft. Lauderdale, with stops in Marathon, Tavernier Key, and Biscayne Bay, Florida
June	Summerfield's Boatyard, Ft. Lauderdale, Florida, *Jacana* sold; family returns to Brookings, South Dakota

COOT, 1991–2006

1991	
September	*Coot* purchased in Newburyport, Massachusetts and shipped to Superior, Wisconsin
1992	
January–August	Pam and Kent teach in China, spring semester. Sail *Coot* to Bayfield and Apostle Islands in Lake Superior and back to Barker's Island Marina, Superior, Wisconsin. Kent returns to teaching in Brookings, South Dakota.

Coot *Timeline and Itinerary, 1991–2006, continued*

1993	
July 15	Pam and Kent sail from Lakehead Marina, Superior, Wisconsin, through Lakes Superior and Huron
August 8	Terror at Whitefish Point, Lake Superior
August 26	Pam and Kent meet Sue and Jeff Grant from Brookings in Midland, Ontario, and cruise Georgian Bay
September 9	Haul *Coot* for the winter at Bayport Marina, Midland, Ontario, Canada. Pam and Kent return to Brookings for the winter. Andy heads to college and Jake to the Peace Corps.
1994	
May 17	Pam and Kent depart Brookings, South Dakota, to live permanently on *Coot* starting in Midland, Ontario, Canada
June 12–July 2	Engine repair, Bobcaygeon, Ontario, Canada, while traversing the Trent-Severn Waterway between Lake Huron and Lake Ontario
July 3–24	Cruise the Thousand Islands with smoking engine
July 25–August 24	Engine repairs, Clayton, New York
August 25– September 3	Through Lake Ontario and the Erie Canal
August 25– September 4	Hudson River. Step mast with Lew and Ann Tucker, Castleton-on-Hudson, NY

September 1	79th Street Boat Basin, New York, NY
September 16–October 2	Baltimore, St. Michaels, Mill Creek, Chesapeake Bay
October 6–November 1	Dismal Swamp, Alligator Bridge, Norfolk, Virginia, to Beaufort, North Carolina. Mail charts, meet *Viking* and *Lady of Spain*, Beaufort (10 days)
November 2–5	Sail from Beaufort, North Carolina to Fernandina Beach, Florida
November 10–19	St. Augustine, Florida
November 22–25	Meet *Viking* again, Lake Worth Entrance to Ft. Lauderdale
December 5–30	Sail to the Bahamas, Lucaya, Nassau, Warderick
1995	
January 1–20	Sail to the Bahamas, Lucaya, Nassau, Warderick Wells, Governor's Harbor. Andy visits December 12–29, rebuild fuel pump, Christmas storm. Depart Georgetown on January 20 for St. Thomas
January 27	Arrive, Charlotte Amalie, St. Thomas, U.S. Virgin Islands and recuperate in Leister Bay, St. John, U.S. Virgin Islands
February 6	Haul *Coot* at Independence Boat Yard, St. Thomas; Hugh Randall arrives
February 21–March 20	Depart Boatyard, St. Thomas, explore Virgin Islands, depart from Road Town, Tortola and cross the Anegada Passage

Coot *Timeline and Itinerary, 1991–2006, continued*

March 21	Arrive St. Maarten/St. Martin
March 27	Explore Saba
April 3–May 26	Explore Lesser Antilles and Windward Islands, Montserrat, Deshaies, Guadeloupe, Roseau, Martinique, Rodney Bay, St. Lucia, Bequia, St. Vincent, Grenada
June 7	Arrive in Trinidad
July 11–September 22	Haul boat at Power Boats, Chaguaramas, Trinidad
October 18–31	San Francisco Bay, Venezuela, to Puerto la Cruz, with stops at Los Testigos, Porlamar, Margarita and other Venezuelan islands
October 31–December 13	Pam is ill; search for doctors, Puerto la Cruz and Blanquilla
December 16	St. Croix, U.S. Virgin Islands, brief stop in Fredericksburg
December 18	Visit doctors in Charlotte Amalie, St. Thomas, U.S. Virgin Islands
1996	
January 16–28	Andy visits at Charlotte Amalie, St. Thomas, U.S. Virgin Islands, St. John
January 28	Lindbergh Bay, St. John, U.S. Virgin Islands
February 1–12	Doctors for Pam in San Juan, Puerto Rico
February 23–March 13	St. Croix U.S. Virgin Islands, Blanquilla, Venezuela

March 17–April 18	Puerto la Cruz, Bahia Redonda. Pam and Kent travel by bus into Venezuela and Colombia to Merida, Bucaramanga, Málaga, and Carcasí
April 18–May 8	Back to the boat in Puerto la Cruz after travel to Colombia. Pam and Kent set sail for Bonaire
May 15	Arrive Bonaire
May 25–June 23	Guanaja, Bay Islands, Honduras
June 24	Enter the Rio Dulce, Livingston, Guatemala
June 29– September 14	Susana's Laguna, Fronteras, Guatemala. Engine repair and overland travel to Mexico and the U.S.
November 14–22	Livingston, Guatemala, to Belize
November 22– December 31	Belize, Placencia, Glover's Reef, Lighthouse Reef, Cays, leave Belize City for Isla Mujeres
1997	
January 6–April 8	Isla Mujeres, Quintana Roo, Mexico, including aborted trip to Cuba, March 29–April 6
April 8–May 2	Isla-Mujeres to Everglades, Florida, with stops at Dry Tortugas and Ft. Myers Beach, Florida

Coot *Timeline and Itinerary, 1991–2006, continued*

May–December	*Coot* at Glades Boatyard, Florida. Pam and Kent travel inland to Black Hills, South Dakota, and other places, launch *Coot* at Glades on November 24, depart for Ft. Myers Beach, Shark River, and Marathon, Florida
1998	
December 24, 1997 –January 6, 1998	Marathon, Florida to Isleta Marina, Puerto Rico; bailed out of rough sail
February 3– March 3	Andy brings sail to Culebra. Sail through the Virgins with Andy.
March 31	Careen boat and paint, Hurricane Hole, St. John, U.S. Virgin Islands
April 25–28	Christiansted, St. Croix
May 3–18	Haul boat at Peake's Boatyard, Chaguaramas, Trinidad, to sandblast and paint the hull
May 25–July 4	Play chess and watch the World Cup at Man-o-War Bay, Tobago
July 13–20	Paint repair at Peake's, Chaguaramas, Trinidad
September 3–16	Chaguaramas to the Macareo River in Venezuela
September 23– November 18	San Francisco Bay, Venezuela, to Cartagena, Colombia, via Los Testigos, Les Aves, Porlamar, and Curaçao, with a rough sail to Cartagena

1999	
November 18, 1998– March 18, 1999	Cartagena, repairs on boat, Norm Bennett's Club Nautico boatyard; Andy visits in the new year and we travel inland to Bogotá, with Pam and Kent departing for Guanaja, Honduras on March 18
March 24	Arrive Guanaja
June 10	Leave Bay Islands, Honduras, for Belize and Rio Dulce
July 14	Enter Rio Dulce at Livingston, Guatemala
August 16– September 11	Vitus Marina, Fronteras, Guatemala, inland travel to Copan, surgery for Pam in Guatemala City
2000	
December 30, 1999– January 15, 2000	Andy arrives in Fronteras and we travel inland to Tikal, Pacaya, and Antigua, Guatemala
January 20– February 24	Pam and Kent leave *Coot* in Fronteras and travel inland to Mexico to visit friends
March 16–April 3	Pam and Kent leave the Rio Dulce for Bahia, Espiritu Santo, Mexico, Pam's encounter with the Barracuda
April 4–June 22	Isla Mujeres, Quintana Roo, Mexico, to Florida and Coan River, Virginia

Coot *Timeline and Itinerary, 1991–2006, continued*

2000–2006	
	Pam and Kent return to Brookings, South Dakota, and Kent works on the boat in Virginia, during the summers
	Kent continues to work on the boat; Pam and Kent explore living in New Mexico, buy a house in Virginia, and then move back to Wyoming, planning to return to *Coot* in the winters.
November 21, 2006	*Coot* put up for sale and sold shortly thereafter, Deltaville, Virginia

Books That Inspired Us
and Books We Used

Bowditch, Nathaniel. *American Practical Navigator:* An Epitome of Navigation, Vol. 1. Defense Mapping Agency, 1984.

Calder, Nigel. *Boatowner's Mechanical and Electrical Manual: How to Maintain, Repair, and Improve Your Boat's Essential Systems.* Camden, ME: International Marine, 1990.

————. *Cuba: A Cruising Guide.* St. Ives Cambridgeshire, England: Imray Laurie Norie & Wilson, Ltd., 1997.

————. *The Cruising Guide to the Northwest Caribbean.* Camden, ME: International Marine, 1991.

————. *Marine Diesel Engines: Maintenance, Troubleshooting, and Repair.* Camden, ME: International Marine, 1987.

Coles, K. Adlard. *Heavy Weather Sailing.* Tuckahoe, NY: John de Graff, 1968.

Cornell, Jimmy. *World Cruising Routes.* Camden, ME: International Marine, 1987.

Cunliffe, Tom. *Heavy Weather Cruising.* Hove: East Sussex, England: Fernhurst Books 1988.

Doyle, Chris. *Sailors Guide to the Windward Islands,* 6th ed. Dunedin, FL: Chris Doyle Publishing, 1992.

Eastman, Peter F. *Advanced First Aid Afloat,* 3rd ed. Centreville, MD: Cornell Maritime Press, 1987.

Guide to Cruising Chesapeake Bay 2000. Annapolis, MD: Chesapeake Bay Communications, 1999.

Hart, Jerrens C. and William T. Stone. A *Cruising Guide to the Caribbean and the Bahamas: Including The North Coast of South America, Central America, and Yucatan.* New York: Dodd, Mead, 1982.

Hiscock, Eric. *Around the World in Wanderer III.* New York: Oxford University Press, 1965.

————. *Cruising Under Sail.* London: Oxford University Press, 1981.

————. *Voyaging Under Sail.* London: Oxford University Press, 1959.

Kerchove, Rene de. *International Maritime Dictionary,* 2d. ed. New York: Van Nostrand, 1961.

Maloney, Elbert S. *Chapman Piloting: Seamanship & Small Boat Handling,* 56th ed. New York: Hearst Marine Books, 1983.

Moitessier, Bernard. *Cape Horn.* London:Coles, 1969.

————. *The Long Way.* Garden City, NY: Doubleday, 1975.

The New Glénans Sailing Manual. London: David & Charles, 1978.

Ocean Passages for the World, 3rd ed.: Somerset: England, Hydrographic Department, Ministry of Defense, 1973.

Roth, Hal. *Two Against Cape Horn.* New York: W.W.Norton, 1978.

————. *Two on a Big Ocean: The Story of the First Circumnavigation of the Pacific Basin in a Small Sailing Ship.* New York: Macmillan,1972.

Sanderson, Ray. *Meteorology at Sea.* London: Stanford Maritime, 1982.

Schumacher, E.F., *Small Is Beautiful: A Study of Economics As If People Mattered.* Harper & Row, 1973.

Sight Reduction Tables for Air Navigation. Bethesda, Maryland: Defense Mapping Agency, 1995.

Slocum, Joshua. *Sailing Alone Around the World.* New York: Century, 1900.

————. *Voyage of the Liberdade.* Boston: Roberts Brothers, 1894.

Smeeton, Miles. *Because the Horn Is There.* London: Grafton Books, 1970.

————. *The Misty Islands.* Tuckahoe, New York, 1969.

————. *Once is Enough.* London: Rupert Hart-Davies,1959 [On the voyage of the ketch "Tuzu Hang." With plates, including a portrait].

————. *The Sea Was our Village.* London: Rupert Hart-Davies,1973.

————. *Sunrise to Windset.* London: Rupert Hart-Davies,1966.

Tangvald, Peter. *Sea Gypsy.* Kimber, 1966.

————. *At Any Cost: Love, Life & Death at Sea : An Autobiography.* Cruising Guide Publications, 1991.

Smith, LeCain W. and Sheila Moir. *Steel Away: A Guidebook to the World of Steel Sailboats.* Port Townsend, WA: Windrose Productions, 1986.

Toghill, Jeff. *Knots & Splices.* London: Fernhurst Books, 1982.

Toss, Brion. *The Rigger's Apprentice.* Camden, ME: International Marine, 198.

Van Sant, Bruce. *The Gentleman's Guide to Passages South: Sailing Directions for Easier Windward Passage Making in the Islands from Florida to Venezuela and a Handbook of Caribbean Cruising.* Dunedin, FL: Cruising Guide Publications, 1993.

Watts, Alan. *Reading the Weather: Modern Techniques for Yachtsmen.* New York: Dodd, Mead, 1987.

Werner, David. *Where There Is No Doctor: A Village Health Care Handbook,* 3rd ed. Palo Alto, CA: The Hesperian Foundation, 1996.

Wilkes, Kenneth. *Ocean Yacht Navigator.* London: Nautical Books, 1976.

Other:

Captains Courageous (1937 film) with Spencer Tracy, Lionel Barrymore, Melvyn Douglas, Freddie Bartholomew, John Carradine and Mickey Rooney. Based on the novel by Rudyard Kipling https://en.wikipedia. org/wiki/Captains_Courageous_(1937_film)

Coot Cook: Recipes by Pamela T. Kedl. Albuquerque, NM: Peartree Books, 2020.

P & K's Mexico (Pam's Blog, 2007–2008): http://gkentkedl.blogspot.com/

Lo Entropy [movie] *The Cuba Connection,* 1997. https://www.journeyman. tv/film/338/the-cuba-connection. Also available through Amazon Prime.

Val Schaeffer, Jr. Obituary, *Washington Post,* 2006 https://www.washington post.com/archive/local/2006/08/19val-schaeffer-jr/6f052ae1-3c11 -4f81-9d51-0efcea8f2cab/.

Acknowledgments

Many people have helped in the writing and publishing of this book.

Friends and writers (some are one and the same) read and offered suggestions both early and late in the process, including Ross Burkhardt, Esther Jantzen, Anne Roberts, Bill Schopf, and Jeanne Whitehouse Peterson. Mark Wuschke from Australia was a helpful early reader.

Sailor and writer, Behan Gifford provided insightful comments and suggestions. Jacquelin Cangro was a helpful developmental editor. Marsha Schaeffer, Tom Cunliffe, and Geoff Boerne (owner of *Lo Entropy*) reviewed the parts of the book and corrected errors.

Sara DeHaan has been an excellent and patient cover and book designer, helping us through the self-publishing process. Jesse Philips contributed the boat logos and many cover designs.

Most of the photographs in the book have been copied from old snapshots taken by friends and family members. Some of Pam's letters were saved by their recipients.

Finally, my wife, Linnea Hendrickson has been the first and last reader, copy editor, proofreader, re-writer, questioner, and instigator, "Yes, people will want to read this! But we have to make it good."

If you enjoyed this book, please take a few moments to write a review of it. Thank you!

PAMELA THOMPSON KEDL
(1944–2009)

Pamela Kedl has spent her life trying to resist other people's schedules and avoiding being a professional at anything. Her work has ranged from the esoteric—a flutist, a potter, and a transoceanic sailor—to the pragmatic: a welfare worker, an English teacher, a librarian's assistant, and a waitress. As soon as she can figure a way to finance it, she wants to travel to the Pacific with her husband, her two sons, and a cat to finish their circumnavigation.[1]

Somewhere along the way, Pam decided against sailing the Pacific, but the letters written during her sailing years make up a large part of *We Ran Away to Sea*. After she and Kent left the sailboat, she took up photography and created stunning collages by piecing together smaller photos to create large landscapes.

---

1. *Women and Houses: An Anthology of Prose, Poetry, and Photography.* Unipress: Brookings, SD, 1988.

GEORGE KENT KEDL

Born on New Year's Eve, 1940, Kent grew up enjoying the out-
doors, competing in football and track, and trying to outdo his
older brother Doug in their hometown of Sheridan, Wyoming.
He quit school during his senior year at the University of Wyoming to serve in the Peace Corps in Colombia. Upon his return,
he completed degrees in mathematics and philosophy, enrolled
in a doctoral program at the University of Oregon, and married
Pamela Thompson. He taught philosophy at South Dakota State
University in Brookings for more than twenty years. After Pam's
death he married Linnea Hendrickson and moved to Albuquerque, New Mexico with his collection of over 100 typewriters.

Made in the USA
Las Vegas, NV
07 November 2024

11300830R00204